'This powerful indictment of state-dictated schoo data-driven performance and education leads into a how things could be. The style combines deep unfailingly lucid analysis. The book is a dis achievement.'

**Tony Edwards, Emeritus ..essor of Education,
University of Newcastle upon Tyne, UK**

'Opportune, imaginative, deeply practical and utterly necessary, this remarkable book offers a contribution of immense national and international importance.'

**Michael Fielding, Emeritus Professor,
UCL Institute of Education, UK**

'After 50 years in English education I thought I knew its history and the reforms it needs. How wrong I was. This book has forced me to question and reject some of my basic assumptions. The process was unsettling and exhilarating, challenging and truly educational.'

**Frank Coffield, Emeritus Professor of Education,
UCL Institute of Education, UK**

BEYOND SCHOOLING

Provocative and engagingly written, *Beyond Schooling* offers a challenging perspective on State schooling in England and the unrelenting increase in centralisation from the late 1960s until the present day. Exploring how the education of our children and young people should be recaptured from the State as the country moves into a precarious future, this book:

- argues that any fundamental reconsideration of schooling has much to learn from an anarchist analysis;
- introduces readers unfamiliar with anarchism to the main themes of this political philosophy and practice and their relationship to the political left and right;
- shows how an anarchist perspective on education raises deep issues about the community and the use of power;
- questions the notions of full-time schooling and age-grading, alongside conventional conceptions of the teaching profession and the potential educational role of parents as work declines or disappears.

In its original reflections on the state of contemporary schooling and the paths to future reform, *Beyond Schooling* is a must-read for anyone seeking a new vision for the future of education and schooling.

David H. Hargreaves is Fellow Emeritus of Wolfson College, Cambridge. He has been Professor of Education in the University of Cambridge and Reader in Education in the University of Oxford. He has also been Chief Inspector of the Inner London Education Authority, Chief Executive of the Qualifications and Curriculum Authority, Chairman of the British Educational Communications and Technology Agency, and Policy Adviser to the Secretary of State for Education. He is a Foundation Academician of the Academy of the Social Sciences.

BEYOND SCHOOLING

An Anarchist Challenge

David H. Hargreaves

LONDON AND NEW YORK

First published 2019
by Routledge
2 Park Square, Milton Park, Abingdon, Oxon, OX14 4RN

and by Routledge
52 Vanderbilt Avenue, New York, NY 10017

Routledge is an imprint of the Taylor & Francis Group, an informa business

British Library Cataloguing-in-Publication Data
A catalogue record for this book is available from the British Library

Library of Congress Cataloging-in-Publication Data
Names: Hargreaves, David H., author.
Title: Beyond schooling : an anarchist challenge / David H Hargreaves.
Description: Abingdon, Oxon ; New York, NY : Routledge, 2019. |
Includes bibliographical references.
Identifiers: LCCN 2018056352| ISBN 9780367187811 (hbk) |
ISBN 9780367187835 (pbk) | ISBN 9780429198229 (ebk)
Subjects: LCSH: Education and state–England. | Anarchism–England. |
Schools–Centralization–England. | Educational change–England.
Classification: LCC LC93.G7 .H33 2019 | DDC 379.41–dc23
LC record available at https://lccn.loc.gov/2018056352

ISBN: 978-0-367-18781-1 (hbk)
ISBN: 978-0-367-18783-5 (pbk)
ISBN: 978-0-429-19822-9 (ebk)

Typeset in Bembo
by Swales & Willis, Exeter, Devon, UK
Printed by CPI Group (UK) Ltd, Croydon CR0 4YY

For Mohan

CONTENTS

ACKNOWLEDGEMENTS

I am deeply grateful to my friend and former colleague Tony Edwards for reading the whole book in draft and for making fascinating comments, insightful reflections and fruitful suggestions, as well as to the publisher's five anonymous referees for their valuable comments and suggestions on the proposal for the book and the selection of chapters they read.

1

THE FUTURE OF SCHOOLING

A distinctively different direction of travel

> Government is nothing but regulated force … The project of a national education ought uniformly to be discouraged on account of its obvious alliance with national government … Before we put so powerful a machine under the direction of so ambiguous an agent, it behoves us to consider well what it is that we do. Government will not fail to employ it, to strengthen its hands, and perpetuate its institutions.
>
> William Godwin, 1793

> It will be observed that the governmental system tends to become more and more complicated, without becoming on that account more efficient and more moral … This complication springs first from legislation, which is always incomplete and insufficient; in the second place, from the multiplicity of functionaries …
>
> Pierre-Joseph Proudhon, 1851, quoted in McKay (2011)

It is impossible to understand, rather than merely describe, the current state of schooling in England (and to some degree in Wales) without looking back to the evolution of the fateful decisions made by politicians in the heady days of the late 1960s. The first rumblings of a deep dissatisfaction with schooling and education more generally were first heard in modern times some sixty years ago. The echoes still resound and, as we shall see, require us to go back to the nineteenth century if we are to understand the full story, much of which has been largely forgotten. The spirit of radical questioning in the 1960s grew steadily until, by the early 1970s, a revolution seemed about to break out, one that would lead to a fundamental and unstoppable rethinking about schooling and compulsory education for the young. It didn't happen. The revolutionary bubble burst so quickly that the age of radical questioning seemed to be over. Yet once again I hear these rumblings among those connected with school education, ones that are strikingly similar to those that

I detected back in the 1960s. Moreover we now live in times of deep disenchantment with politicians and their political parties. Traditional party loyalties are eroding, in France, Italy, Germany, Sweden and other continental countries and in the USA as well as in the UK. Trust in politicians is very low. Brexit, whatever the outcome, seems likely to exacerbate this upheaval.

The discontent with schooling seems strong among younger teachers and people linked to education or otherwise working with young people. To them the 1970s are ancient history, yet as I write this book it is mainly you of this generation I have in mind, because the conditions that present both challenges and opportunities will occur once again, and this time there may be a better chance of facing up to the challenges and seizing the opportunities – if, that is, we choose to learn from history and not repeat the mistakes of fifty years ago, when we did not think through what needed to be done and the action that would realise a finer vision. This is the relevance of the events of so long ago. By looking back we can learn more about how we got here and perhaps what we might do about it if and when we get the chance.

In response to the stirrings of the 1960s' challenges to authority, and the talk of radical reform among school educators, the State fought back and in the simplest and the most effective way possible: in 1972 it raised the school leaving age from 15 to 16, at short notice. Designed officially as a response to youth unemployment, it conveniently distracted attention away from educational reform by immediately sending panic waves through much of the secondary school sector, where most of the radical thinking had taken root in the light of growing numbers of disaffected students caught up in the 1960s' decline in deference and youthful challenges to authority.

I felt these waves as I began my teaching career at the beginning of the 1960s. In the grammar school in which I first taught the rebels were in the sixth form. Rather than being a challenge to my generation, who had just come out of the universities at a time of radical talk about politics (after Suez) and religion (Pope John XXIII), it was thrilling to engage with sixth-formers in just the same questioning. When I moved to a secondary modern school in the slums of Salford, the disenchantment of many of the pupils, whose lives centred around petty crime and the world of the Rolling Stones and the Kinks (not the Beatles, who were for posh kids), was as much a challenge for my generation as for the older teachers. How were the schools going to manage RoSLA – the acronym for the hasty preparations demanded to handle these alienated pupils, yearning to escape into adult life and yet facing another year of much-resented schooling? If revolution was on the agenda, it could hardly come from the teachers whose hands were full just struggling to cope. Radical thinking did not die: it tended to go underground at school level, though it flourished in the relatively cooler and safer waters of teacher training institutions, and in the mouths of a few radicals. The State, once having averted the threats of the early 1970s, continued to strengthen its grip on schooling.

In fact the process of centralisation began in 1870, when parliament initiated the process of mass schooling by the State. It has continued relentlessly for 150 years of State-led change and reform. And it is over the same 150 years that almost all children and young people have been progressively required to attend school for an ever-increasing number of years. State schooling is for so many children and young people by far their most significant experience outside the family, and its grip is, for most young people most of the time, inescapable. Since the turbulence of the 1960s and 1970s, somewhat stealthily, step by scheming step, the pace of the centralisation of schooling quickened, masked by somewhat duplicitous claims about 'school improvement' and 'raising standards'. The long-term impact on schooling of this endless legislation and regulation has, I believe, caused the immense damage that many predicted. Is this damage, as many fear, irreparable? One thing we can be sure of: if Brexit occurs, the slogan of 'taking back control' will not lessen the State's control over schooling – it seems irreversible. A way out may become a clearer possibility if we explore how we came to be here, and pay attention to those who en route not merely opposed this centralisation but sought a very different and distinctive direction for schooling. Since much of this history of school reform is also the history of my professional life, may I be allowed a quick recap?

In the 1970s Her Majesty's Inspectors for schools (HMI) undertook some surveys, concluding that in many schools the curriculum was far too narrow and that many pupils were in consequence being deprived of access to areas of knowledge, skill and experience, all of which was having a negative impact on their choices of more education in school after 16 or, for those leaving school at this age, on their choices of job or further education. It was also discovered that most local education authorities simply did not have policies on the school curriculum, a matter they left entirely to schools, for at this period the *only* compulsory subject on the school curriculum was religious education. The surveys stimulated discussion across the political parties – anxious not to be left out in the cold, Labour Prime Minister Jim Callaghan in a speech at Ruskin College joined calls in the Conservative Party for national action – about the need for some kind of national curriculum to protect standards and ensure children's right of access to a curriculum that should, in the jargon of the time, be 'broad, balanced and coherent' – the word 'coherent' was quickly but quietly discarded as a dangerous hostage to fortune.

The most important eventual outcome was Conservative Education Secretary Kenneth Baker's Education Reform Act of 1988, which established the National Curriculum and schemes of national assessment. Although there had been wide and healthy discussion among the teaching profession and various education bodies about the possible content of such a curriculum, including a series of influential discussion papers by HMI,[1] Baker simply produced the highly detailed draft National Curriculum in a consultation document, which from the teaching profession's point of view came as an unwelcome gift just as they started their summer break in July 1987. It was a major departure from government policy of non-intervention in curriculum matters and in direct contradiction to the then government's previously stated position that 'it would not be appropriate for either the Secretaries of State or the LEA to determine the detailed organisation and content of the programme of any of the pupils of any particular school'.[2] It was conceived in narrow terms as a list of conventional subjects – taking no account whatever of the more sophisticated curriculum conceptualisations of HMI – most of which would be subject to national assessment at ages 7, 11, 14 and 16. The argument was that the test would be a check of whether pupils were attaining the appropriate levels in the various subjects, but in practice it locked in place the main school subjects, since they would be tested, and made schools more accountable since the test results would be published in the form of league tables, ostensibly to help parents to make choices of school for their children. Some argued that the whole purpose of the National Curriculum was to facilitate and legitimate the new testing regime.[3]

Whilst Baker himself could stipulate a content for the National Curriculum, he could not credibly dictate the new assessment system. He assigned this task to an expert committee under Professor Paul Black, which clearly struggled with a difficult brief, but their recommendations were quickly set aside as they gave too much weight to teachers' judgements. This was just one of many subsequent occasions when experts made reports that were then, predictably, selectively set aside to justify what ministers wanted in the first place. As the years have gone by this assessment system has, I believe, grown into a veritable monster, costing an astonishing amount of money and controlling the time and energy of both teachers and pupils, all directed to what by any rational evaluation is a dubious reduction of pupil learning and achievement to crude numbers and predictions, lacking reliability and validity yet having a pervasive and often highly damaging impact on the self of pupils.[4] Most teachers do not believe in these measures and the practices that they require, but have little choice but to implement them and to pretend to unwitting parents that this is all in the interest of their child and good schooling in general.

At a stroke the 1988 Act indisputably turned England and Wales from being one of the least centralised education systems in the world to being one of the most centralised. Many thought the Baker reforms had gone too far – far too far. It was leaked to the press that even Prime Minister Margaret Thatcher preferred a very much simpler reform, but she let Baker have his way.[5] True, schools were given more financial control, at the expense of reduced power for the local education authorities, and head teachers gained additional powers, including the possibility of becoming a grant-maintained school, for they were intended to be at the forefront of improvement efforts.

The Act is particularly significant for two of its many consequences. The first is that the Baker reforms would be very difficult to reverse. Indeed, this was Baker's clear intention and proved to be well founded, for no later Labour government has sought to reverse it, and shows no inclination to do so, for this would obviously entail a sharp reduction in State control. Counter-revolution to the Baker reforms has never been a serious option. The second consequence is that politicians would, from this point on, be unable to resist exercising their new powers over the fine detail of the content of the curriculum and the precise forms of the assessments. No later governments have been willing to reduce ministerial powers: they have increased them, not least by moving to control the way in which teachers teach, which had hitherto been as unthinkable as telling doctors how to deal with their patients in their consulting rooms. In addition, the culling of intermediary bodies that used to stand between the State and the school, initiated by the death of the 20-year-old Schools Council in 1984, became more systematic and continued over the years until Michael Gove dissolved the British Educational Communications and Technology Agency (Becta), aged 13, in 2011 and effectively killed off the National College for School Leadership, also aged 13, by turning it into an executive arm of his Department in 2013. Chris Woodhead was appointed HM Chief Inspector of Schools in 1994 and introduced a much tougher inspection system designed to improve standards, under Woodhead's self-proclaimed banner 'I am paid to challenge mediocrity, failure and complacency', which resulted in a massive bureaucratic burden for teachers.

The 1988 Education Reform Act was the creature of a Conservative government. Tony Blair went into the 1997 election with the famous promise that his priorities were to be 'education, education, education'. Essentially what happened next unleashed a regime that entrenched the Baker reforms ever more firmly into schooling. It happened like this. The new Education Secretary in 1997, David Blunkett, naturally expected some more money for his Department in the light of the new Prime Minister's widely acclaimed priorities. But Blair did not control the money: the Chancellor of the Exchequer, Gordon Brown, did. Brown realised that education – like health – is potentially a bottomless pot into which endless amounts of public money could easily be poured, so he understandably demanded some means of ensuring that any additional money would be well spent, and that schools could be shown to have improved, thus justifying the additional expenditure as value for money. Blunkett, again reasonably, took the point and the assessment system introduced by Baker, as well as public examination results for 16-year-olds, became the means by which he could claim that higher spending meant better schools. The Labour Government, or at least 10 Downing Street, was content with Chris Woodhead as Chief Inspector, though he was much disliked, even hated, by most (but not all) teachers, which he once told me to be a confirmation that he was doing the right thing. Over the following years the regular reports on schools by the Inspectorate (now called Ofsted) have become closely aligned with test performance. In short, schools are now essentially judged as outstanding or good or inadequate (the labels, like most things, keep changing) on the basis of performance in test and examination league tables and an Ofsted grade. Schools with a low ranking in government-imposed measures, also constantly changing, and a low Ofsted grade are taken to be failing and in need of intervention, the forms of which have also changed over the years. It has been very difficult for teachers to keep up with all these changes, let alone parents or employers. The pressure on school governing bodies has been considerable, but this pressure then transfers to head teachers, via them to school staff, and finally to the next level: students. By common consent in the profession, by no means is all this final pressure on students of benefit to learning or to a good education, to say the least.

This brief summary of key events and people helps to remind us of two important facts. First, the degree of change in schooling since the early 1970s, and especially after 1988, has been profound, with some fundamental changes that seem to be largely set in stone. There are no plans by politicians to reverse the process of centralisation and the frequency of intervention to any significant degree. True, schools do not have to follow the National Curriculum if they opt out of local control by becoming academies or are established as so-called 'free schools', but the State's grip over the content of schooling remains tight by means of national tests, public examinations and Ofsted, and the price they pay is coming under the direct control of the Department for Education.

Second, there is the state of the teaching profession. I have had the privilege over this period of working with some outstanding school leaders and teachers doing remarkable things, though much of what they achieve is in spite of the system, not because of it. Much of the quality of what counts as education during the years of schooling depends on classroom teachers. Few would deny that they have, over this long sixty-year period, steadily lost power and autonomy: the teaching profession I entered is simply unrecognisable to today's young teachers. Morale among teachers has steadily deteriorated: 40 per cent of new teachers last less than five years in the profession;[6] and many older teachers tell me that they would prefer to be in some other job. As I look back, I became a teacher in a golden age. If faced with the choice of profession today, I would not for a second consider teaching in a school. This is not on my part a romantic nostalgia for the past: it is simply a recognition that a dispirited teaching profession is working in survival mode, accommodating as best they can a system they so often dislike. Head teachers have inevitably lost power as much of what happens in classrooms on aspects of curriculum and pedagogy is less open to their discretion: they are caught between the pressure on them from the State and the sense of oppression among staff. Whose side are the head teachers on? Moreover their tenure depends on maintaining a very high level of pupil performance in tests and an Ofsted report: if neither is at a high level, they may lose their job, or, should they be lucky enough to survive, keeping tenure depends on rapid improvement. Security for head teachers has evaporated. As one put it recently, 'A head teacher is only as good as his or her last Ofsted.'

As a result of these two facts, there is a severe shortage within the profession of visions for the future of schooling. Politicians have nothing to offer either. The Conservative Party, so rent apart by infighting over Brexit, has even led its MPs to complain about the lack of any kind of vision. The Labour Party, with its general change of direction under Jeremy Corbyn, has had astonishingly little to say about schooling, with no signs that this is about to change. So where must we turn to find visions? My argument is in essence simply stated. To understand the current mess in education we have to go back to the 1970s, and then even further back, to find the root causes of present troubles; but we must also go back to the very same period and before, to re-discover some of the best solutions for getting out of it – and find out why these were never firmly embedded into practice.

My potted history interlaced with some bits of biography will, I hope, explain to you why I have written this book. Will there be a revival of 1960s revolutionary spirit, one stronger and more powerful than it was the first time round? Have we learned any lessons from the ideas that were being canvassed fifty years ago and since? Is there something useful we can draw from the past as well as something new that needs to be devised for the complexities of our current situation?

In *Out of the Wreckage: A New Politics for an Age of Crisis* (2017), George Monbiot says the two most successful political narratives of our age are diametrically opposed: the social-democratic and the neo-liberal. His book offers a new story, based on different principles. In this book I offer a perspective that differs from the social-democratic, the neo-liberal and Monbiot's newly-devised alternative.[7] The lens I adopt to throw light on both what has been happening over the years and on possible paths to the future is a relatively unusual one, despite its long if largely hidden history. I first hit upon this possible tool in the late 1970s, when I moved to Oxford University. One of the advantages of Oxbridge colleges is the opportunity they provide for the Fellows from very different academic fields to mix, especially in conversations over meals. Two of my colleagues were John Gray (the political philosopher, not the educationalist) and Mark Philp, also a political philosopher. Somehow the conversation turned to William Godwin, a name barely known to me, most probably as the husband of Mary Wollstonecraft, and their daughter Mary Shelley of *Frankenstein* fame. They told me about his book on political justice and his interests in education and why he was an important figure in the history of anarchism, of which I knew very little. I read Godwin's *Enquiry Concerning Political Justice* of 1793 and was hooked. Here was a man writing passionately about political justice and in so doing offering a penetrating indictment of the State, including opposition to the still-to-come increase in its role in schooling. William Godwin will assume a major role in my account, because he is the father of English anarchism and his works are more relevant than they have ever been to understanding the damage that centralisation does to education and schooling.

Over the next few years I made a collection of books on anarchism, and especially on those by its major figures, guided by George Woodcock's *Anarchism* (1963) and Daniel Guérin's *Anarchism: From Theory to Practice* (1970). For insight into British anarchism I also turned to *Anarchism Today* (1971), edited by David Apter and James Joll, which remains an important historical document because it charts the move from 'classical' or largely nineteenth-century anarchism to the second wave 'new anarchism'[8] of the 1960s that received a huge impetus from the dramatic unrest that fifty years ago took place in Paris from May 1968, with student occupation and protest as well as general strikes across France – events curiously echoed almost exactly fifty years later in the protests of the *gilets jaunes* or 'yellow vests' in Paris in November 2018. *Anarchism Today* records the changing composition of anarchist groups: they became younger and university educated, so more middle-class and with a significant number of followers in the teaching profession. Richard Sennett makes a useful distinction between the political left and the social left.[9] On the political left, radicals focus on the top-down, whereas those of the social left build change from the bottom up. The political left, especially in Europe, focuses on the State; the social left, especially in the USA, on civil society. Everywhere there was a strong link to youth cultures and, particularly in the USA, to counter-cultures, reacting against consumerism in search of simpler, more permissive and liberated lives.

Anarchism was not one of the major influences on the events in France, where the students drew on an eclectic mix of philosophies; if one influence stood out among the leaders it was Marxism. Forty years later, in Occupy Wall Street (OWS), started in 2011, the balance of influence had decisively shifted, for Marxism now had a much lower profile. According to Mark Bray's (2013) insider account, almost three-quarters of the OWS organisers were explicitly anarchists or held anarchist views, marking a move from the Marxist hierarchical forms of organisation to those of a more 'horizontalist' anarchist organisation,[10] which proved to be difficult to explain to outsiders, especially the ever-present media, who constantly assumed that this was a protest movement with conventional leaders who would make specific demands. Many of the anarchists avoided using the term 'anarchist' or 'anarchism' both to the press and to liberals who associated themselves with OWS, preferring to explain anarchist ideas whilst avoiding the labels that they believed would be both misunderstood and rejected.[11] Bray's research into OWS is interesting in that in order to explain what happened, he is forced to provide readers with an introduction to the history and philosophy of anarchism, demonstrating that even today public understanding of anarchism is not widespread.

Anarchism Today provided me with an extensive reading list. At the time, however, fascinating though all this was, it bore little direct or explicit connection to my work, though it remained a hidden, subterranean influence. I did not know any sociologists who were interested in, and writing about, anarchism applied to education. Was I leading a very sheltered life in academe? Why to my knowledge was so little account being taken of the explosion of anarchist activism taking place all across the globe? Marxism or neo-Marxism was very much alive in universities, but as David Graeber (2004) has pointed out, anarchists have not had much time for high theory, and so their impact on the social sciences with their addiction to theory was relatively slight. Since that period there has been a substantial flow of anarchist writing across the world, not least by younger academics in the 'post-anarchism' wave, which has been even stronger since 2000. For reading, you are not merely more spoiled for choice than

I was; you may not find it easy to find a way through the huge literature in books and in academic and other journals.

Three years ago a brush with bodily limitations forced me to give up the immensely rewarding work I had been doing with school leaders for the Specialist Schools and Academies Trust and the National College as well as directly with schools and local authorities around the country. But it also presented an opportunity to draw on this anarchism lens to engage in some reflections on schooling, past, present and future. It is not the only lens, however, for the challenge to education and schooling in cities is much greater than when the major anarchists developed their ideas.

I must confess to you at once that I am not an anarchist and I am pretty sure anarchists would not wish to count me as one of them. Nor do I make even the slightest claim for expertise in the philosophy or history of anarchism. But I have found anarchist ideas and writings a huge source of reflection and refraction, which has helped me to clarify what I think and what I believe should now be done. One advantage of anarchism is that its philosophy forces one to question what we usually regard as unquestionable, and in particular it questions the very existence of the modern State and its control over schooling. Fifty years ago too few of us asked such fundamental questions and worked out strategies for implementing answers, and I believe we should do so this time. When, armed with this powerful lens, I reviewed our educational history since the 1960s as well as my own professional life, I found it at times a painful process, for anarchism can cut us non-anarchists down to size. Anarchism is now far more relevant than it seemed when first introduced to me, and it has impelled me to conclusions that have taken me by surprise. It is this that I share with you, not an attempt at your political conversion or to impress you with scholarship. By sharing this journey with me you will understand how and why, at the end of the book, my proposals for the future of education and schooling in England have come to assume their particular shape.

If you are the sort of reader I had in mind whilst I wrote, you may know relatively little about anarchism, so I provide some essential background as I go along. There are many splendid introductory books to anarchism[12] and a smaller number on its applications to education, of which the most outstanding is Judith Suissa's *Anarchism and Education* (2006) as well as the older *The Libertarians and Education* (1983) by Michael P. Smith, with its broader canvas.[13] Both books provide detailed discussion of life in anarchist schools and anarchist pedagogy, which I shall therefore treat much more briefly and selectively. If you enjoy my book, you will want to read these books next. I make full reference to the books on which I have drawn, but rarely refer to articles in professional or academic journals since for many readers access to them is far from easy without a foothold in higher education.

For now, I want you to get a feel for the most important writers that I have enjoyed on reading the original sources, rather than in secondary summaries and commentaries. So I have used unusually long extracts from their writings, in the hope that their distinctive voices, not just their thoughts, will be heard. This means I can make only a limited number of points about their views. By the fact of being such good writers, they developed and changed their views over time, so to get a more balanced view of their thought than I provide, you must turn to fuller biographies, of which there are now many.

Books by and about anarchists are mainly by political scientists, philosophers, economists or historians, singly or in combination, and of course I shall draw on them and often commend them. However, I am a social scientist and my bias, with its limitations, will show. My angle is shaped by sociology, anthropology and social psychology, in which anarchism has had a much weaker foothold than other perspectives, such as Marxism.[14]

> Ideas not armies change the face of the world, and in the sphere of social science, too few people with ideas couple them with anarchist attitudes. For the anarchists the problem of the nineteen-sixties is simply that of how to put anarchism back into the intellectual bloodstream, into the field of ideas which are taken seriously.
>
> *Ward (1959)*[15]

This was said almost sixty years ago by one of England's most notable anarchists of the twentieth century. Today it is far less true, but education remains a field in which there remains lots of room for anarchist perspectives – advisedly in the plural, since nowadays there are far more variations in what constitutes an anarchist perspective than when I first took an interest. I use several of these perspectives within my anarchist lens, but it is not the only lens that I use in my reading of past events, my analysis of current problems or my look to the future.

Finally, many of the books on which I draw were written by academics. They too are under government pressure, to publish in academic journals that are refereed by fellow academics. This means that academics have to spend more time writing for fellow academics than for a wider, lay audience, which often includes practising teachers. I have had an unusual career, some of which was in academic life, some in working closely with schools and their leaders, and some with politicians at national and local levels. One hard lesson I learned is that if I write for academics, the books are unlikely to be read by many teachers, apart from those pursuing relevant academic studies. If I write for teachers and a wider readership, such writing is almost entirely ignored by the academic community. If I write for both at the same time, I end up pleasing neither. This book, then, is not primarily for academics, but for teachers and a wider public, though of course I would be delighted if it proved to be of interest in the academic community. If the bias towards non-academic readers does not show, I will have failed. If I succeed, you will, I hope, be lured into further engagement with the more academic literature.

So I want to share with you a distinctively different direction of travel towards what will turn out to be a distinctively different destination for education and schooling in England.[16] It is quite a long journey through anarchism, but if you do not take it you will not understand the rationale for the proposals I make at the end. The trajectory to high centralisation from its beginnings in the 1960s to the decisive and monumental reforms of the 1988 Act took over twenty years of incrementalist softening up, and these were followed by a further thirty years of consolidation for centralisation to reach its present condition. It cannot be changed overnight; indeed, it was designed and carefully nurtured so that it would be virtually impossible to reverse. So what I propose is not a reversion to the status quo ante of a far less centralised schooling system, but a path towards a fundamentally different vision that will also take some time to realise. This vision is deeply fashioned by an anarchist perspective, though of course not by this alone. As you go through the chapters that follow, you might like to reflect at the end of each on how what you have read might affect your ideas for a better future for schooling and education. By the end of the book it will then be evident how and why we agree and/or disagree, but we shall both have clarified our visions, which is what matters most.

Notes

1 The most important of these was probably *The Curriculum from 5 to 15* (1985).
2 *Better Schools,* DES (1985: 11).
3 Aldrich, R., in Lawton and Chitty (1988: 23).
4 The best account of all this is Warwick Mansell (2007), with updates on his website, www.educationbynumbers.org.uk. For a readable overview of these practices in various fields as well as education, see J. Z. Muller (2018).
5 Education correspondents in the press have continued to emphasise this difference between Thatcher and Baker. Will Woodward, 'The legacy of Blue Ken Baker', *Guardian* 25 March 2008, and Peter Wilby, 'Margaret Thatcher's education legacy is still with us – driven on by Gove', *Guardian* 15 April 2013.
6 *The Teacher Labour Market in England: Shortages, Subject Expertise and Incentives*, report of the Education Policy Institute, August 2018. For new teachers of mathematics and physics, the retention rate drops to 50 per cent. An analysis by MP Matthew Pennyhook indicates that more than four out of ten teachers of any subject in London quit the profession within five years (reported in the *Guardian*, 4 October 2018).
7 An anarchist account has some distinct resonances with Monbiot's, since at the heart of his story is the concept of mutual aid (p. 14), though he makes no mention of anarchism.
8 For a comprehensive overview, see Graham (2009).
9 Sennett (2012, especially Chapter 1).
10 On horizontalism, see also Mark Bray's chapter in Franks et al. (2018) as well as Sitrin (2006, 2012).
11 Bray (2013: 113, 123).
12 Apter and Joll (1971), Butterworth (2011), Chomsky (2013), Elzbacher (2004), Franks (2006), Gordon (2008), Guérin (1970), Honeywell (2011), Joll (1964), Kinna (2005), Marshall (1992), Miller (1984), Quail (1978), Ritter (1980), Shone (2013), Taylor (1992), Wolff (1970), Woodcock (1963, 1977).
13 Smith's fine book seems sadly to be out of print; second-hand copies are hard to find and are often expensive.

14 Purkis, Chapter 2 in Purkis and Bowen (2004).
15 Quoted in Goodway (2012: 313) and in Levy (2013).
16 I am not seeking a 'little England' approach, but I recognise that Scotland has its own schooling system, and whilst some of what applies in England also applies in Wales and Northern Ireland, not all of it does. When I was Chairman of a body with a full UK remit, I learned to be careful in this regard. Colleagues from the other three UK countries can take from what I now write as they see fit. At the same time, what happens in England over the next few years will be affected by world-wide changes, not least the move to a 'post-capitalist society' as described by Mason (2015) and the radically reformed capitalism proposed by Collier (2018). Wolfgang Streeck (2016: 38) argues that the disintegration of capitalism, arising not so much from organised opposition fighting for a different social order but from its own internal contradictions, will be followed by 'a post-capitalist interregnum', a long and indecisive transition characterised by deep and unpredictable changes. Should he be right, this would provide a unique opportunity for an anarchist perspective to play a role in shaping an emerging vision.

2

ANARCHISM AND THE ABOLITION OF THE STATE

An intention to murder, Russian-style

> Revolution is overthrow of the State.
>
> Michael Bakunin, 1871, quoted in Maximoff (1953)

> We want to overthrow the government, all government – and overthrow them with violence since it is by the use of violence that they force us into obeying.
>
> Errico Malatesta, 1899, quoted in Richards (1977)

Let us start at the very beginning. The word 'anarchy', surely it is said, is merely a synonym for *disorder, chaos* and *mayhem*, whilst the label 'anarchist' invokes images of men in cloaks lurking in the shadows intent on assassination by bomb or dagger or related forms of terrorism, or perhaps more recently of young bohemian types intent on causing trouble during peaceful demonstrations. Are such labels warranted or are they misrepresentations? 'Anarchism', a term that is much less common than either 'anarchy' or 'anarchist', refers to the political philosophy and practice of those who call themselves anarchists. This philosophy of classical anarchism was developed by six founding fathers. They are certainly anarchism's most influential writers, and arguably the finest; few anarchist writers today might justly claim to be in the same league. Nevertheless their names and works are not widely known:

- William Godwin, English (died 1836)
- Max Stirner, German (died 1856)
- Pierre-Joseph Proudhon, French (died 1865)
- Michael (Mikhail) Bakunin, Russian (died 1876)

and two of a later generation:

- Peter (Pyotr Alexeivitch) Kropotkin, Russian (died 1921)
- Errico Malatesta, Italian (died 1932)

Three of these – Godwin, Bakunin and Kropotkin – will be dealt with in some depth, and the other three much more briefly. To contemporary readers these figures may seem as distant as the world of Charles Dickens, but these are such giants that any newcomer to anarchism will quickly come across them. I shall not be treating them in any systematic way to explain what they have in common and how they differ; that task is done well in many introductory books. You need to be aware that they exert a continuing influence on twenty-first-century anarchist thinkers and writers, but here I shall refer to them only in a partial and selective way. Today's anarchism has rightly been described as the most idealistic, complicated and contradictory of political philosophies, and the seeds of this can readily be detected in the works of the early writers. Few later writers can claim the same combination of passion and clarity that inspired followers in the last century, but for me two, both with a deep interest in education, stand out and will constantly reappear as the book proceeds:

- Paul Goodman (American, 1911–1972)
- Colin Ward (English, 1924–2010)

Socialism and conservatism are useful labels that cover a wide range of views – anarchism embraces even more divergent elements in a less coherent philosophy. Over time anarchist thinking and writing are said to have moved through 'classical anarchism', to 'new anarchism' of the 1960s and 1970s to 'post-anarchism' – categorisations I think rather rough, even simplistic. I have found it more appealing and useful (and for your accessibility if you are relatively new to anarchism) to draw mostly on the so-called first two phases of this development. And of course there is no party membership card, no creed to which one must subscribe. At the same time, this lack of orthodoxy has not inhibited contemporary anarchists from engaging in vigorous debates and disputes, as you can easily discover if you look at post-anarchist discussions,[1] which – be advised – presuppose some knowledge of anarchism's first two waves as well as of post-structuralism and post-modernism. I shall not in this book be troubling you much with this. Anarchists have interesting next-door neighbours, as it were – those who adhere to libertarian views, on both left and right politically. Some of the most interesting writers decline to make a clear affiliation, or change it over time, or are ideologically promiscuous. Indeed, some of these writers to whom I turn have advanced anarchist thinking without being anarchists. In this book I have welcomed them all, as I find tracing common currents between positions under different labels more interesting and worthwhile than demarcation disputes. I will argue in the final chapter that the way out of our problems is for us all to think in more syncretistic, libertarian terms and thus to build alliances for change.

So what do anarchists stand for? What is their philosophy about? The term 'anarchism' derives from the Greek meaning without rulers, without a constituted authority – *without the State*. Could any modern society do what the anarchists were fighting for and simply abolish or murder the State? Is this idea simply risible, meriting instant and unhesitating rejection? There is constant debate about the nature and role of the State, including the distribution of power between local and central government: on the one side, about whether, taken as a whole, the State could improve what it does and whether it could and should do yet more; and on the other side, whether it should do much less, both because it disempowers people and because it is grossly inefficient in its provision. There is lively argument about centralisation on both left and right, but the notion of the *total* abolition of the State is rarely heard or debated. To discover what might be mined from the history and literature of anarchism we need to explore in more detail why so many of its proponents insisted over a long period on the abolition of the State as a major part of their philosophy.

In anarchism there are a few central themes and concepts,[2] but there is no agreed philosophy or agenda for action, no orthodoxy, no party manifesto. Indeed, all these are alien to anarchist thinking and doing, and anarchists seem to revel in the lack of coherence in their writings over the years. For the early anarchists the State is the enemy. Beyond this common ground, most anarchists in their classic form fall into two main groupings. The first one gives primacy to the individual and is wary of, even hostile to, many forms of social organisation, not just the State. The second and larger grouping gives primacy to community and believes strongly in forms of association and cooperation as long as they are not coercive. For them the State not only restricts the freedom and autonomy of the individual, but also damages spontaneous self-organisation and the natural organic communities that flourish on reciprocity and mutual aid. My bias is towards the second communalist grouping, as is much British anarchist writing. Americans are often stronger on the first grouping, and sometimes give pride of place to Max Stirner for his compatibility with and influence on American anarchists and libertarians.[3]

Within any State there is, for anarchists, a constant and ineradicable tension and struggle between the rulers and the ruled, between those who govern and those who are governed. Anarchist philosophy is essentially libertarian, but for the most part does not celebrate the isolated individual. There is always a tension between individual freedom and collective collaboration and the continuing challenge is to resolve such a tension. In Alan Ritter's analysis, anarchists are portrayed as

> seeking to combine the greatest individual development with the greatest communal unity. Their goal is a society of strongly separate persons who are strongly bound together in a group. In a fully-fledged anarchy, individual and communal tendencies, now often contradictory, become mutually reinforcing and coalesce … [This] helps define the target of their

> social criticism; it gives their strategy limits and direction; and it guides their description of an anarchist social order.[4]

Many, but not all, anarchist writers link the two strands, insisting on the indivisibility and the danger of taking the one without the other. Within each of these two strands there is a range of views and advocated practices, just as the tension between them surfaces in particular forms, such as the one between communal use of resources and private property. No British anarchist has been more successful in managing this tension between individual autonomy and communal solidarity than Colin Ward, not least because he took as much a sociological as a philosophical approach to his work.

For some, anarchism is indelibly associated with violence, often linked to the anarchist idea of 'propaganda by the deed' or 'direct action'. Take, for instance, these words of Errico Malatesta, who seems to be struggling with the idea of violence:

> Anarchists are opposed to violence; everyone knows that. The main plank of anarchism is the removal of violence from human relations.[5]

> I think that a regime which is born of violence and which continues to exist by violence cannot be overthrown except by a corresponding and proportionate violence, and that one is therefore either stupid or deceived in relying on legality where the oppressors can change the law to suit their own ends. But I believe that violence is, for us who aim at peace among men, and justice and freedom for all, an unpleasant necessity ... We are on principle opposed to violence and for this reason wish that the social struggle should be conducted as humanely as possible.[6]

Malatesta has an escape clause from the contradiction:

> Anarchists recognise violence only as a means of legitimate defence; and if today they are in favour of violence it is because they maintain that slaves are always in a state of legitimate defence.[7]

Which begs the question of what is meant by the word 'slave'.

In any perusal of anarchist thought it is easy to perceive ambiguity or confusion over the term 'revolution', one that is not always clearly defined in its context.[8] Part of the problem is the number of related words – 'revolt', 'rebellion', 'uprising', 'insurrection' – all of which are concerned with a refusal to accept, or with an act of resistance against, some exercise of power or authority. *Revolution* is widely overused, as for example when a product is advertised as a revolutionary new soap powder or vacuum cleaner, when actually the change is a relatively modest one. It seems best to reserve the word 'revolution' for a deep or substantial change that marks the transition from one state to a fundamentally different one, usually suddenly or over a short period of time. Revolution is often distinguished from reform, which to achieve change uses the processes available in the present system. In reform, opposition to deep change is more easily mobilised; and, for anarchists, mere reform often leaves intact the institutions that need to be abolished.

Another common distinction is one between a political revolution and a social revolution. A *political* revolution usually refers to a violent overthrow of one political system for a very different one. A *social* revolution refers to a radical reordering of social structures and social relationships. A political revolution may or may not intend to create a social revolution, which may or may not come about. In the case of the Marxists the violence is intended to change the control of the State by coercion and thereby usher in a social revolution. Some anarchists appear to want much the same thing; others seem to seek a spontaneous and preferably non-violent revolt that will lead to a social revolution. The Marxists, at least in the short term, want to replace the existing power structure and political system with a very different one of their own design. By contrast the anarchists have often been committed to murdering the State in an absolute sense, with the aim of creating a society without any kind of State, not merely different people at the controls.

In revolutions, depth and speed of social change are often in tension. It seems to be accepted that a sudden revolution is difficult to engineer without violence; and a social revolution without violence is likely to be a very slow, and perhaps uneven, process. In the light of their opposition to coercion and violence, many anarchists support a non-violent social revolution, sometimes impatiently, but also with a belief that a permanent or irreversible change, especially one with a low risk of counter-revolution, is more likely to be achieved by slow rather than sudden change. For many anarchists, it is vital to recognise that the seeds of the social revolution for which they yearn are to be found in present society. In 1970 the American Paul Goodman put it this way:

> In anarchist theory, the word *revolution* means the process by which the grip of authority is loosed, so that the functions of life can regulate themselves, without top-down or external hindrance. The idea is that, except for emergencies and a few special cases, free functioning will find its own right structures and coordination. An anarchist description of the revolutionary period thus consists of many accounts of how localities, factories, tradesmen, schools, professional groups, and communes go about managing their own affairs, defending themselves against the central "system", and making whatever federal arrangements among themselves that are necessary to weave the fabric of society.[9]

In England Colin Ward captured the same spirit at about the same time:

> An anarchist society, a society which organises itself without authority, is always in existence like a seed beneath the snow, buried under the weight

> of the State and its bureaucracy, capitalism and its waste, privilege and its injustice, nationalism and its suicidal loyalties, religious differences and their superstitious separatism … [Anarchism] is a description of a mode of human organisation, rooted in the experience of everyday life, which operates side by side with, and in spite of, the dominant authoritarian trends of our society … If you want to build a free society, the parts are all at hand.[10]

More than thirty years later, in 2006, a contemporary Scottish authority on anarchism, Benjamin Franks, takes the same line, defending revolution-as-process rather than revolution-as-event:

> Revolution is not a single phenomenon but the accumulation of ever expanding and growing incidents of prefigurative anarchist actions. "Rebellion" and "insurrection" refer to less frequent, more geographically contained, incidents of libertarian resistance … Revolutions, according to the anarchist ideal, are not unique acts, being indistinguishable except in scale, from more localised anarchist tactics from which revolution materialises … The anarchist model regards revolution as emerging from escalating, diversely-located acts that interact and interweave.[11]

Anarchists today want to murder the State, but not so much by violent assassination as by slow strangulation or by cutting off the oxygen that keeps the State alive. But it has not always been so, for in the nineteenth century it was commonly assumed that violence would be a necessary part of an anarchist revolution, and this helped to impress on the public mind an indelible link between anarchism and violence. Is this justified? Peter Marshall, perhaps the finest scholar on anarchism, thinks not:

> In fact, only a tiny minority of anarchists have practised terror as a revolutionary strategy, and then chiefly in the 1890s when there was a spate of spectacular bombings and political assassinations during a period of complete despair. Although often associated with violence, historically anarchism has been far less violent than other political creeds and appears as a feeble youth pushed out of the way by the marching hordes of fascists and authoritarian communists.[12]

G. D. H. Cole, the libertarian socialist, economist and historian, who was a conscientious objector during the First World War, points out that for the most part the assassins, even when linked to anarchist bodies, tended to act alone or with just a few others, and this was true even of the outrages of the 1890s, despite attempts to implicate the anarchists.[13] Much of any violence that can be attributed to anarchists, says Daniel Guérin, 'seems to have been a temporary and sterile deviation in the history of anarchism'.[14] Many anarchists would distance themselves from violence, as Gustav Landauer did: 'For what has the killing of people to do with anarchism, a theory striving for a society without government and authoritarian coercion, a movement against the State and legalised violence? The answer is: nothing at all.'[15]

Certainly there are commonalities between Marxism and anarchism in the need for some kind of revolution to bring it about, but the differences between them are far more important than what they share. This is best revealed in the story of Michael Bakunin (1814–1876). He seemed to be heading for a professorship in philosophy but as he became increasingly radical while he travelled around Europe, he fell foul of the authorities and ended up in the notorious St Peter and St Paul Fortress in St Petersburg and was later exiled to a work-camp in Siberia, from which he escaped. In 1868 he joined the socialist International Workingmen's Association, which was to be the site of a great confrontation, the repercussions of which affected the subsequent fate of the anarchist movement.

For Bakunin the difference between the Marxists and the anarchists was fundamental, for the Marxists rejected the anarchists' principled opposition to the State because they wanted to control the State, not be rid of it. He sets out the difference in the starkest of terms:

> Now it is clear why the dictatorial revolutionists, who aim to overthrow the existing powers and social structures in order to erect upon their ruins their own dictatorships, never were or will be the enemies of government, but, to the contrary, always will be the most ardent promoters of the government idea. They are the enemies of the present contemporary governments, because they wish to replace them. They are the enemies of the present governmental structure, because it excludes the possibility of their dictatorship. At the same time they are the most devoted friends of governmental power.[16]

Bakunin recognised that those who take over the State become in turn prey to the very vices that corrupted the State in the first place:

> From whatever angle we approach the problem, we arrive at the same sorry result: the rule of the great masses of the people by a small privileged minority. But, the Marxists say, this minority will consist of workers. Yes, indeed, of *ex-workers*, who, once they become rulers or representatives of the people, cease to be workers and begin to look down on the toiling people. From that time on they represent not the people but themselves and their own claims to govern the people. Those who doubt this know very little about human nature.[17]

Like his fellow anarchists, Bakunin had a very positive view of human nature, but he evidently had no illusions about how power corrupts:

> Nothing is as dangerous for man's personal morality as the habit of commanding. The best of men, the most intelligent, unselfish, generous, and pure will always and inevitably be corrupted in this pursuit. Two feelings in the exercise of power never fail to produce this demoralisation: contempt for the masses, and, for the man in power, an exaggerated sense of his own worth.[18] Take the most radical of revolutionaries and place him on the throne of all the Russias or give him dictatorial powers … and before the year is out he will be worse than the Czar himself.[19]

Bakunin was ever inclined to prolixity and was temperamentally incapable of Lord Acton's concision in his aphorism of 1887 'Power tends to corrupt; absolute power corrupts absolutely.' Acton continued: 'Great men are almost always bad men, even when they exercise influence and not authority; still more when you superadd the tendency or the certainty of corruption by authority.' But Bakunin got there first.

The anarchist ideal, then, is of a decentralised and non-hierarchical society of equals acting in solidarity within federations of independent self-organising communes. A State, Bakunin recognised, operates very differently, and by its nature drifts into colonialism:

> Every State, federated or not, would therefore seek to become the most powerful. It must devour lest it be devoured, conquer lest it be conquered, enslave lest it be enslaved, since two powers, similar yet alien to each other, could not coexist without mutual destruction … It shatters the universal solidarity of all men on the earth, and brings some of them into association only for the purpose of destroying, conquering, and enslaving all the rest. … Since it recognises no rights outside itself, it logically arrogates to itself the right to exercise the most ferocious inhumanity toward all foreign populations, which it can plunder, exterminate, or enslave at will …[20]

Clearly Bakunin understood that the State, whether in the hands of a czar or authoritarian communists, would be committed to violence in achieving, maintaining and then extending its hold. For anarchists, the authority of the State always and ineluctably relies on coercion with an implicit or explicit threat of violence. So what was Bakunin's own position on violence by anarchists? His stance is unclear and reflects his undoubted inconsistency and perhaps ambivalence. Part of him seems to believe that a violent uprising would be against the basic principles of anarchism and would lead inexorably to the re-emergence of the State,[21] but another part openly acknowledges that any uprising is necessarily violent:

> A popular insurrection, by its very nature, is instinctive, chaotic, and destructive, and always entails great personal sacrifice and an enormous loss of public and private property … Revolution requires extensive and widespread destruction, a fecund and renovating destruction, since in this way and only this way are new worlds born …[22]

His preference is that all those who are oppressed by the State should simultaneously rise up against the State and implement an anarchist programme, but the realist in him understands that a spontaneous bottom-up process is unlikely to happen. So at times, in comparison with the Marxists, he looks very naïve. The action he advocates implies violence in the conduct of the revolution itself, but he clings to his idealism by being absolutely clear that in post-revolutionary times violence towards those who resisted the revolution is not acceptable:

> It is clear that the people, longing for emancipation, cannot expect it from the theoretical triumph of abstract right; they must win liberty by force, for which purpose they must organise their powers apart from and against the State … Begin by striking down all who oppose you. And then, having assured your victory and having destroyed the power of your enemies, show yourselves humane towards the unfortunate stricken-down foes, henceforth disarmed and harmless; recognise them as your brothers and invite them to live and work alongside of you upon the unshakable foundation of social equality.[23]

His idealism about the revolution is tempered in another way. Given that he cannot specify in any detail how the spontaneous uprising of the masses will be triggered, he concedes, with evident reluctance but nevertheless to the horror of many anarchists, that some sort of leadership will be needed as

> a sort of revolutionary general staff, composed of dedicated, energetic, intelligent individuals, sincere friends of the people above all, men neither vain nor ambitious, but capable of serving as intermediaries between the revolutionary idea and the instincts of the people. There need not be a great number of these men …[24]

Marxists and anarchists were in broad agreement about what they were against and the need for a revolution to change this world, and at times there were prospects of a common cause. But the deeper differences about both means and ends divided them and these were exacerbated by personality clashes between the protagonists. Roughly between 1869 and 1872 an intense battle of ideas took place between the Marxists and the anarchists over the control and direction of the International Workingmen's Association. Marx of course led for the Marxists; Bakunin was the anarchists' champion. It was a battle that the anarchists were destined to lose.

For Bakunin the strategy of the International could not be a top-down affair in which the natural life of the masses would be forced by a confidence trick into the straitjacket of a new State imposed on them in the creation of what he called a 'fictitious unity'. Neither could Bakunin agree with the Marxists that the revolution should be led by the upper layer of the urban working class, because of all the proletariat they were the most individualist and least social, the closest to the aspirations and pretentions of the bourgeoisie, and because they in turn would become another governing class that would lose touch with the mass of the proletariat. Bakunin, as a Russian, thought rural peasants would necessarily be central to any social revolution, which should include the poor and those in servitude, so he considered the Marx and Engels term 'of the *Lumpenproletariat*' a contemptuous dismissal of most of the players essential to a successful social revolution:

> The revolution must be made not *for* but *by* the people and can never succeed if it does not enthusiastically involve all the masses of the people, that is, in the rural countryside as well as in the cities.[25]

Bakunin was deeply sceptical about Marx's promise about post-revolutionary equality of people. On the contrary, he predicted that the new government would necessarily be larger and more complex because of the scope of the communist ambitions, and thus that it would need many heads to exercise control:

> It will be a reign of scientific intelligence, the most aristocratic, despotic, arrogant, and elitist of all regimes. There will be a new class, a new hierarchy of real and counterfeit scientists and scholars, and the world will be divided into a minority ruling in the name of knowledge, and an immense ignorant majority[26] ... Every State, even the pseudo-People's State concocted by Mr Marx, is in essence only a machine ruling the masses from above, through a privileged minority of conceited intellectuals, who imagine they know what the people need and want better than do the people themselves[27] ... This is a lie, behind which lurks the despotism of the ruling minority, a lie all the more dangerous in that it appears to express the so-called will of the people.[28]

Bakunin would have fully endorsed Voline's judgement that the Marxist approach would require its adherents to follow

> the course of all revolutions which leave intact the statist, centralist, political, governmental principle. This course is a slope. And once [any group is] on that slope, the sliding occurs by itself. Nothing can stop it. At first neither the governing clique nor the governed perceive what is happening. The former (in so far as they are sincere) believe that they are fulfilling their role and carrying out an indispensable salutary work. The latter, fascinated, tightly gripped, and dominated, follow. And when, finally, these two groups, and especially the latter, begin to understand their error, it is too late. It is impossible to go back ...[29]

Anarchist predictions did not persuade the Marxists, of course, though they proved to be devastatingly and chillingly accurate, stretching far into the future to Lenin and Stalin – and Putin. At the time of the International, the arguments were long and sometimes heated and bitter. The two protagonists were very different. Bakunin respected Marx for his learning and his devotion to the proletariat. Marx called him a sentimental idealist, and Bakunin acknowledged that he was right to do so. Not surprisingly, Bakunin totally rejected the Marxian thesis about economic determinism and historical materialism, but he had nothing as intellectually subtle and compelling as an alternative. In reply he called Marx vain, perfidious and cunning – another Bismarck – and said he was right in this too.[30] Marx was more clever, nimble-footed and ruthless than the wild and fiery, eloquent, if sometimes bombastic, but always engaging Bakunin. The battle was lost and history habitually forgets losers. James Joll observes that

> it is unsuccessful revolutionaries who have been the chief victims of those historians who are only interested in success. When a revolution succeeds, historians are concerned to trace its roots and unravel its origins and development, so that, very often, the whole chain of events leading to it over many decades is represented as an inevitable process … On the other hand, the revolutions which failed are treated as blind alleys and the men and ideas that inspired them are rarely studied for their own inherent interest. As a consequence, much that is interesting and curious is neglected and forgotten, and the field of vision of the historian is deliberately restricted. Yet, if the aim of the historian, like that of the artist, is to enlarge our picture of the world, to give us a new way of looking at things, then the study of failure can often be as instructive and rewarding as the study of success.[31]

From this point on, the place of anarchism in academic analysis has been decisively side-lined by Marxism, which has had

> a long and dominating influence in the social sciences and humanities, especially since the 1960s. Anarchism has never achieved more than a toehold in the academic sphere and its intellectual depth has constantly been called into question.[32]

The war between Marxists and anarchists continued in an abated and often underground form after 1872 for another fifty years. In Russia the victorious Marxists, then Lenin and Trotsky and Stalin, had much more work to do in their determination to erase the anarchists completely, to ensure that today you will not find many open anarchists in Putin's sphere of influence. It is worth reminding ourselves of how desperately afraid the Marxists were of the anarchist convictions that would continue to appeal to the people as the new Russian leaders engaged in new horrors.

Fortunately not all accounts of the Bolshevik ruthless elimination of the libertarians and anarchists escaped the historical record, including an event that is much less well known than the Kronstadt rebellion, but which is of much more contemporary interest, because it occurred in southern Ukraine in the years 1917–1921. Caught uncomfortably as ever between east and west, the Ukraine in this period of the Russian civil war as well as during the First World War was at the centre of the battlefield between multiple combatants – the Bolsheviks, the Austro-German armies, the White forces and a local nationalist party led by nobles and landed gentry. All these wreaked material, social and moral destruction on the Ukrainian peasants, whose active resistance was led by Nestor Makhno, and is known as the Makhnovist movement. It was a defensive uprising mainly by peasants who were fiercely independent and were thus experimenting with various forms of self-management. The movement's features were:

> a profound distrust of non-working or privileged social groups; suspicion of political parties; rejection of all dictatorships over the people by any and all organisations; rejection of the principles of the State; complete self-direction of the working people and their affairs.[33]

This was very much the sort of bottom-up movement of the kind that Bakunin admired, and so much of its success and longevity hinged on the charisma, organising skill and courage of the young Makhno himself. There was very little involvement of anarchist thinkers and theoreticians, but as Peter Arshinov's history concludes, it was

> an anarchist movement of the working masses – not completely realised, not entirely crystallised, but striving toward the anarchist ideal and moving along the anarchist path.[34]

Despite fighting hard over a long period, the Makhnovist movement eventually, and indeed inevitably, fell to the Bolsheviks.[35]

By 1947 Voline (the pseudonym of Vsevolod Mikhailovitch Eichenbaum) had published, in French, *The Unknown Revolution*, his searing, detailed indictment of what had happened in USSR, both the direction and character of the revolution and its treatment of dissidents:

> [L]ogically and inevitably, any individual or group who dares not combat the government but simply doubts its infallibility, criticises it, contradicts it, or blames it for anything at all, is regarded as its enemy and therefore as an enemy of the truth … The Anarchists have been exterminated in Russia, they can exist there no longer, simply because they defended the very principle of the Social Revolution, because they struggled for the real economic, political, and social freedom of the people …[36]

For Voline, the anarchist lesson for history is clear:

> Any attempt to achieve the Social Revolution with the help of a State, a government and political action – even though that attempt is very sincere, very energetic, favoured by circumstances, and supported by the masses – will inevitably lead to State capitalism, the worst form of capitalism, which has absolutely nothing to do with the march of humanity toward a Socialist society. Such is the lesson for the world to be drawn from the tremendous and decisive Bolshevik experiment, a lesson that lends powerful support to the libertarian thesis, and which, in the light of events, will soon be understood by all.[37]

This lesson was indeed understood by many of the left and right, though perhaps not by President Putin, who I imagine does not keep Voline and Bakunin among his bedside reading. But where does this leave the anarchists? What lessons have they learned?

There are two plain and painful facts. The first is that nowhere in the world is there a society that has abolished the State. Without question the anarchists' warnings about the dangers of Marxism were prophetic because their understanding about the nature of a State meant they saw through much of the communist rhetoric from a very early stage. But being right about the faults of the communists does not make them right about the alternative that they proffered. Almost 150 years after the death of Bakunin, 100 after the collapse of the Makhnovist movement, and almost eighty after the fall of the Catalonian anarchists in the Spanish civil war, the anarchists have not yet produced a society that has successfully murdered the State, nor are there any indications that such a society is about to be born.

The second unpalatable fact is that the anarchists severely underestimated the resilience of the State, which surely is more firmly entrenched than it was in Bakunin's time. Much of the world is controlled by State communism; Western Europe and the USA are capitalist democratic States; and the rest of the world, notably Africa, South America and the Muslim countries, constitute many other varieties of State formation. And where there is much civil war, as in parts of Africa, it is often held to be a result of a weak central State, not of the State per se. The task of murdering the State has become very much more difficult. As for the ideas about education and schooling propounded by Bakunin and the other founding figures, which we have yet to explore, we must acknowledge that schooling is everywhere under greater State control than it ever was in Bakunin's time.

Interestingly, Bakunin was the most significant anarchist figure to the students at the time of the May 1968 unrest in Paris, which was in parts violent, though it triggered even greater violence in response, especially from the police. James Joll records how the sense of revolution was being experienced:

> The feeling of liberation and excitement which participation in the revolts in Paris produced is documented in every report one reads and in every

> conversation with participants. For these young people, the revolutionary movement is not only the pattern of future society which Bakunin believed that it should be: it *is* future society. Their Utopia is realised here and now in the process of revolution itself.[38]

The idea was put succinctly by German anarchist Gustav Landauer – who died in 1919, when he was murdered by Bavarian counter-revolutionaries – in words so often quoted by the new anarchists that they became virtually their motto:

> The entire system would vanish without a trace if the people began *to constitute themselves as a people apart from the State* … The State is a social relationship; a certain way of people relating to one another. It can be destroyed by creating new social relationships; i.e., by people relating to one another differently.[39]

The enduring significance of this statement is brought out in Charles Maurer's reading:

> Political revolutions may be necessary before a revolution can take place, but the social revolution must be prepared for in advance so that it can take over when the necessary destruction is completed and the task of rebuilding can and must be faced. The preparations must be directed toward the establishment of a new society … For Landauer socialism was both the preparation *and* the social revolution.[40]

In 1900 Landauer set out his personal position more fully in a letter:

> I deem "anarchism" the best term to describe my understanding of life. It is not true that I have abandoned the belief in a future anarchist society. I have only questioned the belief that such a society can be established any time soon by men and women of today.[41]

This conviction was mirrored by Colin Ward in England.

> The task of the anarchist is not … to dream about the future society; rather it is to act as anarchistically as he can within the present society … the choice between libertarian and authoritarian solutions is not a once-and-for-all cataclysmic struggle, it is a series of running engagements, most of them never concluded.[42]

This seems to go further than Landauer, but not so far as David Stafford, who bluntly said, 'There can be no such thing as an anarchist society: or if there can it is such a remote goal that … it becomes a deception.'[43]

This looks like a considerable watering down of Bakunin's position during the period of the 'new anarchism'. Bakunin was a complex figure – with huge personal magnetism and incurable optimism, but a man who could also be illogical, self-contradictory, erratic, unpredictable, devious and secretive[44] – whose reputation today has often been overshadowed by Kropotkin's. Must his idea of an anarchist-inspired revolution be abandoned? Is the answer to the anarchist question *Can the State be successfully murdered?* a firm and incontrovertible negative? All reasonable questions, to be sure, but before reaching any firm conclusions, perhaps we should turn to the USA, where the spirit of rebellion and revolution has deeper surviving roots than in the United Kingdom.

Notes

1 Consider, for example, May (1994), Purkis and Bowen (2004), Rousselle and Evren (2011), Carlin and Wallin (2014), Klausen and Martel (2011) and especially Newman (2016).
2 See Franks et al. (2018) for the best recent overview.
3 See Shone (2013), Chapter 8, for an excellent recent assessment of Stirner's place.
4 Ritter (1980: 3).
5 Richards (1965: 53).
6 Richards (1965: 57).
7 Richards (1965: 59).
8 See Gordon in Franks et al. (2018) for an overview.
9 Goodman, 'Anarchism and Revolution' in Stoehr (2010).
10 Watt (1982: 14 and 16).
11 Franks (2006: 261, 264f).
12 Marshall (1992: iv).
13 Cole (1954: 316, 333).
14 Guérin (1970: 5).
15 Landauer, 1901, in Kuhn (2010: 85). For a current overview of violence for anarchists and anti-fascists, see Bray (2017), Chapter 6.
16 Dolgoff (1980: 329).
17 Maximoff (1953: 287).
18 Dolgoff (1980: 145).
19 Quoted by Guérin (1970: 25).
20 Dolgoff (1980: 133, see also 339).
21 Maximoff (1953: 298).
22 Dolgoff (1980: 334).
23 Maximoff (1953: 376–7).
24 Dolgoff (1980: 155).
25 Dolgoff (1980: 99).
26 Dolgoff (1980: 319).
27 Dolgoff (1980: 338).
28 Dolgoff (1980: 330).
29 Voline (1974: 245).
30 Dolgoff (1980: 25).
31 Joll (1964, second ed. 1979: viii).
32 Purkis in Purkis and Bowen (1997: 40).
33 Arshinov (1974: 81).
34 Arshinov (1974: 241).
35 For what Stalin did to the Ukraine in the early 1930s, see Applebaum (2018).

36 Voline (1974: 350, 387).
37 Voline (1974: 389).
38 Apter and Joll (1971: 217).
39 Landauer in Kuhn (2010: 214, original emphasis). This is most commonly quoted, in a slightly different translation, from Ward (1973, 1982 ed.: 19), for which no source is cited.
40 Maurer (1971: 96).
41 Landauer in Kuhn (2010: 303).
42 Ward quoted by David Stafford in Apter and Joll (1971).
43 Apter and Joll (1971: 94).
44 All words used by Anthony Masters in his biography of Bakunin (1974).

3

MURDERING THE STATE, IN AMERICAN DESCHOOLER STYLE

> Truth consists in nothing other than man's revelation of himself, and thereto belongs the discovery of himself, the liberation from all that is alien, the uttermost abstraction or release from all authority, the re-won naturalness. Such thoroughly true men are not supplied by school; if they are nevertheless there, they are there *in spite* of school.
>
> Max Stirner, 1842

> Everywhere to this day children are forced almost by violence to go to school and parents are forced, by the severity of the law or by cunning – the holding out of advantages – to send their children to school; whereas the common people everywhere study of their own accord and regard education as good.
>
> Leo Tolstoy, 1862, quoted in Pinch and Armstrong (1982)

In most countries the abolition of the State seems further away than ever: the common solution to the flaws in current models of schooling has been yet more State intervention, more centralisation. Indeed, in England since the 1970s governments of all colours have regularly introduced Acts of Parliament on schooling that have massively increased the work of government education ministries (under various names) and their associated agencies (ever increasing under a bewildering variety of names, usually with short lives). All of this was done in the name of educational improvement and the constant appeal to the raising of standards. Some of this government activity was not well received, some was widely welcomed, yet there was relatively little opposition *in principle* to this continuing extension of State involvement in education.

All anarchism's founding fathers, for whom the State and its abolition was a central tenet of their faith, were dead before the Second World War and the introduction of the famous 1944 Education Act that transformed secondary schooling in England and Wales and then the 1988 Education Reform Act that extended State control over the school curriculum and means of assessment. Had they lived, they would have been utterly appalled at this persistent interference by the State and its repeated tinkering in educational provision. But the anarchists are not alone in this regard, for most politicians of all parties at the beginning of the twentieth century would have been equally dumbfounded at the extent of later centralisation. It is much harder than it was in Bakunin's time to imagine what life would be like if the State were to be abolished, because it is simply a taken-for-granted part of our lives. Apart from the anarchists, few people think that the question *Could and should the State be abolished?* is worth a moment's consideration. The agreed issue is *How can we make the State work better?* and perhaps also *Should and could the State be smaller?* If we are to get to the heart of anarchism we shall have to ask many questions about the State that at first sight appear to defy common sense.

We are all to some degree prisoners of our present, and the further away we move back in time the harder it is to capture what the common sense was 100 years ago, or 500, or 5,000, or 10,000. We are not, of course, entirely trapped by our present, because we have evidence about the past and how life was lived then and we have imagination to project how life might be lived in the future. Both the distant past and the distant future can be seen, as once famously said, only through a glass darkly. To do so is to some degree to stand outside the frame we use to make sense of our everyday lives. There is always an understandable tendency to use the lens by which we interpret and act in the present to view and make sense of past and future. We so easily impose on people of the past or imagined future a way of thinking that is not theirs at all and indeed may be utterly alien and incomprehensible to them. What is common sense to us today was not common sense to people in the past, and vice versa. The common sense that people will develop in future will not be our common sense either.

So an interesting question arises: is there an underlying *structure* to common sense that is shared by all forms of common sense – past, present or future – despite the huge variations in the content of common sense that is shaped by the enormous varieties of culture, circumstances and experiences in which humans are embedded? Alfred Schütz was an Austrian philosopher who brought together sociology and phenomenology in a way that throws light on this, by analysing the nature of common-sense thinking in everyday lives. Our lives are enacted for the most part without having to do much hard thinking, because our routines save us the trouble. These become troublesome only when something very unexpected happens and our usual way of making sense breaks down. For most of the time daily life proceeds smoothly enough. If it were not so, life would be exasperating and difficult to manage. Schütz puts it this way:

> Only a very small part of my knowledge of the world originates within my personal experience. The greater part is socially derived, handed down to me by my friends, my parents, my teachers and the teachers of my

> teachers. I am taught not only how to define the environment (that is, the typical features of the relatively natural aspect of the world prevailing in the in-group as the *unquestioned but always questionable* sum total of things taken for granted until further notice), but also how typical constructs have to be formed … [which include] ways of life, methods of coming to terms with the environment, efficient recipes for the use of typical means of bringing about typical ends in typical situations.[1]

These recipes lie behind our ways of making sense of events and in particular of what and why other people do what they do. The recipes also furnish us with the options for how we can behave normally.

In a brilliant short essay Schütz took the situation of a stranger to expose when the taken-for-granted recipes on which we rely for life-as-normal break down. Strangers find themselves in groups or situations with which they are unfamiliar, and where they find it difficult to know what is going on and how to behave. The more remote the culture of the approached group is from the strangers', the more difficult they find it to cope, because their own recipes for negotiating everyday life do not work, and the recipes being used by the members of the approached group make little sense.

So one way in which to explore the taken-for-granted common sense of any group of people in any place and at any time in history is to treat that common sense as questionable, to act as if we do not understand what is going on so that their recipes for managing life can be unpacked. This is what social anthropologists must to some degree do in studying people in other and often very different settings or cultures. By close and careful observation and enquiry, and by participation in the life of the chosen group, anthropologists dissect how life in a different culture, which at first meeting is often puzzling and difficult to understand for the stranger-anthropologist, actually does make sense and has its own rationality, if one very unlike the stranger's own. Anthropologists cannot trust their own common sense, for this may mislead them into thinking that they understand behaviour or events, when in reality by using their own recipe they are misunderstanding. Anthropologists need access to the recipes of others if they are to make proper sense of what they witness.

We shall look later at a number of anthropological studies to see what light they throw on anarchism and education, but the anthropologist's method can be adopted within our own culture, by treating it as *anthropologically strange*, that is, treating what is actually familiar as if it were unfamiliar, treating what goes on in schooling as if one were an anthropologist or a visitor from another planet. The stranger may be handicapped in getting by in an unfamiliar situation, but he has some advantages too, for he achieves a kind of objectivity that derives from

> his own bitter experience of the limits of the "thinking as usual", which has taught him that a man may lose his status, his rules of guidance, and

> even his history and that the normal way of life is always far less guaranteed than it seems. Therefore, the stranger discerns, frequently with a grievous clear-sightedness, the rising of a crisis which may menace the whole foundation of the "relatively natural conception of the world", while also those symptoms pass unnoticed by the members of the in-group, who rely on the continuance of their customary way of life.[2]

Anarchists constantly insist that there are alternative ways of making our social lives; treating the way we normally do things as 'anthropologically strange' exposes the essential fragility of life-as-usual. What anarchism offers is more realistic and realisable than it seems to those who do not recognise just how soft and unstable is the ground of their common-sense rejection of anarchist ideas as unrealistic. The State must not be treated as unquestioned and unquestionable.

A parallel approach to that of Schütz is taken by the Australian philosopher Charles Taylor in his development of the concept of *social imaginary*.[3] Its general concern is with the intellectual schemes people use when they think about social reality, but more specifically with

> the ways in which they imagine their social existence, how they fit together with others, how things go on between them and their fellows, the expectations which are normally met, in the deeper normative notions and images which underlie these expectations.[4]

In any epoch its social imaginary is shared by most people in that society. It is their taken-for-granted world, the layman's sociology and psychology, which are normally and routinely both unquestioned and unquestionable, and which allow them to have enough in common to carry out their collective life without much trouble. From time to time there is a major disruption – such as a war or a revolution – that undermines the social imaginary, forces a questioning of what was previously unquestioned, and leads to a new social imaginary with a better fit to the new circumstances. Taylor's books trace the transition from a hierarchical social imaginary of the Middle Ages to the later more egalitarian one of the modern Western world, though Keith Thomas's books on early modern England, exploring continuities and discontinuities in shifting imaginaries, are in some ways of greater relevance to my arguments in this book.[5]

It is of course more difficult to unpack the social imaginaries that dominate in contemporary society. One of these is bureaucracy. The German sociologist Max Weber argued that bureaucracy was the rational way in which to run an organisation, since it promoted efficiency and reduced the risk of favouritism, nepotism and similar forms of corruption.[6] In a bureaucracy, tasks are specialised, within a hierarchical structure of authority, and are filled through a process of selection by qualification for office, the holders of which follow set rules and requirements. The American anthropologist David Graeber has argued that by now this bureaucratic spirit has run riot: it pervades so much of our lives that he calls this the age of total bureaucratisation. Yes, there are benefits of bureaucracy as Weber pointed out, but at the same time there are aspects of bureaucratisation that we all complain about or even use as part of political campaigns. A key element of the argument for Brexit was the complaint about the bloated European Union (EU) bureaucracy with its allegedly petty rules and excessive regulations. But all the talk about restoring sovereignty and 'taking back control' was about removing one form of State control, the EU, for an increase in another State control, our own. There was never a question of getting rid of the EU and our own State at the same time. Politicians may claim they are against 'red tape', but when in office spend much of their time drafting legislation that creates yet more rules and regulations:

> Bureaucratic practices, habits, and sensibilities engulf us. Our lives have come to be organised around the filling out of forms. Yet the language we have to talk about these things is not just woefully inadequate – it might as well have been designed to make the problem worse. We need to find a way to talk about what it is we actually object to in this process, to speak honestly about the violence it entails, but at the same time, to understand what is appealing about it, what sustains it, which elements carry within them some potential for redemption in a truly free society which are considered the inevitable price to pay for living in any complex society, which can and should be eliminated entirely.[7]

In his own life as a university teacher Graeber has felt the impact of this bureaucratisation:

> [T]he last thirty years have seen a veritable explosion of the proportion of working hours spent on administrative paperwork, at the expense of pretty much everything else. In my own university, for instance, we have not only more administrative staff than faculty, but the faculty, too, are expected to spend at least as much time on administrative responsibilities as on teaching and research combined … The result is a sea of documents about the fostering of "imagination" and "creativity", set in an environment that might as well have been designed to strangle any actual manifestations of imagination and creativity in the cradle.[8]

Much the same would be said by university teachers in the UK, but in my experience it is teachers in schools who have borne a far greater burden of such bureaucratisation in the form of lesson plans, assessments of student progress and achievements, the setting of targets, plans for their own professional development, and so on. Graeber observes that much of the bureaucratisation has grown through State control of what was originally undertaken in non-bureaucratic ways outside the State.[9] For instance, the welfare state, now infamously bureaucratic, arose as the State took over from trades unions, neighbourhood associations, cooperatives and working-class parties and organisations of various sorts. This was also to become a core argument of English anarchists such as Colin Ward, as we shall see in the next chapter.

How could we break free from something so deeply pervasive? Is unpacking the welfare state and seeking to return it to its origins, whilst maintaining its benefits but losing the excessive bureaucracy, a feasible project? An anarchist might argue that if the State is left intact, wrenching a part of it from the State would never be more than a temporary measure, for in due course the State would reassert itself in a recreation of the welfare state. Is this an argument for revolution rather than reform?

At the time of a revolution, be it actual, hoped for or predicted, people in that pre-revolutionary society are caught in their current social imaginary and will be poorly placed to imagine or predict the form of the post-revolutionary social imaginary. History does not suggest we have had much success in foreseeing the consequences of deep change, whether planned or not. The failure of early anarchists and Marxists to say much about post-revolutionary change exposes their own unavoidable but unrecognised difficulty in somehow standing outside their own social imaginary. It is particularly acute for the anarchists, because they were more vague than the Marxists about how the transition to the new society would be managed. When the transition did take place in Russia under the Marxists, their incapacity to think ahead about the management of the transition was soon exposed. The French and Russian revolutions were started in the name of the people against oppressive rulers, but both ended up with a reign of terror. The outcome of the French Revolution did not cure the later anarchists of their hopes of a revolution and it did not stimulate the necessary hard thinking about how their revolution would avoid a similar fate. The inescapable complexity of the transition from one social imaginary to another means all social revolutions are destined to fail at least to some degree and in ways that are not, and could never be, anticipated.

Karl Popper came to a similar conclusion, but for different reasons. In his powerful critique of Marx and Plato, he made a distinction between *utopian engineering*, of which he took Marx and Plato as exemplars, though each of a different kind, and *piecemeal engineering*, which he regarded as the only rational alternative. He argues that the utopian blueprint requires a strong centralised rule of the few, and which therefore is likely to lead to a dictatorship and authoritarian rule,[10] just as Bakunin suggested. The case for piecemeal social engineering is based on several advantages. Instead of fighting to achieve some rather abstract ideal, the piecemeal engineer identifies and seeks to rectify the outstanding evils, an approach that is more likely to command common consent. If the remedy goes wrong, the damage is likely to be limited and continuous readjustments can be made relatively easily. By contrast, utopian engineers do not like to admit and learn from mistakes and retain a dogmatic attachment to the blueprint. For Popper, utopian engineering is

> the reconstruction of society, i.e. very sweeping changes whose practical consequences are hard to calculate, owing to our limited experiences. It claims to plan rationally for the whole of society, although we do not possess anything like the factual knowledge which would be necessary to make good such an ambitious claim. We cannot possess such knowledge since we have insufficient practical experience in this kind of planning, and knowledge of facts must be based upon experience. At present, the sociological knowledge necessary for large-scale engineering is simply non-existent.[11]

Both Taylor's social imaginary and Popper's utopian engineering expose flaws in the notion of a deep revolution, and point to a preference for reform over revolution. A programme of reform is slower and less likely to engage the passions, especially among the young and impatient, but is less likely to go disastrously wrong. Some bits of the State can be amputated, but then if unintended consequences reveal the loss to have been mistaken, the bits can be grafted back. New practices can be tried and tested, and if the test result is negative, they can be abandoned as failed experiments before it is too late.

The question for the anarchists then becomes this: can something as deeply embedded and as resistant to change as the modern State be abolished by piecemeal engineering and a range of reforms designed to eliminate current ills? You may, like me, have mixed feelings about the State. In recent years there has been widespread disaffection from the main political parties; cynicism about the integrity of politicians and political leaders; a growing gap between rich and poor and obscene levels of pay and bonuses to the bosses of large companies, both private and public, including universities; an increasing level of child poverty and a worrying reliance on food banks for so many of the poor. Would these and other problems be solved by the abolition of the State? Moreover there are today many benefits of the State, such as a national health service and some powerful protections of individual liberty. The danger in entirely abolishing the State is one of throwing out the baby benefits with the bathwater failings. To many people the abolition of the State will seem today to be more out of the question than it was at the time of anarchism's founding fathers, not least because today the State provides so many more valued services than it did then.

The modern State seems to be here to stay; it might be, and indeed often is, modified to varying degrees and in different ways, but I believe much more is needed in this regard than the main political parties are prepared to offer, or more precisely more in practice than in their promises that too often are shamelessly broken. Piecemeal social engineering along anarchistic lines, that is, a relatively slow social revolution without any sudden political revolution, and based on anarchism's core principles and ways of operating, has an obvious attraction and a distinctive place in the possibilities for the future of society. Some of today's anarchists go along with gradualism as the only sensible route to a better society. The American anarchist Paul Goodman, of whom much more shortly, certainly took this line:

> In anarchist theory, "revolution" means the moment when the structure of the authority is loosed, so that free functioning can occur. The aim is to open areas of freedom and defend them. In complicated modern societies it is probably safest to work at this piecemeal, avoiding chaos, which tends to produce dictatorship. To Marxists, on the other hand, "revolution" means the moment in which a new State apparatus takes power and runs things its own way. From the anarchist point of view, this is "counter-revolution", since there is a new authority to oppose. But Marxists insist that piecemeal change is mere reformism ...[12]

Arguably any revolutionary approach, then, places too much stress on the destructive part of change and assigns insufficient importance to the creative or constructive aspect of change, all the new practices that need to be designed as replacements for what has been discontinued. In other words, change demands an essential innovative component, which ought to be at the very heart of its appeal, especially in education. Bakunin early in his career said, 'The passion for destruction is a creative passion too',[13] but never clarified the relation between the two passions.

Joseph Schumpeter, however, did exactly that in his conception of 'creative destruction'. Although he was cautious about transitions from one social structure to another without doing damage to human values, he understood that the success of capitalist economies depended on the incessant drive to innovation. When their innovations dwindle, firms begin to die, and this so easily happens to large and established firms whose leaders tend to be much more risk-averse than those of smaller, newer enterprises. The creative destruction of innovation constantly sweeps out old products, old enterprises and old organisational forms. For Schumpeter, the painful destruction of products, practices and companies is the essential complement of the vital innovative processes that fuel capitalism. Is there a lesson for anarchists here, not least in the matter of the future of schooling?

> Destruction, however painful, is the necessary price of creative progress toward a better material life. But the current sequence is vital: creative innovation first, then the destruction of obstacles that lie in its way.[14]

Anarchists must first and foremost be innovators. Adoption of piecemeal engineering, with a Schumpeterian twist that puts innovation first, as a prerequisite and precursor of larger radical change, is potentially what anarchism can best offer as strategy for social improvement. The welfare state, for example, cannot be dismantled through a restoration of its smaller-scale predecessors, but it could be removed if it were accompanied by an explosion of new forms of potential replacements that were innovated as appropriate to the changed conditions. If the aim is to reduce State control of schooling, then alternatives to schooling will have to be devised even whilst the State control of schooling continues.

There is thus be a five-fold challenge for anarchists:

1. Which bits of the existing State should be eliminated?
2. Which bits of the existing State should be preserved, preferably outside State control?
3. Which elements of the desired anarchist society need to be innovated, and how?
4. How much of the innovation in 3 might be a development of what is in 2?
5. How far do we need to go with 2, 3 and 4 before dealing with 1?

There are some obvious objections to this line. How could one be assured that there would be sufficient innovation of high quality to generate replacements for what is to be dismantled? Why would the State invest in innovation that was designed to replace the State? Moreover the State might attempt to incorporate any innovations into itself in order to control them. This is exactly what happened to some of the best bottom-up educational innovations, such as Records of Achievement and Assessment for Learning, both of which were simplified, distorted and ruined once the State took over. All this is, of course, the very danger that Bakunin correctly detected in the Marxist refusal to abolish the State. A State does not let go easily and has many ways of resisting alternative forms, the most favoured of which is to praise the practices that have emerged outside the State, to claim that it is stepping in to disseminate them more widely, and then to adjust them to fit existing State policies. Control is reasserted or, in today's terms, 'taken back'. States might fear abolitionists, but it knows from long experience exactly how to deal with would-be reformers. The bigger or more radical in scope any newcomer idea might be, the less likely the State can incorporate it, and so the most favoured responses are to ignore it or to ridicule it as unworkable and lacking in public support.

Is this what happened to school reformers in the USA and to all the proposals that emerged from the flowering of the critiques of schooling and of the wider society during the decade from the beginning of the 1960s to the early 1970s? The man who can justifiably be called the inspirational pioneer here is Paul Goodman, who died in 1972, just as the great wave of new ideas for schooling was at its peak and his voice was most needed. Although Goodman's writing covered an astonishing range, including city planning, psychiatry, literary criticism, politics and poetry as well as education, he first came to wide public attention in 1960 with a book of startling originality and an arresting title, *Growing Up Absurd*.

The context for the writing was 1957 and Sputnik, which had, to the consternation of the Americans, been launched by the Russians. Feeling deeply humiliated, the politicians began to question the quality of the education system. The Carnegie Corporation invited James B. Conant, a distinguished diplomat and former President of Harvard, to investigate. His first report of 1959, *The American High School Today*, failed to please conservatives, but a key recommendation asserted that the high schools were not doing enough to identify, challenge and support the academically talented, some 15 per cent of the school population. A lengthy battle was about to start in the USA between radical reformers in education and the flustered forces of conservatism. It is said that in the rest of his life Conant did much to set in train the standards and accountability movement that still dominates today.

Growing Up Absurd is in typical Goodman style – a passionate indictment of the ills of his society and their impact on people, especially the young. His concern lies between what he calls the Organised System, that is, government, large corporations, advertising, etc., and the growing disaffection of the young people who came to characterise the 1960s generation throughout the Western world. He aims his attack at a wide range of targets that provide the conditions in which people have to live but deny them anything that might qualify as the good life:

> These conditions are absurd, they don't make sense; and yet millions, who to all appearances are human beings, behave as though they were the normal course of things … It then becomes necessary to stop short and make a choice: Either/Or. Either one drifts with their absurd system of ideas, believing that this is the human community. Or one dissents totally from their system of ideas and stands as a lonely human being … For many young people, however, the difficulties of growing up have been so great that they do think that they are faced with a critical choice: Either/Or. They have this picture of themselves and of the world. And then unfortunately, whichever way they choose tends to create in fact the very metaphysical crisis that they have imagined. If they choose to conform to the organised system, reaping its rewards, they do so with a crash, working at it, marrying it, raising their standard of living, and feeling cynical about what they are doing. If they choose totally to dissent, they don't work at changing institutions as radical youth used to, but they stop washing their faces, take to drugs, and become punch-drunk, or slaphappy. Either way they lose the objective changeable world. They have early resigned.[15]

Goodman's narrower focus on education took two more years to mature, with *Compulsory Miseducation* in 1964 (but not published in the UK until 1971). He singles out James Conant for attack, since his work represented a kind of watershed in educational thinking that 'puts us back to the ideology of Imperial Germany, or on a par with contemporary Russia'.[16] Some extracts give a flavour of his full-frontal assault:

> I doubt that, at present or with any reforms that are conceived under present school administration, going to school is the best use of the time of life of the majority of youth.

> Education is a natural community function and occurs inevitably ... it by no means follows that the complicated artifact of a school system has much to do with education, and certainly not with good education.

> There is a mass superstition, underwritten by additional billions every year, that adolescents must continue going to school ... Like any mass belief, the superstition that schooling is the only path to success is self-proving.

> If we are going to experiment with real universal education that educates, we are going to have to start by getting rid of compulsory schooling altogether ... There are thinkable alternatives.

> When, at a meeting, I offer that perhaps we already have too much formal schooling ... the others look at me oddly and proceed to discuss how to get more money for schools.

> I would suggest that ... we experiment, giving the school money directly to the high-school-age adolescents, for any plausible self-chosen educational proposals, such as purposeful travel or individual enterprise. This would also, of course, lead to the proliferation of experimental schools.

Few people were ready for this. The last extract above shows him to have been an early advocate of what later became known as education voucher schemes, though Goodman had a much more liberal and more interesting view on how the money might be spent, since it is far more radical than simply choice of school. It is clear that his proposals would be the death knell of State schooling as hitherto known, for the survival of post-primary schools would depend on their responsiveness to student demand and preference, and schools might lose out on a potentially massive scale if students preferred the many other options to conventional schools. At this period Goodman alone was able to stand outside the dominant social imaginary about schooling: it took seven more years before school critics of comparable stature were to emerge in 1971.

Before this remarkable year there were other, if less radical, critics of schools. One of the most trenchant was an ordinary teacher, John Holt (1923–1985) who kept an extraordinary diary, published as *How Children Fail* (1964), reporting his observations of life in his elementary school classroom, which he often treated as 'anthropologically strange', noticing things that for the most part teachers regard as quite unremarkable, just the ways things are in the daily routines of working with children. He made himself stop looking at his pupils through the lens of what they were supposed to be doing or not doing, to disclose what they were really thinking and doing, and why. Holt's style is deceptively simple. It is as if through his observations he is having a conversation with himself, expressing his surprise, even dismay, at what he has observed, or almost unwillingly inferred from observation:

> It has become clear ... that these children see school almost entirely in terms of the day-to-day and hour-to-hour tasks that we impose on them ... For children, the central business of school is not learning, whatever this vague term means; it is getting these tasks done, or at least out of the way with a minimum of effort and unpleasantness. Each task is an end in itself. The children don't care how they dispose of it. If they can get it out of the way by doing it, they will do it. If experience has taught them that this does not work very well, they will turn to other means, illegitimate means, that wholly defeat whatever purpose the task giver may have had in mind.[17]

So pupils develop coping strategies. If, for instance, a teacher asks a question and you don't know the answer, check first how many hands go up. If many go up, put yours up too, since there is a low chance of being invited to answer, but you will give the impression at best that you know, and at worst, well, at least you are being keen. Holt skilfully unmasks such strategies, which entirely defeat the point of what the teacher is trying to do:

> A year ago I was wondering how a child's fears might influence his strategies. This year's work has told me. The strategies of most of these kids have been consistently self-centred, self-protective, aimed above all else at avoiding trouble, embarrassment, punishment, disapproval, or the loss of status. This is particularly true of the ones who have had a tough time in school.[18]

It is with some reluctance that Holt decides why these 10-year-old children do this. And his conclusion goes absolutely against the very atmosphere that he and other teachers wanted to create in the classroom:

> These self-limiting and self-defeating strategies are dictated, above all else, by fear. For many years I have been asking myself why intelligent children act unintelligently at school. The simple answer is, "because they're scared".[19]

Does Holt exaggerate just how fearful children are in classrooms? It is hard to say, but the difficulty in deciding is that the fear is hidden: the pupils do not want their fear to show, and this determination not to show it grows with age. Armed with Holt's insights, I once followed two girls aged 14, considered to be 'difficult' by their teachers, as they moved from class to class in their seven-period day. How, from my observation, was their day? They had by this stage in their school careers learned not to be afraid because they no longer had the remotest interest in pleasing the teacher:

> School lessons for them appeared to be like seven very dull television programmes, which could not be switched off. They did not want to watch and made little effort to do so; occasionally the volume rose to a very high level, so they listened; occasionally the programme became sufficiently interesting to command their attention, but it was never more than a momentary diversion from the general monotony. Part of the problem appeared to be that they were not, in fact, seven new independent programmes: all of them were serials, which demanded some knowledge of earlier episodes. Indeed, most of the teachers generously provided a recapitulation of earlier episodes at the beginning of every lesson. But the girls had lost track of the story long ago. Two of the programmes were, in fact, repeats; since their first broadcast had aroused no interest in the girls, it is not surprising that the repeat evoked no new response. So these two girls responded as most of us do when faced with broadcasts of low quality that we cannot switch off: they talked through the broadcast whenever they could. The easiest form of resistance was to treat the lessons as background noise, which from time to time interrupted their utterly absorbing sisterly gossip. And of course they made the most of the commercial breaks, as it were: they were the first to leave each lesson and the last to arrive at the next one.[20]

Were these girls afraid? No, they were not cowed by their teachers, but they were indeed afraid of being of being made either to look stupid or like a good student, both of which were possible risks of behaving well. It is a self-protective fear, always to be kept well hidden for it must never show, and so teachers often don't see it.

It is never easy for a teacher, especially in the early years of a career, to capture the pupils' perspective on the demands of a classroom and to grasp the problems they have in learning. The result of Holt's scrutiny is a penetrating study of what it is like to be a child in school from the inside. For a practising teacher his diary contains more insights than many a book on educational psychology and will remain a classic long after the psychology books are out of date.

At this stage Holt believed that what he had observed could be corrected by better classroom practice by teachers with a better insight into the pupils' perspective. He has no interest in murdering the school, let alone State schooling; this came later, as we shall see, when the urge to assassinate had time to mature within him.

If one puts Goodman and Holt together, it is clear how the ground had been prepared for Neil Postman and Charles Weingartner's *Teaching as a Subversive Activity* (1969), which is overtly and dramatically radical, as the title indicates. Following the national dramas of Cuba and Vietnam, whilst they claim to be 'simple and romantic' men, they believe in the improvability of the human condition through intelligent, daring and revitalising innovation in education. School is 'inflicted' on pupils and they explain this use of the word 'because we believe that the way schools are currently conducted does very little, and quite probably nothing, to enhance our chances of mutual survival'.[21] They point to the assertions of many of their contemporaries about the negative impact of schooling – explicitly including Holt's claim that it is based on fear and Goodman's that it induces alienation – and so conclude that schooling must be radically changed if students are to be prepared for a rapidly changing world, a task that demands a fundamental shift in the purposes of schooling. Their proposals would certainly change schools and classrooms as they had hitherto been conceived, since they would eliminate:

- all 'subjects' or 'courses'
- all use of textbooks
- all requirements of students
- all tests and grades
- all questions to which the teacher knows the answer.

They claimed that these proposals had been successfully implemented somewhere and their wish is to create schools where *all of them* take effect in one place.

The book was a best-seller among teachers, who delighted in some of their ideas, such as the need to develop in learners the art of 'crap-detecting' – the title of their first chapter – but no more than a very small number of their ideas could ever be adopted in State schools. The main flaw was that they stripped away from schools almost everything that was recognisably schooling, whilst leaving the institution of the school intact. Twenty-five years later Postman was to write another book with a good title: *The End of Education* (1995). Was this to be a report on how schools had carried out the earlier vision? Did it mean that the school could no longer survive the advocated reforms? Sadly, the title misleads, for the book is about the *ends* of schooling, that is, its purposes, not its demise, a forlorn hope that State schooling could be saved by a rethinking of its aims.

Deep reform of the kind proposed by Postman and Weingartner, if ever implemented in full in State schools, an extremely unlikely event, would inevitably kill the school after a short spell on a life support system, so why not go straight for an assassination? This logical conclusion was drawn a mere two years later and bluntly expressed in Everett Reimer's title, *School Is Dead* (1971), a stark proclamation of the murder of the State's favourite child, the school, even though this announcement proved to be a touch premature.

The same year – 1971, *annus mirabilis* – saw the publication of Ivan Illich's *Deschooling Society*, which with Reimer's book caused a sensation with their dramatic titles. The two men had worked together for many years and the books are so very similar that one wonders why they did not collaborate on the one book. Both acknowledged a debt to Paolo Freire, whose *Pedagogy of the Oppressed* appeared in the previous year.[22] Was this a competition to get published first? Illich, I think, reached the largest readership. His advantage over the others was two-fold: he set his critique of schooling in a broader social framework and he had a more captivating style, writing with a passion and hyperbole worthy of a Bakunin. His apocalyptic prophecies fitted the ethos of the period, even if they never happened in his predicted time-scale. Illich's arguments for educational change are not merely radical but set within a critique of society, since 'welfare bureaucracies claim a professional, political and financial monopoly over the social imagination':[23] society as a whole, not just education, needed to be deschooled. Yes, he wanted to murder the school, but would this not require the State to be murdered too?

He starts with a phenomenology of the school, refusing to make the taken-for-granted assumption of many educational critics that schools and education are inextricably intertwined. He rejects the basic premises: that children belong in school; that they learn in school; and that they can be taught only in school. The credibility of schooling rests on the assumption that learning is a result of teaching by a professional:

> In school we are taught that valuable learning is the result of attendance; that the value of learning increases with the amount of input; and, finally, that this value can be measured and documented by grades and certificates ... A person who is self-taught or taught by a non-professional outside the school is immediately rendered suspect.

The book is littered with provocative and memorable aphorisms:

> The school system is a modern phenomenon, as is the childhood it produces ... If there were no age-specific and obligatory learning institution, "childhood" would go out of production.

> Only by segregating human beings in the category of childhood could we ever get them to submit to the authority of a schoolteacher.

> School initiates young people into a world where everything can be measured, including their imaginations.

> To deschool means to abolish the power of one person to oblige another person to attend a meeting.

Illich's solutions were ahead of his time, in his advocacy of much out-of-school learning, the creation of skill centres and networks ('learning webs') that connect those who want to learn with people ready and willing to help them to do so. His solutions rested heavily on his faith in technological developments – the internet, mobile devices – that lay many years into the future.

For Reimer, the State's monopoly of schooling had to be terminated, and replaced by a plurality of alternatives, ones that would be more integrated with life and work. He explores how his vaunted alternatives could be paid for. Like all those, anarchists or not, who want to abolish the State's control over schooling and education, he sees no alternative but to move the money directly to learners and to other providers. He uses the term 'personal educational account' rather than 'voucher', but the idea is similar: it would be provided to each individual at birth, with choices about how to spend it, or supplement it, throughout life. He writes well of the importance of skill models for young people. They are potentially in plentiful supply but the way schooling works is to make their availability too scarce a resource: schools bar skill models who are not qualified teachers from access to the young people who could learn much from them.

In the UK, some teachers, especially those in initial training, responded with excitement and an enthusiasm to debate the Illich/Reimer diagnosis as well as at least some of their solutions, even though both offered the most fundamental of challenges to their careers as teachers. The insights of both men so often touched raw nerves, reservations and concerns that teachers had about their work but were too remote from the daily grind to be acknowledged or debated with colleagues in staffrooms.

Paul Goodman was as brilliant a writer as Illich, but in a very different way. His thinking was ahead of Illich's, if expressed in a less organised and coherent a form. Both men were prophetic: Goodman's style was that of a passionate conversationalist, displaying his huge personal charisma that attracted followers among the young. Illich's style had a finer apocalyptic grandeur, which increased the apparent novelty of his message, but underplayed the extent to which he relied on insights made previously by others. Illich and Reiner evidently knew Paul Goodman, but neither drew explicitly on *Compulsory Miseducation*, though clearly it had been very influential on them.

Illich's critique of the State was thought to be too radical: deschooling was not limited to educational institutions, but extended to de-institutionalising much more widely in society. Going far beyond a programme of educational reform made many feel uncomfortable. Illich fully recognised that his was a cause without a party. Those on the mainstream left had policies that would entail greater intervention by the State, not its abolition or reduction. Moreover, Illich fell foul of the old problem of lacking clarity about the transition process. His book, he said, 'is not the place to elaborate on the political, social, economic, financial, and technical feasibility'[24] of his proposals, and he took exactly the same line in *Tools for Conviviality* (1973), which is closer to an anarchist philosophy. But that is exactly what was needed if his proposals were to be taken seriously and certainly what a political party might expect from him. By declining to elaborate as he knew many readers would expect, he risked consigning his work to longer-term oblivion, despite its having raised for many working in education both challenges to conventional thinking and fresh ideas on how things might be very different.

Reimer explicitly assigned a revolutionary role to schools, though not a violent one:

> Effective alternatives to schools cannot occur without other widespread changes in society. But there is no point waiting for other changes to bring about a change in education. Unless educational alternatives are planned and pursued there is no assurance that they will occur no matter what else happens. If they do not, the other changes are likely to be superficial and short-lived. Educational change, on the other hand, will bring other fundamental changes in its wake.[25]

This simply fails to do justice to the very complicated relationship between societal change and educational change. The first sentence is true, though the main obstacle to the creation of alternatives is the State's control over schooling. The claim in the last sentence in the above paragraph strikes me as false. The extent of educational change is heavily constrained by what the State allows, and the more the State centralises its control over schooling, the less scope there is for teachers to innovate within schools, let alone create or support more radical alternatives. Moreover, even when school leaders and teachers do manage to innovate in spite of State control and surveillance, the innovations tend to die out when the innovator leaves or moves on: the system rarely allows such innovation to become institutionalised and so resistant to the departure of their originators. There is no evidence that innovations in schools, even those that prosper despite the lack State approval, lead to fundamental changes in society at large. The closing pages of Reimer's book turn to the pressing need to rethink the nature of community. Both Reimer and Illich are weak on this, whereas to anarchists this is an absolutely central part of their vision for a society without the State and its control over schooling, as we shall see later.

In short, Reimer and Illich badly misjudged how the revolution they sought might ever come about. They were not short of admirers, but they did not recruit able disciples to advance the deschooling argument in more persuasive but less rhetorical detail. More importantly, they lacked serious followers and allies, both in education and in the wider society, which is so essential to the success of any social revolution. As stars in the firmament of educational reform they faded with surprising speed. Their wonderful core idea of networks for peer matching, skill exchanges and easier access to resources did come about, sadly not in education but in the wider society in the form of manifold adult dating agencies, social media and innovations such as Wikipedia. No fundamental reform of schooling will ever take place that does not, in some degree, draw on ideas that they first floated.

In the UK a few academics in the education field, notably Ian Lister at the University of York, became enthusiastic supporters of deschooling,[26] but most simply enjoyed the rough and tumble of debate that had been aroused, since some deep questions about the purposes and value of schooling had been raised and were worth discussion. But were they to be taken seriously? An alarmed ex-headteacher, Harry Judge, then at Oxford University, fired off *School Is Not*

Yet Dead (1974) – did anyone really think the murder had taken place or was even about to? Robin Barrow offered an incisive claim-by-claim and idea-by-idea dissection of the deschoolers as part of his *Radical Education: A Critique of Freeschooling and Deschooling* (1978). Determined to see them off the territory defended by serious educationists, Barrow had little patience with their 'emotionalism, contradiction and incoherence', rejecting what he saw as

> the steady flow of reductionism, argument by analogy, retreat into metaphor, obscurity masquerading as profundity, jargon, assertion without the backing of evidence, and conceptual ambiguity.[27]

Barrow, irritated by the polemics, misses the point that this is in part what makes their books and ideas so stimulating to read and think about. He scores some good points, not least in turning 'crap-detecting' back onto the concept's inventors, but there are so many minor cavils and so much trivial nit-picking that the book becomes as overblown as those he attacks. This is an academic conservative's defence against barbarians at the gates of the academy. This is a demolition job – and a telling one – from a philosopher, not a sociologist.

Neither Judge nor Barrow was an Edmund Burke reflecting on the education revolution in America, but then was one really needed? Revolutionary deschooling was dying, not the schools, which seemed to be as resistant to attempted murder as the State itself. The tragedy of deschooling's demise was that some of the best radical writing was bundled up with deschooling, particularly that of Goodman and Holt, which deserved more careful scrutiny, and was in danger of being decanted along with Reimer and Illich.[28]

As for the anarchists themselves, it is not clear whether Illich felt he might find a home with them despite their not being a party, and as a Catholic priest he might well have been given the cold shoulder. In any event, at this time the anarchists were far more comfortable with a man whom they could count as 'one of us', namely the self-identified anarchist and atheist Paul Goodman, who is also a much finer thinker and writer. At the time Illich was barely mentioned in anarchist books, but Colin Ward took him seriously:

> Nothing could be more mistaken than the tendency to dismiss the ideas [deschoolers] represent as a passing fad. They have raised questions which may change the whole course of the continuing debate on education.[29]

Younger writers on anarchism, such as Emily Charkin (2014), are not making this mistake. Was Illich an anarchist? As far as I know he did not so self-identify, but Judith Suissa[30] is surely right that he 'belongs to the same broad dissenting tradition as many anarchist thinkers'. Had Illich openly identified himself with the anarchists, or shown how his ideas related to theirs, he would have influenced subsequent anarchist writing on education and probably found a more permanent place in their history. Illich strikes me as too egocentric for that.

The Marxists did not ignore or take the risk of underestimating Illich, who unintentionally provided them with a golden opportunity to make their own case. They acknowledged the rapturous reception given to his writing in some quarters and moved quickly to offer a neo-Marxist attack in the form of Herbert Gintis's radical critique published in the high-status *Harvard Educational Review* in 1972. In Britain this piece was later given a high profile among teachers by its inclusion as the opening chapter in an Open University (OU) education course reader entitled *Schooling and Capitalism: A Sociological Reader* (Dale et al., 1976), but with no extract from any of Illich's own writing or any balancing defence of him, or indeed a response from an anarchist. It all caused something of a sensation because at that time very large numbers of non-graduate teachers were pursuing an OU degree as the profession moved towards becoming an all-graduate one. There were inevitable complaints that the course was inappropriately biased towards neo-Marxist perspectives and the OU was forced to conduct an investigation.[31]

From the point of view of many practising teachers the neo-Marxist account had little in the way of practical advice, whereas Illich gave them a much clearer vision of what might be done. Gintis rejected Illich's analysis as simplistic and therefore his programme as a diversion from the immensely complex and demanding political, organisational, intellectual and personal demands of revolutionary reconstruction. It is crucial, he suggested, that educators and students who had been attracted to him should move beyond him.[32]

Most teachers, however, wanted something more satisfying and usable than suggestions that they wait for the Marxist revolution, as was also the case with Labour Party politicians. The Samuel Bowles and Herbert Gintis full-scale argument in *Schooling in Capitalist America: Educational Reform and the Contradictions of Economic Life*, published in the same year as the OU course reader, was of no greater practical value to teachers. Nobody at the time expected to see the imminent collapse of the Soviet Union, or the subsequent embrace of capitalism by the Russians and the Chinese, in a desperate attempt to retain control of the State whilst suppressing any notion that the State itself might be partially to blame for communism's evident failures.

So has there been a loss of faith by anarchists and their sympathisers in the idea of a direct abolition of the State, certainly for anything that resembles a Bakunin-style revolution? If it be the school rather than the State that should be murdered, why would the State consent? Is Bakunin's revolutionary fervour utterly out of date in today's USA and UK, where the State is much more deeply entrenched in the social imaginary than in Bakunin's time? Is the State's life now safe from assassination? Is piecemeal social engineering the accepted way forward?

As the 1970s came to an end, what was the considered response of the English to the ferment abroad and at home of the previous decade? After the collapse of Edward Heath's government in March 1974 the Conservatives spent five years waiting impatiently for a return to government and had time to develop their ideas. So how would they respond when Margaret Thatcher took power in 1979? Or had the anarchists taken heart by the turmoil of the previous decade and were they ready for battle against her?

Notes

1 Schütz in Natanson (1963: 312 emphasis added).
2 Schütz in Brodersen (1964) and Cosin et al. (1971: 32).
3 Taylor (2004, 2007). In his development of the concept Taylor draws on the work of Benedict Anderson and Cornelius Castoriadis.
4 Taylor (2007: 171, 2004: 23).
5 Thomas (2009, 2018).
6 Weber (1922).
7 Graeber (2015: 44).
8 Graeber (2015: 133–4).
9 Graeber (2015: 153).
10 Popper (1945: 159).
11 Popper (1945: 161–2).
12 Goodman in Stoehr (2010: 93).
13 Dolgoff (1980: 57).
14 McCraw (2007: 501).
15 Goodman (1960: 113–14).
16 Goodman (1964: 21).
17 Holt (1964: 37–9).
18 Holt (1964: 91).
19 Holt (1964: 92).
20 Hargreaves (1982: 3).
21 Postman and Weingartner (1969: xiii).
22 Richard Kahn and Douglas Kellner (2007) offer an interesting comparison between Freire and Illich. Freire's 'critical pedagogy', which is often closer to neo-Marxism than to anarchism, was taken up particularly in Mexico and South America, but has had a more limited following in the UK.
23 Illich (1971: 3).
24 Illich (1971: 83).
25 Reimer (1971: 137).
26 Lister (1974).
27 Barrow (1978: 177).
28 Smith (1983: 142).
29 Ward and Fyson (1973: 5).
30 Suissa (2006: 153).
31 See the discussion of pro-Marxist bias in Hammersley, M., 'Accusation of Marxist bias in the sociology of education during the 1970s: academic freedom under threat?' No date. Available online: www.open.ac.uk/blogs/History-of-the-OU/?p=2584.
32 Gintis in Dale et al. (1976: 8).

4

ANARCHISM ENGLISH-STYLE

State murder by other means

> Since government, even in its best state, is an evil, the object principally to be aimed at is that we should have as little of it as the general peace of human society will permit.
>
> William Godwin, 1793

> The best government will be the one which most steadfastly sets before itself the ideal of preparing its own euthanasia.
>
> Victor Branford, 1914

The rapid development during the 1960s of the youth movements and youth subcultures[1] and their challenges to the traditional deference to authority that culminated in student riots in France may in some quarters have seemed to be an opportunity for anarchist thinking and writers to move into the mainstream, for they were closer to the zeitgeist than the main parties of left and right. But it did not happen. British anarchist writing was a valuable if rather neglected baby, one with some distinguished forebears, but it was thrown out with the American deschooling bathwater. The anarchists, never mainstream, had been writing critically about education in the 1960s, but were too often lurking in the sidelines of educational debate during the 1970s.

In England some of the unease over student unrest focused on the alleged domination of the education system by a vague and ill-defined 'education establishment', and especially those who were training the next generation of classroom teachers in teacher education, which allegedly consisted of left-wing idealists, even Marxists, with ideas championing 'progressive' education and spreading a gospel of 'teaching as a subversive activity' and even deschooling.[2]

At the same time the secondary school sector was in turmoil. Back in 1965 the government had required all local education authorities to submit plans for the conversion to comprehensive schools and this was now taking place. This was seen as a threat to the grammar schools and Prime Minister Harold Wilson tried to calm troubled waters by claiming, disingenuously, that comprehensive reorganisation meant 'grammar schools for all'.[3]

All this was said to amount to a dangerous assault on traditional schools and traditional education, so inevitably precipitating a fall in *education standards* – a notion that was to become the watchword, in the UK as much as in the USA, and the litmus test of every idea and every change for the next half-century.

A life-threatening virus was supposedly spreading throughout the system, and especially the universities, and like any virulent plague it needed to be eradicated as quickly and firmly as possible. Student sit-ins in English universities were the spark that ignited the flames of a fierce right-wing counter-revolution, for such was apparently needed. The response took the form of pamphleteering in the 1970s, initially with C. Brian Cox's Black Papers, the first two of which were published in 1969 and were without doubt the most influential of a series that continued for several years. Each of these pamphlets consisted of articles, mainly short, penned mostly by distinguished figures in intellectual, academic and literary circles. As well as student sit-ins and the panic they created among some vice-chancellors and senior administrators in the universities, the targets for the contributors were: progressive teaching, especially but not only in primary schools (A. S. Neill's Summerhill was a particular target for disseminating what were called 'utopian simplicities and progressive ideology'); the plans to abolish grammar schools and replace them with comprehensive schools; the expansion of higher education by which, in the Black Paper words of Kingsley Amis, 'more has meant worse'; and so-called *egalitarianism*, which was assumed to have a commonly agreed meaning and which was thought to be behind many of the ideas and actions of those who were threatening to ruin the education system as well as wider society.

The first Black Paper was entitled *Fight for Education*: the ambiguity of whether the first word was a noun or a verb in the imperative was probably intentional. The pamphlet's tone was militant, as captured in publicity about it sent to teachers:

> Much of this agitation could be dismissed as extremist nonsense, if it were not that major administrative decisions are resulting from these so-called "liberal" views. The new fashionable anarchy flies in the face of human nature, for it holds that children and students will work from natural inclination rather than the desire for reward. It also, like other anarchisms [*sic*], tends to be more authoritarian than the system it seeks to replace. Parents, children, students and teachers are to be forced to accept the new changes whether they like them or not. Our purpose is not to resist the exciting challenges of new ideas but to make clear that certain theories thought to be new and progressive are in fact old-fashioned and products of a bankrupt romanticism.[4]

Publication of the first two Black Papers caused a storm that spread from educational and academic circles into wider political circles and the media. They led later to a regular flow of pamphlets by Caroline Cox (no relation of Brian) and John Marks, as well as by Sheila Lawlor at the think tank Centre for Policy Studies and then Politeia, all of which heavily targeted university teachers in schools of education and local education authorities. The political right was by this means setting much of the agenda, including Prime Minister Callaghan's famous Ruskin College speech of 1976 that marked a shift in education policy making in the Labour Party.

The pamphleteers' longer-term reward was Kenneth Baker's Education Reform Act of 1988, which was a massive act of centralisation in education with the introduction of an extensive national curriculum and elaborate schemes of pupil assessment. A small sop of decentralisation was included: schools would have more control over their budgets, but this was decentralisation from the local authorities, not central government. The Act was built on what was largely a political consensus between left and right on how best to maintain and improve 'education standards' and ensure schools' accountability for reaching them. These are the issues that came to dominate debate about schooling from 1988 to this day. It was no longer worth talking about scaling down schooling or listening to the pleas in some quarters for a reduction in the minimum school leaving age; how to gain control over the operation and direction of the school system was the territory on which education's war was to be fought. This was not a case of taking back control, but of seizing it on an unprecedented scale.

Just as 100 years earlier Bakunin's anarchism had lost its duel with Marxism and so faded as a major international force, so yet again anarchism lost its post-1960s opportunity when the first battle in the new war about 'education standards' after the Black Papers was triumphantly won. Illich and deschooling were not the only casualties. Two important British anarchist writers were quietly sliding out of view, though not as a direct result of being subjected to right-wing denunciation, which would have oxygenated them with needed publicity.

Herbert Read (1893–1968), a Yorkshire man, acquired a global reputation for his championing of modern art, about which he was a prolific writer. He writes very well, and is readable to this day. Who now could fail to warm to what he wrote in 1951?

> The most terrifying object in the world today is not the atom bomb but the political cliché … To listen to the purveyors of clichés, the so-called statesmen, the politicians, generals and journalists, has become an inescapable infliction.[5]

Two years later he was knighted, for his contribution to literature not art, and unsurprisingly he was then shunned by many of his fellow anarchists. In fact, he wrote well too about his commitment to anarchism, but without originality. Was he up for murdering the State? No. He accepted Bakunin's view that a violent revolution simply changes the people who control the State, whereas an anarchist favours a spontaneous uprising that would kill the State:

> When we have got hold of the right principles of social relations, there will then be the problem of putting them into practice. The idea that this can be done by some kind of revolutionary *coup d'état* is really very childish. You cannot readjust individuals to society, or society to individuals, by purely external measures of control … The only way a biological or organismic change can be induced is by training or education. The word *revolution* should largely disappear from our propaganda, to be replaced by the word *education* … This is fundamental anarchism – anarchist fundamentalism. It discards for ever the romantic conception of anarchism – conspiracy, assassination, citizen armies, the barricades. All that kind of futile agitation has long been obsolete: but it was finally blown into oblivion by the atomic bomb. The power of the State, of our enemy, is now absolute. We cannot struggle against it *on the plane of force*, on the material plane. Our action must be piecemeal, non-violent, insidious, and universally pervasive.[6]

In the First World War he had won a DSO and MC; the impact on him of the Second World War and Stalin's rule in Russia were immense:

> When Stalin and his works are trampled into the dust by new generations of men, the poetry of Pasternak and the music of Shostakovich will still be as real as on the day they emerged from the minds of their creators[7] … In my lifetime I believe we have suffered a decisive disillusion in this respect: we have once more experienced the truth that revolution carried out by force leaves force in command of the ensuing situation. We should abandon the rhetoric of revolt, not changing anything in our hearts or our understanding. Our ideals must be as bold as ever, and our strategy must be realistic.[8]

He became a pacifist – 'anarchism naturally implies pacifism'[9] – and a supporter of nuclear disarmament. On the first day of June, 1942, looking through his window at the golden rain falling from the laburnum trees as he thought about the RAF bombing of Cologne and the two armies in the Ukraine counting their dead, he started to write the final chapter of *Education Through Art* (1925), with its conclusion 'The necessary revolution' and an epigraph from Tolstoy. Read's legacy and his reputation as an anarchist rest in part on his educational theorising. Whilst much of his writing on art is not much read today, his philosophy of education through the arts has deservedly exerted a lasting influence, for the simple reason that he is the most eloquent and persuasive champion of arts education in the whole of the twentieth century.

The book reflects his deep interest in Plato (but carefully discounting the fascist-leaning aspects) as well as many psychologists and philosophers of his day, now mainly forgotten. Plato, he says, understood the purpose of education, and the thesis of the book is Plato's idea that art should be the basis of education. Immediately he sets this thesis within the central tension of anarchism, between the individualist and the communalist:

> It is assumed, then, that the general purpose of education is to foster the growth of what is individual in each human being, at the same time harmonising the individuality thus educed with the organic unity of the social group to which the individual belongs. It will be demonstrated in the pages which follow that in this process *aesthetic education* is fundamental.[10]

> All the possible words we may use to express the purpose of education – tuition, instruction, upbringing, discipline, the acquisition of knowledge, the inculcation of manners or morality – all these reduce to two complementary processes, which we can best describe as "individual growth" and "social initiation".[11]

By 'art' he often means 'the arts', which are listed as follows:

Visual education – EYE – design
Plastic education – TOUCH – design
Musical education – EAR – music
Kinetic education – MUSCLES – dance
Verbal education – SPEECH – poetry and drama
Constructive education – THOUGHT – craft

He thus places the arts and design-technology at the centre of the curriculum, and spends nearly 300 pages justifying this. Over the years many people have been persuaded by his argument, as I was in 1982 by placing community studies and the arts at the core of a recommended curriculum in the comprehensive school.[12] Read also understands the role played by the arts in the nurturing of creativity:

> We begin our life in unity – the physical unity of the mother and child, to which corresponds the emotional unity of love. We should build on that original unity, extending it first to the family, where the seeds of hatred are so easily and so often sown, and then to the school, and so by stages to the farm, the workshop, the village and the whole community. But the basis of unity at each successive stage, as at the first stage, is creativity. We unite to create, and the pattern of creation is in nature, and we discover and conform to this pattern by all the methods of artistic activity – by music, by dancing and drama, but also by working together and living together, for, in a sane civilisation, these two are arts of the same natural pattern.[13]

Since the Baker reforms of the 1988 Act, however, the arts have been squeezed further and further out of the curriculum as the separate (and somewhat misleadingly called) 'academic' subjects hold sway within a curriculum that has lost touch with the purposes of education that Read rightly set out before he even turned to curriculum content. Despite political talk about the value of creativity, in the light of the paramount importance assigned to it both by our flourishing arts industries and, significantly, by employers who understand its relevance for innovation in the workplace, governments merely reflect the word back without showing the slightest sign that they have in fact reflected on Read's message.

Read never loses sight of the individual learner in the anarchist fusion of individual and community. As a result, he is wary about the claims of the school to cater for it, since the State tends to enforce uniformity:

> Mankind is naturally differentiated into many types, and to press all these types into the same mould must inevitably lead to distortions and repressions. Schools should be of many kinds, following different methods and catering for different dispositions.[14]

And even so, it is essential to accept the limitations of what school alone can ever achieve:

> The first essential institutions [to a process of revitalisation] will be educational institutions. By "educational institutions" I do not necessarily mean "schools", certainly not the abattoirs of sensibility which go by that name today. To achieve "the greatest lucidity, purity, and simplicity" – that should be the aim of education. Such an achievement is likelier to come from the workshop and the playing field than from the academy or grammar schools – in the context of work and the context of play, of work-play.[15]

He would not, I think, have been an enthusiast for comprehensive schools retaining their pupils for ever longer years.

Read's contribution to anarchism in Britain is well summarised by Carissa Honeywell in her fine portrait of his life and work:

> Read did not see anarchism as alien to British cultural and political traditions. He utilised anarchism in order to draw these national traditions into a vital political programme with which to challenge the pernicious erosion of liberties in an era of war, mass consumerism and state growth. In so doing he attempted to revive the anarchist tradition of highlighting its pertinence to contemporary radical dilemmas regarding the exercise of individual conscience, war, nationhood, the growth of the state and the commitments of the socialist tradition.[16]

Read had much in common with his friend, thirty years his junior, Colin Ward (1924–2010), including their admiration for Peter Kropotkin,[17] the other Russian founding father of anarchism. Together they established a distinctive English variation on anarchist themes and their application in education. Ward, whose life and work are now gaining increased recognition,[18] left school at 15 and was a classic autodidact. He was, as a result, a man of considerable breadth of interest and accomplishment, so his writing covers many fields and the links between them, and unlike that of Illich, it displays his personal modesty. Happily, an anthology of his work that illustrates his enormous breadth of interest is now available.[19]

Ward, like John Holt, observed children very closely and so wrote insightfully about childhood with its inbuilt curiosity and creativity. He worked in architectural practices and for the Town and Country Planning Association and also spent five years as a teacher of general studies in a technical college. He was a key player in the field of environmental education, by which pupils were to be directly involved in the exploration of the urban spaces in which they lived – an inherent part of his commitment to improving life and education in the city, in London, its streets, architecture and buildings, neighbourhoods, parks, public places and, most of all, planning and housing – in a deeper crisis now, if in a different form, than when Ward was writing.

In his short *Anarchy in Action* (1973, second edition 1982) – one of the best introductions to the subject by a modern British writer – he says that his book

> is not about strategies for revolution and it is not involved with speculation on the way an anarchist society would function. It is about ways in which people organise *themselves* in any kind of human society, whether we care to categorise those societies as primitive, traditional, capitalist or communist ... We win over our fellow citizens to anarchist ideas, precisely through drawing upon the common experience of the informal, transient, self-organising networks of relationships that in fact make the human community possible, rather than through the rejection of existing society as a whole in favour of some future society where some different kind of humanity will live in perfect harmony.[20]

From the start, he makes clear his position on the State: he is no utopian yearning for paradise, nor a revolutionary hatching plots for a quick murder. Indeed, he quotes the founding fathers of anarchism showing how in the Russian revolution the Marxists took over the State, not to create liberty and justice but to exercise a new centralising authoritarianism. For Ward, as for Read, a violent revolution would be incompatible with the firmly held objection to coercion.

Ward cites Malatesta's statement that revolution is the destruction of coercive ties and their replacement by 'the autonomy of groups, of communes, of regions, revolution is the free federation brought about by a desire for brotherhood'.[21] This sentiment lies behind much of Ward's work. He defends himself against a charge of utopianism and says he wants to build on this same 'common experience and common knowledge' because 'for an anarchist, a society which organises itself without authority, is always in existence like a seed beneath the snow, buried under the weight of the State'.[22]

The future, then, is built upon what people do in the present, where lie the seeds of better things not far ahead:

> Once you begin to look at human society from an anarchist point of view you discover that the alternatives are already there, in the interstices of the dominant power structure.[23]

This attitude is in stark contrast to one that sees an unbridgeable disjunction between present oppression and misery and an altogether different and better future that has yet to be experienced. It is the positive version of piecemeal engineering, looking not so much for ills to be remedied but for a future-already-in-the-present that with the right treatment can be made to flourish. It is in this present that he resolves the tension between anarchism's individualist and communitarian strands, as Carissa Honeywell notes:

> The individualist notion of self-help and the more communitarian emphasis on mutual aid combined comfortably in the writing of Ward to form the underpinning for his notion of freedom as socially responsible autonomy. Ward highlighted the anarchist tradition as relevant to contemporary concerns and an appropriate approach to modern politics.[24]

Ward felt very strongly about education, which, though integral to his thinking, forms only a portion of his writing. He is conversant with Illich, Reimer and Holt. In his 1973 anarchist primer, he reveals parallel concerns in the chapter entitled 'Schools no longer':

> An immense effort by well-intentioned reformers has gone into the attempt to manipulate the education system to provide equality of opportunity, but this has simply resulted in a theoretical and illusory equal start in a competition to become more and more unequal. The greater the sums of money that are poured into the education industries of the world, the smaller the benefit to the people at the bottom of the educational, occupational and social hierarchy. The universal education system turns out to be yet another way in which the poor subsidise the rich.[25]

He is naturally strongly drawn to Paul Goodman's writing, on both education and wider social issues. Goodman and Ward were brothers in arms. Why do I say this? Both had deep interests in housing, architecture and urban planning, as well as in education. Indeed, Ward was to spend much of his energies in promoting the active participation of people in the planning decisions that affected their lives. Admirers of Goodman often forget that his brother Paul was an architect and they jointly wrote *Communitas: Means of Livelihood and Ways of Life*, a guide to the planning of cities from basic principles, first published in 1947 to rave reviews. Consider this:

> The best defense against planning – and people do need defense against planners – is to become informed about the plan that is indeed existent and operating in our lives; and to learn to take the initiative in proposing or supporting reasoned changes. Such action is not only a defense but good in itself, for to make positive decisions for one's community, rather than being regimented by others' decisions, is one of the noble acts of man … For a community is not a construction, a bold Utopian model; its chief part is always people, busy or idle, en masse or a few at a time. And the problem of community planning is not like arranging people for the play or a ballet, for there are no outside spectators, there are only actors; nor are they actors of a scenario but agents of their own needs – though it's a grand thing for us to be not altogether unconscious of forming a beautiful and elaborate city by how we look and move, that's a proud feeling. What we want is style. Style, power and grace. These come only, burning, from need and flowing feeling; and that fire brought to focus by viable character and habits.[26]

This is classic Paul Goodman style. Ward would have entirely shared the sentiment, but would have expressed it differently. He could, however, be equally forceful about the involvement of the young in urban decision making. Consider this:

> Education for participation in planning is not education about aesthetics, or about cost-benefit or central place theory, it is education about power … The only way a child learns to ride a bike is by riding one, and the only way that anyone, child or adult, learns to participate in environmental decision-making is by doing so … People, young or old, learn through involvement, and not through being told … participation does not consist of having ready-made decisions explained to you, it implies *making* decisions. In school this means that we are not educating for participation if we just pour in information about planning legislation and its background; we can only do it by involving the young in real issues and real controversies.[27]

Ward's and Goodman's concern with education and schooling was thus integral to their much wider fascination with life in cities and how they could be better designed and used to enhance the life of the communities within them. For both, the city environment was a powerful resource for learning that was ignored by the schools, which too often did not know how to draw on it. At the same time, the informal education of learning outside the school was an education in and for better citizenship in adult life. How could Ward not be attracted to the indictment of schools in *Compulsory Miseducation* for failing to provide the young with an adult world in which to grow up, which would mean

> experimenting with different kinds of school, no school at all, the real city as school, farm schools, practical apprenticeships, guided travel, work camps, little theatres and local newspapers, community service. Many others, that other people can think of, probably more than anything, we need a community and community spirit, in which many adults who know something, and not only professional teachers, will pay attention to the young ...[28] Throughout the educational system there is a desperate need for institutional variety and interims in which a youth can find himself. If we are going to require as much schooling as we do, we must arrange for breaks and return-points, otherwise the schooling inevitably becomes spirit-breaking and regimentation. In my opinion, however, a much more reasonable overall pattern is to structure all of society and the whole environment as educative, with the schools playing the much more particular and traditional role of giving intensive training when it is needed and sought.[29]

At this stage Ward's optimism was boosted by the student unrest that upset those on the political right:

> The students' revolt was a microcosm of anarchy, spontaneous self-directed activity replacing the power structure by a network of autonomous groups and individuals. What the students experienced was that sense of liberation that comes from taking your own decisions and assuming your own responsibilities. It is an experience that we need to carry far beyond the privileged world of higher education, into the factory, the neighbourhood, the daily lives of people everywhere.[30]

He did not remove this paragraph from the 1982 edition, after events were taking a different turn: his faith in the young did not falter.

In the fateful year of 1971, Colin Ward and Anthony Fyson were appointed straight from the classroom to initiate the Town and Country Planning Association's *Bulletin of Environmental Education*. The first book they produced was *Streetwork: The Exploding School* (1973).

> It is a book about *ideas*: ideas of the environment, as *the* educational resource, ideas of the enquiring school, the school without walls, the school as a vehicle of citizen participation in environmental decisions, ideas above all about a "problem-oriented" approach to environmental education.[31]

This is indeed 'anarchism in action' applied to school-age education. And it is a clear parallel to Paul Goodman's injunction in *Compulsory Miseducation*

> to use the city itself as the school – in streets, cafeterias, stores, movies, museums, parks and factories … it is the model of Athenian education.[32]

In 1969 Goodman conceptualised this out-of-school or in-the-community learning as *incidental learning* that occurs unselfconsciously and almost unnoticed as part of young people's activities outside school in their interactions with one another, with adults and with places and things, in contrast with the *intentional pedagogy* of the schoolroom:

> The chief occupation of educators should be to see to it that the activities of society provide incidental education … If necessary, we must invent new useful activities that offer educational opportunities.[33]

This is precisely what Ward did with astonishing energy and ingenuity. Incidental education and informal learning continue to be undervalued, despite a recent reminder of their importance in the UK by Frank Coffield.[34]

A neat way in which to capture the spirit of Ward's writing is through the parable he tells, that of the adventure playground. We are all familiar with the piece of ground that contains the ubiquitous swings and roundabouts. This is well-intentioned public provision, but one often not much used by children. The one in my village that I can see through my study window is an example: a child is rarely to be seen there. Ward points out why. Swings and roundabouts can only be used in one way: they cater for no fantasies, no developing skills, no emulation of adult activities, and call for no mental effort and very little physical effort. Very little is added by supplementing a climbing frame (we have one of those too; do you?), which is also unattractive to older children. Ward then compares these with what children do for pleasure when the right opportunity occurs or, more to the point, when it is provided for them:

> That there should be anything novel in simply providing facilities for the spontaneous unorganised activities of childhood is an indication of how deeply rooted in our social behaviour is the urge to control, direct and limit the flow of life. But when they get the chance, in the country, or where there are large gardens, woods or bits of waste land, what are the children doing? Enclosing space, making caves, tents, dens, from old bricks, bits of wood and corrugated iron. Finding some corner which the adult world has passed over and making it their own.[35]

These are the activities that help to develop all the qualities that are neglected in publicly provided play spaces. The challenge then is, armed with the knowledge of what children do when they get the chance, to make similar provision in towns and cities. Ward provides actual examples, in which the children are given low-cost materials, often essentially waste or scrap, especially wood, and then the tools by which they might build, dig, sculpt and so on, but as the children themselves see fit, not as directed by an adult.

Yes, initially there was some egocentric behaviour as individuals argued over who possessed what, some squabbling, pushing and shoving, some destruction. But all this soon gave way, even in the least propitious of circumstances, to the formation of groups, of mixed age and sex, engaging happily in collaborative activities, even in the least propitious ones, of surprising size and ambition. Notably, there is less vandalism and fewer accidents. It is clearly a story as parable:

> The adventure playground is a free society in miniature, with the same tensions and ever-changing harmonies, the same diversity and spontaneity, the same unforced growth of co-operation and release of individual qualities and communal sense, which lie dormant in a society devoted to competition and competitiveness.[36]

Colin Ward was more concerned with education outside school rather than within it, with complements to the classroom rather than to what the deschoolers conceived as alternatives to, and competitors for, schooling. There were, however, serious attempts at a kind of alternative *within* State schooling, that is, successful attempts to create schools that would win approval from anarchists. The space for this was in the secondary modern schools, which before the development of comprehensive schools were attended by two-thirds or more of the pupil population. One such school was St George-in-the-East, in Stepney, East London, whose head teacher in the post-war period from 1945–1955 was Alex Bloom, whose achievements have been celebrated by Michael Fielding, in a book celebrating Colin Ward. Bloom was unusual in banning all punishment, especially corporal, and competition, streaming by ability/achievement, and the awarding of individual prizes. 'For Bloom, at the root of much bad education, in both its broad and narrow senses, is the utilisation of fear, either as a motivating device for good behaviour or as a deterrence for its opposite'.[37] He pioneered innovations that today would be called 'student voice' and 'personalised learning'. It is no surprise that on his death Colin Ward penned an obituary.

Significantly it was a secondary modern school that Bloom was able to run based on such a philosophy. Throughout the post-war period secondary modern schools enjoyed what to a contemporary eye is an astonishing degree of autonomy, with very little oversight by the local education authorities. Inspections by HMI were rare events and secondary moderns in very poor areas were not interfered with unless there was some kind of scandal. Today this space has been closed and it is virtually impossible to imagine that St George-in-the-East could now survive. The State removed the freedom that Bloom enjoyed in two ways. The first was the reorganisation of secondary schooling along comprehensive lines, the result of which was the takeover of senior staff roles, including that of the head teacher, by former grammar school teachers, with much more traditional views and practices. The second was the later control over the curriculum and student test performance exercised by the State, as well as pressures from regular Ofsted inspections and ratings. These two changes had some beneficial consequences. Some secondary modern schools that, even at this period, were falling well short of high standards, as illustrated in studies of individual schools by Partridge (1966) and Hargreaves (1967), were simply squeezed out. But it also eliminated the possibilities of different conceptions of schooling and experimentation with less conventional methods. The new social imaginary of schooling began to reduce diversity of provision in favour of homogeneity.

From the late 1960s various kinds of free school (that is, free from local authority control) were established, partly under the influence of the student unrest, and partly as a product of working-class community dissatisfaction with conventional schooling. They were all small, and run according to the principles of libertarian education – a maximum of student freedom and choice, no set lessons, few explicit rules if any, staff who behaved in ways quite unlike the conventional teachers the students resented. The only one I ever visited, the White Lion Free School in Islington, London, was famous in part because it became the subject of a book.[38] Most had a very short life: the White Lion closed in 1990. The school reforms of 1988 ensured the death of these free schools, until the term was revived by the Conservative Government in 2010 as the designation for a different kind of school. By this time most people had forgotten about the original free schools and the vast majority of teachers in schools today are completely unaware of their existence. We gratefully rely on John Shotton, who captured valuable evidence about them.[39]

Twenty years later, did the next generation of British radical thinkers build on the ideas of their British predecessors, such as Read and Ward, as well as Paul Goodman and the deschoolers? The change of government in 1997 provided an opportunity. Although anarchists always jealously guarded their distinct identity, they were always closer to socialism than to conservatism. However, a quarter of a century had passed, so to younger members of the left the deschoolers were no more than a dead bit of history, and in any event the new government's direction of travel was not heading in an anarchist direction. Indeed, many in the Labour Party did not regard New Labour as socialist at all. Herbert Read had detected this much earlier, in 1938, in disturbingly prescient words:

> Socialism is dynamic; it is a movement of society in a definite direction and it is the direction that matters most. In our conception of socialism, are we moving towards centralisation, concentration, depersonalisation; or are we moving towards individualisation, independence, and freedom? It seems to be that there can be no possible doubt as to which direction is the more desirable; and I am afraid that, at the moment, everywhere in the world we are moving in the wrong direction.[40]

Tom Bentley was director of the think tank Demos, appointed in 1998 aged 30 to this prestigious post. After an exhilarating eight years he moved to Australia. In 1998 he published *Learning Beyond the Classroom: Education for a Changing World*. At the beginning of the book we are told that:

> Effective education will have to extend beyond the classroom, using a broader range of resources – cultural, social, financial and physical – than we usually associate with education services … [The book] shows that creating a *revolution* in education requires us to think *far more radically* about the role of young people and the kinds of learning opportunities we offer them.[41]

What would this 'far more radical thinking' amount to? More radical than Ward or Goodman or Illich? Bentley refers to many projects designed to support 'active learning', particularly outside school. These projects, which are without question ones that would cultivate active learning, are mostly not linked directly to schools or teachers. Unlike Ward's books, this one is not in any way a resource book of ideas or practical activities for teachers, so it not clear how these projects would change anything that happens in and around schools. Indeed, schools are held at a rather discreet distance: they are not in the least under threat. Nor, of course, is the State. How could it be, for Bentley was soon appointed as a policy adviser to David Blunkett, New Labour's first Education Secretary.

Does this explain why there is not a single mention of Read or Ward, or of Goodman or Holt or Reimer? Were these simply too radical for Bentley? Or had he forgotten about them, since his favourite American sources are the more recent Howard Gardner and David Perkins? Or is it possible he was not familiar with their work? After all, *Compulsory Miseducation* had been published before he was born. Illich is mentioned just once, in acknowledgement of the similarity of some of his ideas, but then Bentley adds that 'this revolutionary vision was quickly dismissed'.[42] In fact, Illich's conception of networks of reference services, skill exchanges, peer-matching are far more imaginative than Bentley's notion of 'neighbourhood learning centres', an idea that is unelaborated despite the highly relevant earlier work of Ward and his friends and associates.

In a follow-up publication, *The Creative Age* (1999), written with Kimberly Seltzer, Bentley argues that in the age of the knowledge economy a key challenge for schools is to develop students' creative capacities. This involves a considerable degree of restructuring of schools, since students will need new skills, including the ability to:

- identify new problems, not just solve old ones
- transfer knowledge between different contexts
- combine knowledge from different disciplines

On the basis of studies of projects in several countries, Bentley makes the following recommendations:

- reduce the National Curriculum contents by half
- develop a curriculum model that includes project-based learning
- appoint school–community brokers for out-of-school opportunities

- make work placements integral to 50 per cent of degree courses
- develop inter-disciplinary teaching and learning

He concedes that such changes would 'provoke controversy and resistance'. Indeed, but in my experience the resistance would come less from teachers than from politicians, including the New Labour ministers, who would have thought such proposals a distraction from the standards agenda or feared the right-wing media attacks that such ideas would inevitably have provoked. None of the suggestions could be implemented in any depth or breadth without ministerial willingness to re-think schooling and the State's tight control of it. So none were.

Bentley was never in a position to make such a challenge. On appointment as Secretary of State, David Blunkett immediately brought Michael Barber into the Education Department as head of the Standards and Effectiveness Unit (SEU). Barber had earlier written his book *The Learning Game: Arguments for an Education Revolution* (1996) and was now a key figure in the writing of the White Paper, *Excellence in Schools* (1997), that was issued within weeks after the general election. Here are a few snippets to indicate the direction of policy:

> The preoccupation with school structure has absorbed a great deal of energy to little effect.
>
> There will be unrelenting pressure on schools and teachers for improvement.
>
> We are setting challenging targets which must be met.
>
> The first task of the education service is to ensure that every child is taught to read, write and add up. [There are] challenging national targets for the performance of 11 year-olds in English and maths.
>
> We are firmly committed to the regular inspection of schools by OFSTED.
>
> From September 1998, each school will be required to have challenging targets for improvement.
>
> We now have sound, consistent, national measures of pupil achievement for each school at each Key Stage of the National Curriculum.
>
> The publication of performance data benefits parents and acts as a spur to improve performance. We will publish more such data than ever before.

In short, the new government's education was not so much a break with policies established by Kenneth Baker but in many ways an extension of them – not a revolution by any standard. The approach was commonly summed up in three words: *standards not structures*. This left little fertile ground in which Bentley might plant something new. And the ground remained hostile to his ideas for the duration. Barber soon left the Department at Blair's request to head up a new Delivery Unit to be the progress-chaser or enforcer on other government departments. He was succeeded in the SEU by David Hopkins, but without any detectable change in policy.

Perhaps Bentley's closeness to government and the need for his think tank to influence government policy with practicable solutions limited his ability to challenge government control and its conservative conception of schooling. Even as a New Labour insider, he dared not stand very far outside the dominant social imaginary, and so schooling, let alone the State, could never be fundamentally questioned, let alone murdered. As a result, Bentley is unable to offer a radical vision of a different system in which to set his ideas: radical ideas always disappear quite fast if the framework in which they are intended to operate is not itself reconceptualised. What the anarchist or anarchism-leaning thinkers I have discussed in this chapter had in common was a vision of a fundamentally different society within which reconstructed schooling and education flow from the new model of society rather than being somehow grafted onto the existing one, in which the built-in antibodies naturally react with the very resistance that Bentley expected. Locked in the dominant State-centred social imaginary, Bentley's imagination founders and the magic that is the essential ingredient of persuasive visions is lacking. His ideas are undoubtedly part of the solution to the flaws in mass schooling, but in themselves they are insufficiently radical for the task at hand.

Whilst I would not wish to under-value some of the Blair government's policies or their commitment to increase education spending, one does have to ask: do the limitations of Bentley's book also characterise the whole of New Labour's readiness to think radically about education? I was very much around central government during the New Labour years and my impression was that there was indeed more radical thinking among ministers and advisers and among some civil servants. The complication was that Tony Blair was a strong centraliser *within* government. Any significant policy development nurtured in a Department had to be cleared by 10 Downing Street, which had its own policy advisers for each important area of government. In education, Number 10's education man was Andrew Adonis, an able and creative thinker, who whenever we met gave the impression of sharing New Labour's notorious worries about how the press or public might perceive any education policy and damn it as 'loony left'. Is this why the opportunity to re-think a more integrated examination system for the 16+ examinations was so tragically botched with the rejection of the Tomlinson Report?[43] Is this why, despite changes in government over the last forty years, education policy, from the point of view of a would-be radical reformer, has turned out to be more a history of continuity than of change?

From the late 1960s to the end of the century, then, the English anarchists had few opportunities to implement their ideas. They had no stomach for a direct attack on the State, not least because, except in the case of self-defence, violence was against their principles. They had mixed feelings about schools, recognising their weaknesses, but gave no more than half-hearted support for radical deschooling. So they looked for spaces in the interstices of State control over schooling where they could introduce positive innovations compatible with their values as well as opportunistic resistance to this control when they might get away with it – quietly seeking to tame the State through the milder versions of direct action. Rather than abolishing the State, they preferred constructively colonising the gaps in State control. Ambush would be better than assassination, a slow bleeding to death rather than a stab in the heart. As Colin Ward put it:

> Our task is not to gain power, but to erode it, to drain it away from the state … There is no final struggle, only a series of partisan struggles on a variety of fronts.[44]

Just how far have these 'partisan struggles' taken the anarchists since Ward wrote these words almost half a century ago? Some advances in the battle against the State and its control over schooling were fought on fronts quite other than those Ward had in mind; indeed, ones that might have dismayed him. One of these was started on English soil and the other in the USA. We cannot say, of course, how Ward would have reacted, but we can show some continuity between these two new fronts, English and American, through the anarchist writing of England's greatest anarchist thinker, who unbeknown to them was a unifying force. This means going back briefly to the end of the eighteenth century.

Notes

1 Hall and Jefferson (1975); Centre for Contemporary Cultural Studies (1981).
2 For an examination of the various publications of the Hillgate Group, see Chitty (2004 and later editions).
3 The phrase was first used by Emmanuel Shinwell in a letter to the *Times* in July 1958 but was later used as a campaign slogan by Wilson. See Chitty (1989: 36).
4 Cox (1992: 146).
5 Read (1994: 153).
6 Read (1994: 122–4, original emphasis).
7 Read (1974: 91).
8 Read (1974: 31).
9 Read (1974: 102).
10 Read (1925: 8, original emphasis).
11 Read (1994: 66).
12 Hargreaves (1982).
13 Read (1994: 94).
14 Read (1994: 89).
15 Read (1974: 186).

16 Honeywell (2011: 69).
17 Read (1994: 8) and Honeywell (2011: 37).
18 Warpole (1999), Honeywell (2011), Wilbert and White (2011b), Goodway (2012), Levy (2013), Burke and Jones (2014).
19 Wilbert and White (2011b). The introduction provides a good critical overview of Ward's work. A very good longer overview that includes wider social policy as well as education is that of Honeywell (2011).
20 Ward (1982: 4–5, original emphasis).
21 Ward (1982: 25).
22 Ward (1982: 14).
23 Ward (1982: 16).
24 Honeywell (2011: 138).
25 Ward (1973: 83).
26 Goodman and Goodman (1947: 10, 19).
27 Ward (1976: 124ff, original emphasis).
28 Goodman (1964: 117).
29 Goodman (1964: 106).
30 Ward (1982: 87).
31 Ward and Fyson (1973: Preface).
32 Goodman (1964: 32).
33 Goodman (1969: 86).
34 Coffield (2000).
35 Ward in Wilbert and White, 2011: 40).
36 Ward in Wilbert and White, 2011: 44).
37 Fielding in Burke and Jones (2014: 89). See also Fielding and Moss (2011).
38 Wright (1989).
39 Shotton (1993).
40 Read (1974: 103).
41 Bentley (1998: Blurb before the preface, emphasis added).
42 Bentley (1998: 182).
43 Inquiry into A Level Standards, December 2002.
44 Ward (1982: 22 and 26).

5

THE STATE AND SCHOOLING

Some old and some new assailants

> The time may come when men shall exercise the piercing search of truth upon the mysteries of government, and view without prepossession the defects and abuses of the constitution of their country … Government was intended to suppress injustice, but its effect has been to embody and perpetuate it.
>
> William Godwin, 1793

> The most violent institution in our society is the State and it reacts violently to efforts to take away its power.
>
> Colin Ward, 1973

England's finest anarchist, William Godwin, was born in Wisbech, Cambridgeshire, in 1756. He shot from relative obscurity to instant fame with the publication in 1793 of his *Enquiry Concerning Political Justice and its Influence on Modern Morals and Happiness*, which with its vast scope and great length made him the father of English anarchism and one of greatest anarchist thinkers of all time. He is 'the first man to present an elaborated criticism of political institutions as such and to produce a justification for a libertarian society',[1] and 'the English philosopher of freedom who eclipsed all the others as visionary for the new post-Revolutionary political and social order'.[2] It is worth our spending some time with him, for his *Political Justice* is 'the first major work which indubitably belongs in the anarchist tradition'[3] and 'the most complete and worked out statement of rational anarchist belief ever attempted'.[4] It is very serious stuff, not relieved by any humour. As James Joll puts it,

> His utopia, like that of so many British political thinkers, is redolent of the non-conformist chapel, even though religion had been banished from it.[5]

His novels have a slightly lighter touch. Mary Wollstonecraft, author of *A Vindication of the Rights of Women* (1792) and advocate of co-education in schools, was Godwin's first wife. Although in *Political Justice* he advocated the abolition of marriage, he in fact married Mary in March 1797 to ensure the legitimacy of their child, Mary, who was born on 31 August 1797. The mother died of complications just ten days later. Godwin's fame did not last: he died in 1836.

This is not the place, nor is there space, to discuss Godwin's theory of justice in relation to modern theories of justice, such as those of John Rawls or Robert Nozick. Here the importance of Godwin lies in his opposition to the State and his passionate views on education. The social injustice that Godwin seeks to remedy lies in the inequitable distribution in wealth, which is the product of the inequitable distribution in property. The accumulation of property gives rise to power by which 'one man obtains an unresisted sway over multitudes of others'[6] that results in the oppression of the majority. This cannot be eliminated by the State, for that would involve coercion, to which Godwin is fundamentally opposed. The equality he has in mind is of a different kind:

> This is not an equality introduced by force, or maintained by the laws and regulations of a positive institution. It is not the result of accident, of the authority of a chief magistrate, or the over-earnest persuasion of a few enlightened thinkers; but is produced by the serious and deliberate conviction of the public at large. It is one thing for men to be held to a certain system by the force of laws, and the vigilance of those who administer them; and a thing entirely different to be held by the firm and habitual persuasion of their own minds … Equality of conditions cannot begin to assume a fixed appearance in human society till the sentiment becomes deeply impressed, as well as widely diffused, that the genuine wants of any man constitute his only just claim to the ultimate appropriation, and the consumption, of any species of commodity.[7]

For Godwin the abolition of the State is not an end in itself but a means to a more just society, not just a different and better one. The equality justice demands emerges when people become more rational and share the relevant values. A redistribution of property cannot be imposed, but must arise naturally because people have come to see that this is for the common good.

His views on the State and government, so central to anarchist thought, are frank and fierce, as best shown in his words rather than any jejune summary:

> Government is nothing but regulated force … All government corresponds, in a certain degree, to what the Greeks denominated a tyranny.[8]

> There is no satisfactory criterion marking out any man, or set of men, to preside over the rest[9] … No man must encroach upon my province, nor I upon his. He may advise me, moderately and without pertinaciousness, but he must not expect to dictate to me … Force may never be resorted

> to but in the most extraordinary and imperious emergency … To dragoon men into the adoption of what we think right is an intolerable tyranny. It leads to unlimited disorder and injustice.[10]

> The stronghold of government has appeared hitherto to have consisted in seduction. However imperfect might be the political constitution under which they live, mankind have ordinarily been persuaded to regard it with a sort of reverential and implicit respect … The time may come which shall subvert these prejudices. The time may come when men shall exercise the piercing search of truth upon the mysteries of government and view without prepossession the defects and abuses of the constitution of their country … Bad government deceives us first, before it fastens itself upon us like an incubus, oppressing all our efforts.[11]

Abolition of government would naturally entail the abolition of the legal system. He spots one of its central problems, the never-ending increase in rules and regulations as new cases require adjustments:

> One result of the institution of law is that the institution, once begun, can never be brought to a close. Edict is heaped upon edict, and volume upon volume. … As new cases occur, the law is perpetually found deficient. How should it be otherwise? … The volume in which justice records her prescriptions is forever increasing, and the world would not contain the books that might be written.[12]

His conclusion is scathing:

> From all these considerations we can scarcely hesitate to conclude universally that law is an institution of the most pernicious tendency … A lawyer can scarcely fail to be a dishonest man.[13]

Godwin had witnessed the outcome of the French revolution and learned the lessons. His commitment to reason and his aversion to coercion were thereby strengthened. He sees nothing but drawbacks to a sudden and violent revolution:

> Revolution is instigated by a horror against tyranny, yet its own tyranny is not without peculiar aggravations … Any attempt to scrutinise men's thoughts, and punish their opinions, is of all kinds of despotism the most odious; yet this attempt is peculiarly characteristic of a period of revolution … During a period of revolution, enquiry, and all those patient speculations to which mankind are indebted for their greatest improvements, are suspended. Such speculations demand a period of security and permanence; they can scarcely be pursued when men cannot foresee what will happen tomorrow.[14]

> The most dreadful tragedies will infallibly result from an attempt to goad mankind prematurely into a position, however abstractly excellent, for which they are in no degree prepared[15] … The interests of the human species require a gradual, but uninterrupted change … we shall have many reforms but no revolution … Revolutions are the produce of passion, not of sober and tranquil reason.[16]

We see in *Political Justice* the tensions, and perhaps contradictions, with which Godwin struggled, those between anarchism's individualist and communitarian strands. So he insists on the sanctity of the individual as the essential unit in a world without coercion. We even find a statement not unlike one notoriously made by Margaret Thatcher:

> Society is nothing more than an aggregation of individuals. Its claims and duties must be the aggregate of their claims and duties.[17]

Individual talent, however, must be deployed not for egocentric ends, but for the general good. Society is at the same time essential for the expression of individuality, for the pleasures of the company of others, and for the informal social controls that are needed in the absence of law:

> In the same manner as my property, I hold my person as a trust in behalf of mankind. I am bound to employ my talents, my understanding, my strength and my time, for the production of the greatest quantity of general good. Such are the declarations of justice[18] … Without society, we shall probably be deprived of the most eminent enjoyments of which our nature is susceptible. In society, no man possessing the genuine marks of a man can stand alone … On the other hand, individuality is of the very essence of intellectual excellence.[19]

Godwin is nevertheless stronger on the individualist than on the communalist side, in part because the social aspects of life are always a potential threat to the autonomy and independence of the individual. Social pressure to engage with others beyond what is necessary for a good life is to be resisted:

> Everything that is usually understood by the term co-operation is in some degree an evil … All supererogatory co-operation is to be avoided … We ought to be able to do without one another. He is the most perfect man to whom society is not a necessity of life, but a luxury, innocent and enviable, in which he joyfully indulges.[20]

It becomes evident that for Godwin 'small is beautiful' because it is in only these conditions that the State-free society can work. In the absence of law, people must behave rationally and sincerely by which inappropriate behaviour may be brought into line. With boundless confidence in his fellow human beings, he assures us that they can, under the right conditions, do the right thing by one another:

> Man is perfectible ... By perfectible, is not meant that he is capable of being brought to perfection. But the word seems sufficiently adaptable to express the faculty of being continually made better and receiving perpetual improvement; and in this sense it is here to be understood.[21]

So he is startlingly optimistic that even bad behaviour can be reformed by the right sincere treatment:

> Sincerity, upon the principles on which it is here recommended, is practised from a consciousness of its utility, and from sentiments of philanthropy. It will communicate frankness to the voice, fervour to the gesture and kindness to the heart. Even in expostulation and censure, friendliness of intention and mildness of proceeding may be eminently conspicuous. The interest of him who is corrected, not the triumph of the corrector, should be the principle of action. True sincerity will be attended with the equality which is the only sure foundation of love, and that love which gives the best finishing and lustre to the sentiment of equality.[22]

When it comes to education, Godwin cannot speak with the voice of experience, for his attempt to establish a school in 1783 failed to attract pupils. This did not, however, discourage him from thinking deeply and writing about the subject. He defines education as of three kinds: accidental or incidental education; political education, the way in which ideas are shaped by a society's form of government; and education in the more commonly used sense.[23] On political education he recognises the difficulty of a teacher who wants to rescue his pupils from the influence of a corrupt government. When a teacher's own character has been shaped by the same political influences, ones that Godwin says must infect us all, the pedagogic task is 'nearly impossible'.

By recognising the significance of incidental education, he can reject placing too much weight on the impact of heredity on educability – the 'differences we are supposed to bring into this world':

> One of the principal reasons why we are so apt to impute the intellectual difference of men to some cause operating prior to their birth, is that we are so little acquainted with the history of the early years of men of talents. Slight circumstances at first determine their propensities to this or that pursuit. These circumstances are irrecoverably forgotten and we reason upon a supposition as if they never existed.[24]

Small environmental factors are always at work. He provides an example of two children walking together. One walks hand in hand with an adult, the other plucks flowers or chases butterflies. Such minor accidental differences may have consequences of a relativist kind:

> Two men view a picture. They never see it from the same point of view, and therefore strictly speaking never see the same picture. If they sit down to hear a lecture or any piece of instruction, they never sit down with the same degree of attention, seriousness or good humour. The previous state of mind is different, and therefore the impression received cannot be the same.[25]

So distinction in later life – what he calls 'illustrious exceptions' – may well be the result of 'the most trivial circumstance'. But intentional education by a teacher is likely to be the more influential. Children, he claims,

> are a sort of raw material put into our hands, a ductile and yielding substance, which, if we do not ultimately mould it in conformity to our wishes, it is because we throw away the power committed to us.[26]

He is thus acutely aware of the role of intrinsic motivation in learning:

> The best motive to learn is a perception of the value of the thing learned. The worst motive, without deciding whether or not it be necessary to have recourse to it, may well be affirmed to be constraint and fear.[27]

When he writes on education, the fierceness he displays attacking the State is put aside as we discern the gentle and generous side of his character. The first chapter of his wonderful work, *The Enquirer: Reflections on Education, Manners and Literature in a Series of Essays* (1797), is entitled 'Of awakening the mind', and the opening sentences capture mutual aid as the very essence of anarchism and the importance that anarchists assign to education:

> The true object of education, like that of every other moral process, is the generation of happiness. Happiness to the individual in the first place. If individuals were universally happy, the species would be happy. Man is a social being. In society the interests of individuals are intertwined with each other, and cannot be separated. Men should be taught to assist each other. The first object should be to train a man to be happy; the second to train him to be useful, that is, to be virtuous.[28]

Unlike many of today's politicians, he is against attempting to jam too much knowledge into infantile heads at too early a point:

> The purpose of early instruction is not absolute. It is of less importance, generally speaking, that a child should acquire this or that species of

> knowledge, than that, through the medium of instruction, he should acquire habits of intellectual activity.[29]

We hear much complaint today of the excess of passive learning by pupils under the pressure of testing, which reduces the opportunities of active learning. Godwin valued active learning and understood what this entailed:

> Activity is a mental quality. If therefore you would generate habits of activity, turn the boy loose in the fields of science. Let him explore the path for himself. Without increasing his difficulties, you may venture to leave him for a moment, and suffer him to ask himself the questions before he asks you, or, in other words, to ask the question before he receives the information.[30]

It is the absence of such practice, both then and now, the ensuing damage of the teaching is often irreparable, and is especially marked on the children of the poor:

> Examine the children of peasants. Nothing is more common than to find in them a promise of understanding, a quickness of observation, an ingeniousness of character, and a delicacy of tact, at the age of seven years, the very traces of which are obliterated at the age of fourteen … It is the greater slaughterhouse of genius and of mind. It is the unrelenting murder of hope and gaiety, of the love of reflection and the love of life.[31]

With great empathy he puts himself in the role of the child to make a protest that John Holt and the deschoolers would, 170 years later, echo with equal passion:

> Of all the sources of unhappiness to a young person the greatest is a sense of slavery. How grievous the insult, or how contemptible the ignorance, that tells a child that youth is the true season of felicity, when he feels himself checked, controlled, and tyrannised over in a thousand ways? I am rebuked, and my heart is ready to burst with indignation. A consciousness of the power assumed over me, and of the unsparing manner in which it is used, is intolerable. There is no moment free from the danger of harsh and dictatorial interruption … There is no equality, no reasoning, between me and my task-master. If I attempt it, it is considered as mutiny. If it be seemingly conceded, it is only the more cutting mockery. He is always in the right; right and power in these trials are found to be inseparable companions. I despise myself for having forgotten my misery and suffered my heart to be deluded into a transitory joy. Dearly indeed, by twenty years of bondage, do I purchase the scanty portion of liberty, which the government of my country happens to concede to its adult subjects![32]

Godwin's stance on the possibility of a State-led national system of schooling, which at the time was under discussion, is not surprising. He agrees, of course, with the need for the young to be educated and recognises arguments for its extension. Is, however, State provision the best solution? He is firmly against it on several grounds. In the first place, such an education would be dangerously conservative, emphasising past knowledge rather than subjecting it to scrutiny and examination, and thus reinforcing the status quo. He favours an education that will help learners to question and challenge:

> Public education has always expended its energies in the support of prejudice; it teaches its pupils, not the fortitude that shall bring every proposal to the test of examination, but the art of vindicating such tenets as may chance to be established … No vice can be more destructive than that which teaches us to regard any judgement as final, and not open to review … Teach them neither creeds nor catechisms, either moral or political … All this must be unlearned before we can begin to be wise.[33]

Second, the idea of national education is guilty of 'inattention to the nature of mind', that is, it has a faulty psychological foundation, a failure to acknowledge the essential motivation for both learning and teaching.

> What I acquire only because I desire to acquire it, I estimate at its true value; but what is thrust upon me may make me indolent, but cannot make me respectable.[34]

And then his final, lethal blow:

> Thirdly, the project of a national education ought uniformly to be discouraged on account of its obvious alliance with national government. This is an alliance of a more formidable nature than the old and much contested alliance of church and state … Government will not fail to employ it, to strengthen its hands, and perpetuate its institutions … It is not true that our youth ought to be instructed to venerate the constitution, however excellent; they should be led to venerate truth; and the constitution only so far as it corresponds with their uninfluenced deductions of truth.[35]

In a despotic society, he argues, it may be impossible to stifle truth entirely, but it would strive very hard to deploy 'the most formidable and profound contrivance for that purpose that imagination can suggest'. He may not have seen that in his lifetime, but we know how accurately he predicted the Nazi propaganda machine and its effect on the Hitler-Jugend.

Godwin's arguments went unheeded, of course. If there was an official opposition at the beginning of the nineteenth century to a scheme of national education it was based on the fear that education would lead the working classes to resist their station in life, not an objection in principle. But opposition, not least from those most affected, the working classes, did not die; it had to be crushed, and it was. If the opposition resurfaced, it was not only with Paul Goodman and the American deschoolers. One of Britain's creative thinkers about State schooling systems, who was almost entirely overlooked amid all the post-1970s turmoil, was an English academic who had, in 1965, just before the full-scale education wars broke out, published a book as original as *Deschooling Society* and of just as much potential interest to anarchists: E. G. West's *Education and the State* (1965, second edition 1970).

Edwin West examines the nineteenth century history of education that fundamentally reshaped the relationship between education and the State, especially through the momentous 1870 Education Act, which later led to the establishment of compulsory education and which has underpinned the education system ever since. The Act was intended to ensure a basic education of the working classes so that they would be better able to contribute to the national economy and the needs of the rapidly increasing industry that was undermining the old low-skill rural economy. West argued that up to 1870 the basic education of most people was successfully carried out without State intervention and mostly by the payment of very low fees to a wide range of small independent schools. There was a choice to be made. The existing state of education could be supplemented by the State to ensure its improvement, or it could be replaced. The question West raises is this: was the replacement that took place over the years really necessary and, when we make an assessment of it from today, has it worked? (I pose this question on the day the UK government announces yet another multi-million-pound drive to boost literacy in schools. Any bets that it will be the last?)

Much of West's historical account was later given much greater depth and colour by Phil Gardner's *The Lost Elementary Schools of Victorian England* (1984). Gardner sees the nineteenth century as an arena of class conflict in which an independently generated working-class alternative to official State prescription was firmly crushed. Some deep currents of working-class culture flowed into its own networks of practical educational activities: the well-established tradition of working-class private schooling. It was a *class-based* refusal of the equation of education with State schooling. Like West before him, Gardner points out that many historians and reformers of education simply did not want to recognise this, because of their understanding, their social imaginary that 'educational development worked its way downwards, from above, *in spite of* the working class and certainly not *because of* them'.[36] Consequently what the working classes provided could not legitimately be called schools at all. Some of what was provided warrants being called schools, but they were self-financing and beyond the reach or control of the Inspectorate: quite simply they were *working-class private schools*, and he insists that this term has greater descriptive accuracy and analytical utility than misleading and dismissive labels, such as a 'dame's school', implying worthlessness.

Gardner reveals the insurmountable difficulties in discovering just how many children attended these private schools, but he himself is convinced that 'working-class private schooling was a numerically strong, ubiquitous and resilient feature of an independent working-class culture'.[37] Most of the schools were small, and the teachers' qualifications were inevitably rather limited, but certainly required a mastery of the basic skills, since that was what the parents were paying for. Some of the teachers also had other sources of remuneration and the additional job reinforced the consonance between the culture of the home and that of the school, which reformers wanted to fracture in order to increase the moral education of the working classes. The move to the training of teachers for State schools marked the beginning of the distinction between teachers (now professionalised) and real or ordinary people (from the local community), a distinction that is still alive and well in pupil perceptions.

After the 1870 Act the official view was that the evident superiority of State schools would wean parents away from the working-class private schools – another example of an assumption that something undesired would wither away naturally. It did not. The reformers tried to explain the working-class loyalty to their private schools as apathy and ignorance, when it was in fact driven by factors such as the close link between home and school and the school's proximity to the home. The State had more work to do and the favoured tactic was not so much a direct attack – for example, from a reluctance to require inspectors to declare schools unfit (a tactic modern States use with nonchalance) – but something more subtle and indirect:

> This was no grand political battle fought out to a climax between two well-organised interest groups in the glare of the public spotlight. It was instead a fitful, intensely localised process of harassment, warning and threat, in which representatives of local education authorities sought to redirect working-class preference from private to public schools. In this they utilised a range of indirect sanctions passed down through successive legislative actions. Against these, parents who were faced with many other material problems, and who had no organised support, must have found sustained resistance very hard. There were to be no celebrated set-piece encounters in this long and bitter fight, but only a numberless succession of isolated skirmishes. The vast majority of these have no record.[38]

The State could perhaps use the idea of a school having to prove that it was 'efficient' as a means of attack, but this raised the problem of what exactly constituted a school, for the State had earlier insisted that the so-called dame schools were not really schools in the first place. The final blow to parental support was legislation in 1876 by which children/young people would not be able to gain employment without obtaining a certificate to prove attendance at a school, which could only be a State, not a private, school. Parents were still nominally free to send their children to schools which were not 'certified efficient' if they chose. But the price for most had simply become far too high – their children would not be able to get jobs.[39]

> The schools themselves were not all the working class lost. The link between the working class and a network of independent schools under their direct control was severed not only in fact, but also in popular perception. Thereafter, the legitimacy of the concept of the 'private school' was annexed in a very short space of time as an exclusively middle-class educational preserve. Indeed, the association came to be somehow inappropriate, even unnatural or illogical. In effect, working-class private schooling disappeared from history almost as if it had never been.[40]

The way in which Gardner tells this story is both enthralling and terrifying. It is no surprise that Colin Ward loved the book. It should be much better known.

Gardner does not explicitly draw policy recommendations from his account, but Edwin West did. Like the anarchists (whom he ignores in the book apart from one reference to Godwin[41]) and the later deschoolers, West makes the sharp distinction between education and schooling, as is recognised in the 1944 Education Act, which makes education, not schooling, compulsory: if parents object to schooling, they can ensure that their children are educated *otherwise*, which is as crucial to anarchist conceptions of the education of school-age children as it is to West's own view on the future. He refers approvingly of Mill's preference for making education, not schooling, compulsory, a position that all anarchists should treasure and all freedom-loving education ministers should ponder:

> Were the duty of enforcing universal education once admitted, there would be an end to the difficulties of what the State should teach, and how it should teach … If the government could make up its mind to *require* for every child a good education, it might save itself the trouble of *providing* one. It might leave to parents to obtain the education where and how they pleased, and content itself to pay the school fees of the poorer classes of children, and defraying the entire school expenses of those who have no one else to pay for them. The objections which are urged with reason against State education do not apply to the enforcement of education by the State, but to the State's taking upon itself to direct that education; which is a totally different thing.[42]

The State has failed the poor in so many ways. West addresses the poverty problem by striving to get rid of poverty directly by simply increasing their incomes. For justifying State schooling on the grounds that the poor cannot afford to send their children to school is to turn a problem of incomes policy into an education policy.[43] To de-couple education and schooling, argues West, a system of vouchers is needed, for this would restore parental control over their children's education and give them much wider choices between schools than the thin choices currently available, as well as between other-than-school educational options, perhaps through subsidising alternative agencies from the money saved from a much smaller education budget. Of course, this is, at least in part, a market solution, which is anathema to most of the political left, though West has shown that one of the idols of the left, Tom Paine, also wanted money to go to parents rather than schools in a voucher-like scheme.[44]

We have so many families in poverty, through low pay or low welfare support for unemployment, whose children it is that so often do less well in (State) schools and in turn end up locked in the same cycle of deprivation. We struggle to find solutions other than trying to attract better teachers to deprived areas and additional funding in terms of the pupil premium and maintenance grants for those beyond the school leaving age. West raises serious alternatives of directly raising the incomes of the poorest families and in place of a 'free' State education providing parents with education vouchers.

West's book did not advocate the abolition of the State, but by attacking the State record in schooling and proposing alternatives, his work should have had some appeal to anarchists because of the centrality of liberty in their philosophy. 'I find it difficult,' West admits, 'to accept any political philosophy in which the individual is not the primary philosophic entity',[45] so he is naturally suspicious about State interventions unless they can be shown to be better than some other alternative. West's similar suspicion of centralisation makes him a champion of decentralisation, which is equally crucial to the anarchist creed. Yet both West and Gardner provide a telling and, for me, unanswerable dissection of how a largely effective, if imperfect, decentralised schooling system was from 1870 steadily and increasingly transformed into an expensive, bureaucratised and centralised one, with a consequent loss of power to parents and pupils. The anarchist urge to reclaim education from the State has no better supporting argument.

West's review of the history of schooling since the nineteenth century, amplified by Gardner, makes a persuasive case for challenging State control of education, and with some positive ideas for change. There are parts that anarchists would shun, but there are aspects, in both diagnosis and remedy, that anarchists would warm to. More importantly, anarchists are peculiarly rich in ideas for alternative provision to schooling and from which West's supporters and followers could benefit.

On publication the book was as always released for reviews. The *New Statesman* chose as reviewer A. H. Halsey, the most distinguished, indeed revered, social scientist in the UK with an established track record on educational research. Halsey's review in 1965 savaged the book, trashing it with unusual vituperation:[46]

> Of all the verbal rubbish scattered about by the Institute of Economic Affairs [the right-wing think tank] this book is by far the most pernicious … a crass and dreary imitation of those published several years ago by Professor Milton Friedman … Mr West is a man who knows nothing about psychology or sociology and has less understanding of economics than first-year students …

Edwin West knew that his book risked annoying potential readers who might have different grounds for rejecting his analysis and ideas:

> For their very definition of education may be one which is so bound up with their political philosophy that the absence of a central role of government is inconceivable to them.[47]

This anticipation of criticism turned out to be an accurate prediction about Halsey, who not long before had become the Director of Oxford University's Department of Social and Administrative Studies, and a research and policy adviser to Anthony Crosland, who was Labour's Secretary of State for Education from 1965–1967. West's book undermined everything that Halsey stood for: it threatened to shatter his dearly held social imaginary, and in retaliation it had to be pilloried lest the contagion spread. Halsey's political commitment blinded him to West's historical analysis. Yet many of the schemes favoured by Halsey, such as Education Priority Areas and other versions of compensatory education beloved by many of his generation, have proved to be an expensive waste in terms of making enduring reforms designed to make a real difference.

Halsey's dismissive review may have damned the book in the eyes of many potential readers on the political left who may have missed positive reviews elsewhere. Sadly it never made it into the OU's *Schooling and Capitalism*. West's book has dated in parts, but he raises deep questions that remain with us because mainstream ideas from the political left have not produced satisfactory answers. However, while the Labour Party contemptuously cast aside West's book, it nevertheless found a British admirer who sought to apply its insights in imaginative ways.

The opening pages of James Tooley's *Reclaiming Education* (2000) sound like textbook anarchism:

> This book makes out a case for reclaiming education from the State ... There are solutions to the fundamental challenges facing education. The solutions do not require much more from government other than that it leaves [*sic*] education well alone ... This book ... shows how all the supposed justifications for State intervention in education melt away ... [and] also lays out why we should reclaim education from *the tyranny of schooling* ... The fundamental question of education policy is what role should there be for the State in education. This book sets out why I believe there is no justified role.[48]

So has the UK found an assassin ready to end the State's control of schooling? The opening may have sounded like anarchism, but Tooley makes no mention whatever of anarchism, or even of Godwin. Nor do they appear in his *Education Without the State*, which was published by the right-wing Institute of Economic Affairs as a paper in 1996. Perhaps he simply did not know of them; perhaps they were ideologically alien to him. In any event, he neglected some potentially useful allies for his argument.

Tooley fully understands just how difficult it is to challenge the common assumption that the State's position on school is unquestionable, and he shows how many school reformers end up somewhat naively expecting the State to relax its grip and commit even the first tentative steps towards suicide. For these well-intentioned reformers simply cannot escape the dominant social imaginary in which they are trapped. It is essential for Tooley to show that escaping the social imaginary – this is not the term he uses – is necessary not merely to sustain his thesis, but more importantly to show that this is a perfectly rational thing to do. To this end he uses an imaginary focus group where in essence the members discard their existing assumption about schooling and instead explore how they would devise, from scratch as it were, education for the young.[49] They do not come up with or reinvent our present school system, so the point is made that there are ways of stepping out of our educational imaginary.

As a doctoral student, Tooley had a Damascene experience when he discovered, entirely by accident, E. G. West's book, which changed his intellectual and political position. (Curiously he utterly neglects Gardner's book, which in my view would have provided more detailed and vivid support for his thesis.) Yet Tooley rejects voucher schemes, which in any event still leave a role for the State in approving and regulating where the voucher can be spent, and he accepts the flaws in similar ideas of giving money directly to learners with their potential for extensive fraud. He also rejects simply privatising the whole of schooling, by which the State might contract out schooling to private companies, not least because although there might be some gains in quality and cost, it preserves far too much of the status quo and State involvement. The heady promises of the opening pages begin to fall rather flat as the book progresses.

The book is set not within the wider range of West's work, but in the context of education writing of the late 1990s. His proposals are prefaced with a rehearsal of his critiques of several other philosophers of education, which are intellectually impressive and which worked well in their original academic journals, but seem somewhat out of place here and would be difficult for many readers to follow. His most obvious allies are Illich and Reimer for they are so close to the themes he announces in the opening pages. Yet Illich barely gets a mention and Reimer is ignored completely. Perhaps they were dismissed as old hat.

So in place of deschoolers he calls on his contemporaries in education reform, and of these he is most sympathetic to Tom Bentley and his *Learning Beyond the Classroom* (1998) and, with more reservations, Michael Barber and his *The Learning Game: Arguments for an Education Revolution* (1996). Neither could ever make a comfortable bedfellow for Tooley. Barber, as we have seen, had been the key figure behind New Labour's education policy and after 1997 played a major role in expanding educational centralisation by the State. Bentley's proposals, as again we saw earlier, were in the Illich tradition and in many respects of the kind to win approval from anarchists. Such ideas would inevitably become important if

State control were to be reduced, but Bentley assigned to the State the role of midwife to such alternatives to conventional schooling. Tooley talks of competing chains that would manage Centres of Learning, Quiet Zones and Places Apart. These sound fine but remain seriously under-developed as innovations and fall far short of the imaginative suggestions offered by earlier reformers, including the deschoolers.

To the end Tooley's wish to terminate the State's role in schooling remains intact, but he does not see how this could ever be achieved other than by slow erosion. He opts for gradualism, taking incremental steps in the fissures that exist in the State system – much the same as what Colin Ward called the interstices of the dominant power structure – such as existing private education companies, chains of private schools, problems of provision for excluded pupils, supplementary provision, home schooling. He was optimistic that the fissures would soon widen – and into these he wants to tuck bits from Bentley and rather fewer from Barber – but they never did, even after the Conservatives regained power in 2010. His ideas lack the imaginative bravado of an Illich, and his blindness to anarchism means that he cannot draw on the ideas of Colin Ward or the many other forms of radical alternative practice that would have given greater substance to his proposals.

Most of all, Tooley lacks what was so important for Godwin, Goodman and Illich, the wide conception of society and the necessity for it to be different, for he could then show that the schooling system helps to block the path to such a society. Tooley focuses too narrowly on education, betraying his true starting position, which is not the State as such, but a conviction that private provision, if given a more pivotal role, will deliver a more effective and cheaper education. His reports on the work he has done in developing countries along the lines of lost-cost private schools in poor areas is impressive, especially in the readable, moving and at times terrifying *The Beautiful Tree* (2009), where he repeatedly finds that in these nations the leading authorities in education simply deny such schools exist, when he has found them in significant numbers, or if compelled to admit their existence, insist that the quality is unacceptably poor. There is an unnerving parallel with the official attitudes to working-class private schools in England in the mid-nineteenth century as reported by Phil Gardner. It seems that it is not just in western society that educators find it difficult to escape the social imaginary about State education: we have exported it to places where it does even more damage than it does here.

Tooley's work is inspirational for developing countries if only the authorities can be persuaded to listen to him, and perhaps in parallel to Colin Ward's ideas of a bottom-up approach to social welfare.[50] There were poor schools, poor private schools, not only in nineteenth-century England but also in the USA at precisely the time that the explosive books from Goodman to Illich were raining down on American educators with radical leanings. I find an interesting parallel between Tooley and Jonathan Kozol (born 1936) and George Dennison (1925–1987), who have been two of the best American writers on schooling in this period: as with Tooley, their stylish books are driven by anger, passion and with a no-holds-barred frankness derived from their experience with schooling in deprived areas.

Kozol had published *Death at an Early Age* in 1967 and it deservedly became a bestseller. Here I turn to his book *Free Schools* (1972), a handbook on how to establish and run a free school. He had been sacked from his Boston school, allegedly for reading to his students a poem by Langston Hughes, a black American poet and social activist. So he and a dozen parents decided to start a little school of their own outside the State school system, to be available for free for families that had no money. At the time they thought that this was an unprecedented move: they were soon disabused and learned that there had been such schools in the past and many new ones were now being established as a consequence of the educational ructions created in the late 1960s and early 1970s. Some of these were affiliated or associated with public (i.e. State) schools, and as such they were necessarily still part of the system, not a genuine alternative to it:

> The school that flies the flag is, in the long run, no matter what the handsome community leader in the startling Afro likes to say, *accountable to that flag* and to the power and to the values which it represents. This is, and must remain, the ultimate hang-up of all ventures which aspire to constitute, in one way or another, a radical alternative "within the system".[51]

Kozol's type of free school was not. The pupils were poor black and Hispanic children and the free schools designed for them had a different rationale:

> Their function is as much political as pedagogic. They are enormously significant in community organisation. They are not, however, a sound or reasonable context for active and conspicuous participation on the part of white men.[52]

It was to be small, permanently so, not just at the beginning, with eighty to 100 students, as Goodman had advocated with his 'mini-schools'. In short, this school and the ones like it would have five distinctive features:

1. outside the public education apparatus,
2. outside the white man's counter-culture,
3. inside the cities,
4. in direct contact with the needs and urgencies of those among the poor and dispossessed, who have been most clearly victimised by public education,
5. as small, "decentralised" and "localised" as we can manage,
6. as little politicised as possible.[53]

Moreover, the location for the free school was not in some delightful place away from the inner city – not at all:

> The ideal location for a Free School born of the frustrations and the discontents of ten years' struggle to transform or liberate the public school is not across the city but *across the street* from the old, hated, but still-standing and still-murderous construction. I know that such an appropriate and explicit sense of physical confrontation is not always possible; nor, of course, does the visible reminder of the miserable and monolithic enemy assure the radical integrity or the revolutionary perseverance of the Free School on the opposite corner ... The farther the distance from the place of pain, the less the reason to remember the oppressor's eyes or to be cognizant of his abiding powers.[54]

Kozol had visited and talked with Illich and Reimer. Returning to Boston, he was not in a situation where he could simply ignore credentialism or curriculum in deschooler fashion, much as he might agree with the deschoolers' criticisms of them. He could not ignore the system in the hope that it would fall to pieces: it would be insanity to behave as if it were not there. He could not dismantle the framework in which he, his students and their families lived and had to survive. He had to carry his own 'campaign of guerrilla actions'. His school was outside the State system, but would not ignore the 'basic skills'. He accepted, with the deschoolers, that some children would pick up the ability to read quite naturally without much adult intervention. But others had resisted the ways they had been coerced in the public schools, without success, to learn to read, and now needed active teacher help, and this could be done with 'a visible presence of high energy and fun, pupil irreverence and adult unprotectedness'.[55] He did not want teachers with ideas of 'organic' and 'spontaneous' philosophies of learning, for this was not the way in which to learn calculus, Latin grammar, physics, brain surgery or engineering. He did not want to recruit

> rich white kids who speak three languages with native fluency, at the price of sixteen years of high-cost, rigorous and sequential education, who are the most determined that poor kids should make clay vases, weave Indian headbands, play with Polaroid cameras, climb over geodesic domes.[56]

Kozol's free school was not strictly free, for it did not receive money from the State and it needed to be funded. Kozol devotes much of the book on how his and other free schools raised money for the buildings, the teachers and other resources: this was a very difficult task, consuming much time and energy from the staff, from parents and the community – just as in the schools in Gardner's and Tooley's accounts. The American free schools were free: free from the State. To exist at all, they had to be *private* schools, even though in many cases the parents did not, and could not, pay direct fees.

George Dennison's *The Lives of Children: The Story of the First Street School* (1969, UK publication 1972) runs in parallel with Kozol's story, since his free school was also free from the State, being funded from a private foundation until the grant ceased. The school, in a shared building in New York's Lower East Side, had taken Goodman's mini-schools as the model. There were 23 students, black, white and Hispanic, all from low-income families, half on welfare. The pupils had all had bad experiences in State schools. There were three full-time teachers and one part-timer, and a few others for specialised fields, such as music. All the staff lived within a few blocks of the school and saw themselves as part of the local community. They all rejected 'the present quagmire of public education [that] is entirely the result of unworkable centralisation and the lust for control that permeates every bureaucratic institution'.[57] So there were no administrators, no report cards, no testing of a comparative or competitive kind, no schedules. Instead, they sought to create

> a new order, based first on relationships between adults and children, and children and their peers, but based ultimately on such truths of the human condition as these: that the mind does not function separately from the emotions, but thought partakes of feeling and feeling of thought; that there is no such thing as knowledge *per se*, knowledge in a vacuum, but rather all knowledge is possessed and must be expressed by individuals; that the human voices preserved in books belong to the real features of the world, and that children are so powerfully attracted to this world that the very notion of their curiosity comes through to us as a form of love; that an active moral life cannot be evolved except where people are free to express their feelings and act upon the insights of conscience.[58]

Dennison points out that, with two exceptions, the parents were not libertarians:

> They thought that they believed in compulsion, and rewards and punishments, and formal discipline, and report cards, and homework, and elaborate school facilities. They looked rather askance at our noisy classrooms and informal relations. If they persisted in sending us their children, it was not because they agreed with our methods, but because they were desperate. As the months went by, however, and the children who had been truants now attended eagerly, and those who had been failing now began to learn, the parents drew their own conclusions. By the end of the first year there was a high morale among them and great devotion to the school.[59]

The school did not get written approval from the Board of Education, which had no jurisdiction over private schools. The school would never have met the official criteria for recognition, which included the prescribed course of study and textbooks. How fortunate to be able to escape a formal inspection.

The book is an account of the school's short history in the form of a diary, like that of John Holt. It is a rich, moving and exhilarating story that naturally defies summary. Like Kozol's, Dennison's school was similar to those run on explicitly anarchist lines, as we shall see later. But the State showed no real interest. They were left alone because they were doing work with youngsters who could not easily be contained within the State's schools. They were tolerated as long as they lasted; they offered no challenge to the State, not even a few lessons from which the State might learn.

At the end of the book, where he speaks glowingly of the influence of John Dewey, he draws an explicit comparison with Jerome Bruner, at that time perhaps the most eminent of psychologists in the education field, with a global reputation. He takes Bruner to task for asking the wrong question, namely *how can we improve our schools?* This is, of course, the very same question that, in England, we – I use the first person advisedly – have for nearly half a century been asking ourselves, in our State's Department for Education, in the local education authorities, in teachers' centres, in professional development consultancies, and in institutes of higher education and research units and countless teacher conferences. For Dennison, who has stood outside the dominant social imaginary of the State and schooling, the real question is different: *how can we educate our young?*

> Bruner is not interested. He speaks, rather, of instruction, and is concerned to improve its efficiency within the existing framework of the schools ... How odd, really, our educationists are! They proclaim a reverence for facts, and immure themselves for years in experimental labs, from which they emerge in a haze of abstractions, agreeing chiefly on one thing: that more research is needed. And when this research brings them to the truisms known to every mother, and they might at least rest, they haven't the modesty to admit it and hold still.[60]

Dennison leaves me with a disturbing thought. What if university faculties of education were to put to one side, if only for one year, the work of Bruner and the thousands of academics in the field of education – which of course includes me – and instead adopted Holt and Dennison and Kozol, who as far as I know were not anarchists, as well as a few who were, such as Goodman, Read and Ward, and put their books at the core of their courses for initial teacher training and advanced study? How would this affect the course members' perspective on their chosen profession? How might it influence the place in which they would choose to exercise their profession, with what colleagues and with what central purpose? I cannot answer these questions, either for myself or for them, but I suspect I would be shaken but also excited by the outcome.

Godwin has had so much to say about society and education that the neglect or ignorance of him by so many of those I have discussed in this chapter is as sad as it is startling. Kozol and Dennison were not self-identified anarchists, which must excuse them. But during this same period of the late 1960s and early 1970s, there was in the USA a group of anarchists of a rather peculiar kind who might well have been fascinated by William Godwin, though they were not. Who are they?

Notes

1 Woodcock (1989: 257).
2 Krammick, Introduction to Godwin (1793: 11).
3 Miller (1984: 4).
4 Joll (1964: 31).
5 Joll (1964: 16).
6 Godwin (1793: 733).
7 Godwin (1793: 741–2).
8 Godwin (1793: 242, 550).
9 Godwin (1793: 231).
10 Godwin (1793: 198, 262).
11 Godwin (1793: 256–8).
12 Godwin (1793: 685f).
13 Godwin (1793: 689).
14 Godwin (1793: 269–71).
15 Godwin (1793: 262).
16 Godwin (1793: 252f).
17 Godwin (1793: 176).
18 Godwin (1793: 175).
19 Godwin (1793: 757).
20 Godwin (1793: 758, 761).
21 Godwin (1793: 144).
22 Godwin (1793: 320f).
23 Godwin (1793: 111).
24 Godwin (1797: 25).
25 Godwin (1793: 111).
26 Godwin (1793: 112).
27 Godwin (1797: 78).
28 Godwin (1797: 1).
29 Godwin (1797: 5).
30 Godwin (1797: 82).
31 Godwin (1797: 16f).
32 Godwin (1797: 66f).
33 Godwin (1793: 614f).
34 Godwin (1793: 616).
35 Godwin (1793: 616f).
36 Gardner (1984: 4, original emphasis).
37 Gardner (1984: 50).
38 Gardner (1984: 192).
39 Gardner (1984: 206).
40 Gardner (1984: 88).
41 But see a fuller treatment of Godwin in his essay 'Liberty and education: John Stuart Mill's dilemma' (1967), in Tooley and Stanfield (eds.) (2003).
42 John Stuart Mill (1859), *On Liberty*, Book 5, original emphasis.
43 West (1965, second edition 1970: xxxvi).
44 West, 'Tom Paine's voucher scheme for public education' (1965), in Tooley and Stanfield (eds.) (2003).
45 West (1965: 70).
46 The full story is told by James Tooley, in his book entitled *E. G. West,* Continuum 2008 and Bloomsbury 2014, page 194f.
47 West (1965: 230).
48 Tooley (2000: 1, 16, 22, original emphasis).
49 This device is a variant of philosopher John Rawls's 'veil of ignorance' in *A Theory of Justice* (1971).

50 See Honeywell (2011: 162ff) and Wilbert and White (2011: xxiv).
51 Kozol (1972: 14, original emphasis).
52 Kozol (1972: 14).
53 Kozol (1972: 16).
54 Kozol (1972: 50, original emphasis).
55 Kozol (1972: 74).
56 Kozol (1972: 33).
57 Dennison (1969: 12).
58 Dennison (1969: 11f).
59 Dennison (1969: 10).
60 Dennison (1969: 200–2).

6

ANARCHIST CHALLENGES TO STATE SCHOOLING FROM THE RIGHT, AMERICAN-STYLE

> The subject of property is the keystone that completes the fabric of political justice.
>
> William Godwin, 1793

> Property is theft.
>
> Pierre-Joseph Proudhon, 1840

A fresh impetus to the case against the State's control of schooling in the USA came from an unexpected quarter, the *anarcho-capitalists*. Isn't their name an oxymoron? Who are they and what do they stand for? What is their relation to anarchism and how do they envisage a State-free future for schooling?

Their name sounds less oxymoronic, even for right-wing libertarians, when one remembers that the concept of liberty became deeply rooted in the American soul after they threw off their colonial chains, and if they were to be drawn to any one of anarchism's founding fathers it would be Max Stirner, the key figure in the individualist strand of anarchist thought. The particular stress he placed on individual liberty has an obvious appeal for the libertarian right. His major work, *Der Einziger und sein Eigentum*, published in 1844, is usually translated as *The Ego and Its Own*, but a better sense of it might be in a more literal translation as *The Unique Individual and His Property*. The word 'egoism' in English has connotations of egocentricity or selfishness, which is not quite the same.

Much of what Stirner wrote was embedded in the issues and writings of his day, many of which make little sense to today's readers. His concern is that individuals should achieve freedom from the dominant ideologies of his times, including religion and the State, which result in internal and external constraints that oppress and enslave and so inhibit the achievement of autonomy. In 1842 he published a short paper, *The False Principle of Our Education*, which was in part a preview of his more famous book. Stirner had himself been a schoolteacher for five years, so his deep concerns about the negative effects that schools have on pupils, as well as his convictions about what education should do, all spring from direct experience. He understood that schools are an agent of social control, subjecting the learner to the authority of teachers that demands submission to authority that brooks no opposition. A flavour of his passionately held convictions is evident in the following extracts:

> In the pedagogical as in certain other spheres freedom is not allowed to erupt, the power of *opposition* is not allowed to put a word in edge-wise: they want *submissiveness* … nothing but *subservient* people … When then will a spirit of opposition be strengthened in place of the subservience which has been cultivated until now, where will a creative person be educated instead of a learning one, where does the teacher turn into a fellow worker, where does he recognise knowledge as turning into will, where does the free man count as a goal and not the merely educated one?[1] … In a word, it is not knowledge that should be taught, rather, the individual should come to self-development: pedagogy should not proceed any further toward civilising, but toward the development of free men, sovereign characters … the school is to be life and there, as outside of it, the self-revelation of the individual is to be the task. The universal education of the school is to be an education for freedom, not subservience: to be free, that is the true *life*.[2]

Although the anarcho-capitalists rarely cite Stirner directly, his ideas resonate throughout their writing, as well as more evidently in that of their other philosophical predecessors, including Spooner and Tucker, whose names, unknown to most UK readers today, sound more like a TV comedy duo.

The man who is usually acknowledged as the central figure of the anarcho-capitalists, and who coined the label, is Murray Rothbard (1926–1995), a political economist and historian and leader of right-libertarianism. His core philosophy is set out in *For a New Liberty: The Libertarian Manifesto* (1973), commissioned in 1971 – the remarkable year that brought Illich and Reimer to international fame – as a powerful challenge against growing statism in American political life. The book has been described as the intellectual, moral and strategic core of modern libertarianism. Of particular relevance here are *Education: Free and Compulsory* (1979) and the shorter *Anatomy of the State* (2009). Much of Rothbard's polemical writing is in a dramatic, punchy style that Bakunin would have relished:

> The libertarian creed rests upon one central axiom: that no man or group of men may aggress against the person or property of anyone else. This may be called the "nonaggression axiom". Aggression is defined as the initiation of the use or threat of physical violence against the person or property of anyone else.[3]

He knows what he is up against if he is to attack the State on this basis. He starts where most of his readers now stand:

> The State is almost universally considered an institution of social service. Some theorists venerate the State as the apotheosis of society; others regard it as an amiable, though often inefficient, organisation for the achievement of social ends; but almost all regard it as a necessary means for achieving the goals of mankind.[4]

Only then does he make his first strike, based on his first axiom:

> Briefly, the State is that organisation in society which attempts to maintain a monopoly of the use of force and violence in a given territorial area; in particular, it is the only organisation in society that obtains its revenue not by voluntary contribution or payment for services rendered but by coercion.[5]

Property is a central idea: property of the self – shades of Stirner – and private property of things, which are the basis of free exchange and contract:

> Freedom is a condition in which a person's ownership rights in his own body and his legitimate material property are *not* invaded, are not aggressed against. A man who steals another man's property is invading and restricting the victim's freedom, as does the man who beats another over the head. Freedom and unrestricted property right go hand in hand … Crime is an invasion, by the use of violence, against a man's property and therefore against his liberty. Slavery – the opposite of freedom – is a condition in which the slave has little or no right of self-ownership; his person and his produce are systematically expropriated by his master by the use of violence.[6]

Doesn't this put Rothbard into direct conflict with Pierre-Joseph Proudhon, one of the most important figures in nineteenth-century classical anarchism, whose most famous saying is 'Property is theft'? Actually Proudhon's position is much more subtle than this, as a reading of his *What Is Property?* (1840) shows. In his introduction to an English translation of the book, George Woodcock says that the three-word maxim hung around Proudhon's neck like a verbal albatross:

> Ironically, Proudhon did not mean literally what he said. His boldness of expression was intended for emphasis, and by "property" he wished to be understood what he later called "the sum of its abuses". He was denouncing the property of the man who uses it to exploit the labour of others without any effort on his own part, property distinguished by interest and rent, by the impositions of the non-producer on the producer. Towards property regarded as "possession" the right of a man to control his

> dwelling and the land and tools he needs to live, Proudhon had no hostility; indeed, he regarded it as the cornerstone of liberty, and his main criticism of the communists was that they wished to destroy it.[7]

So far, so much agreement in principle with Rothbard – except that Rothbard presumably, as a capitalist, would not be at all upset if what a person produces is in fact produced by an employee, whereas Proudhon certainly would.

Had Rothbard been familiar with William Godwin, who offers him more than do Stirner or Proudhon, he could have drawn on *Political Justice* to support his argument, and in a forthright style that Rothbard would have relished:

> The first idea of property then is a deduction from the right of private judgement; the first object of government is the preservation of this right. Without permitting to every man, to a considerable degree, the exercise of his own discretion, there can be no independence, no improvement, no virtue and no happiness … Thus deep is the foundation of the doctrine of property. It is, in the last resort, the palladium [protection or safeguard] of all that ought to be dear to us, and must never be approached but with awe and veneration. He that seeks to loosen the hold of this principle upon our minds, and that would lead us to sanction any exceptions to it without the most deliberate and impartial consideration, however right may be his intentions, is, in that instance, an enemy to the whole[8] … We should set bounds to no man's accumulation [of property] … men ought to be protected in the disposal of the property they have personally acquired[9] … how pernicious the consequences would be if government were to take the whole permanently into their hands, and dispense to every man his daily bread … [laws] which have been invented for keeping down the spirit of accumulation deserve to be regarded as remedies more pernicious than the disease they are intended to cure.[10]

All anarchists can agree with Godwin that the root cause of injustice lies in the huge gap between the rich and the poor, but one faction, the anarcho-communists, who believe in the abolition of private property, would have detested Godwin's line as much as Rothbard's basic axiom. At least as a starting position, I know which side I am on – do you?

Godwin did not pretend that his position on property would not have undesirable consequences. He admits, more readily than the anarcho-capitalists, that

> it will be difficult to set bounds to the extent of an accumulation in one man, or of poverty and wretchedness in another … If one individual, by means of greater ingenuity or more indefatigable industry, obtain a greater proportion of the necessaries or conveniences of life than his neighbour, and, having obtained them, determine to convert them into the means of permanent inequality, this proceeding is not of a sort that it would be just or wise to undertake to repress by means of coercion.[11]

With obvious reluctance, Godwin concedes that in extreme cases coercion may be used, but only as a temporary and local measure in order to protect the general principle. For less extreme cases, he falls back on an appeal to rationality:

> Persuasion, and not force, is the legitimate instrument for influencing the human mind; and I shall never be justified in having recourse to the latter, while there is any reasonable hope of succeeding by the former[12] … Hence it follows that the distribution of wealth in every community must be left to depend upon the sentiments of the individuals in that community.[13]

Godwin is clearly here thinking of a small community in which his solution might work. In the larger community or society, however, his approach is hopeless at restraining the greed of, for instance, the owners or directors of Carillion, whose directors were branded for their 'recklessness, hubris and greed' in a parliamentary report and whose accountants and lawyers are set to earn millions from managing the collapse.[14] He would, as we would too, certainly consider them as cases where coercion might be justified. Where he, or the anarcho-capitalists, or we ourselves, would draw that line is a moot point.

On the basis of his central axiom, Rothbard then shows to what extent and in what ways the State is an aggressor, indeed the aggressor par excellence. The State's power hinges on its ability to compel citizens, under threat of violence, to pay the taxes on which the government decides. The income from taxes is what provides the State with the immense power to control and organise so much of our lives. He quotes Lysander Spooner's 1870 assertion that

> It is true that the *theory* of our Constitution is that all taxes are paid voluntarily; that our government is a mutual insurance company, voluntarily entered into by the people with each other … But this theory of our government is wholly different from the practical fact. The fact is that the government, like a highwayman, says to a man: "Your money or your life." And many, if not most, taxes are paid under the compulsion of that threat. The government does not, indeed, waylay a man in a lonely place, spring upon him from the roadside, and holding a pistol to his head, proceed to rifle his pockets. But the robbery is none the less a robbery on that account: and it is far more dastardly and shameful.[15]

Here we see the deep-rooted objection in some long-standing American thinking to the very idea of taxes, not merely high taxes, as is common in most cultures. For anarcho-capitalists, as with other Americans, it is taxes, not property, that are theft. To add insult to injury, the State's use of the money derived from taxes is then too often wasted on inefficiency, bureaucracy and regulation. Proudhon took much the same view. Edward Hyams, in his biography of Proudhon (1979), makes the point that also explains why Proudhon and Marx, who at first was a great admirer of *What Is Property?*, eventually parted company:

> If property could be defined as the exploitation of the weak by the strong, then communism must be defined as the exploitation of the strong by the weak; and both led either to ruin or to an intolerable tyranny … It is very clear that Proudhon, using the long, clear foresight of genius and the device of extrapolation, perceived that the State as arch-proprietor could not avoid becoming the monstrous tyrant which arch-economist Joseph Stalin made of the Soviet bureaucracy. Stalin halted the Revolution at the stage which Lenin called state capitalism which, in Proudhonian language means the State as proprietor, that is, as Thief.[16]

Prophetic words indeed of Putin's Russia.

An important axiomatic feature of Rothbard's thinking is his celebration of human diversity. This involves a rejection of egalitarianism – that notoriously slippery word – which equates equality with an unjustified uniformity:

> The development of individual variety tends to be both the cause and the effect of the progress of civilisation … With the development of civilisation and individual diversity, there is less and less area of identical uniformity, and therefore less "equality". Only robots on the assembly line or blades of grass can be considered as being identical with respect to all their attributes … It is evident that the common enthusiasm for equality is, in the fundamental sense, anti-human.[17]

Since some people are going to be better at the processes of production and exchange, there will inevitably be differences in accumulated resources or wealth. As we shall see, this assumption also has significant implications for his views on both the failures of State schooling and on what for him is the desirable future of education.

A similar line is adopted by David Friedman in his *The Machinery of Freedom: A Guide to Radical Capitalism* (1973), a book that is a loose collection of pieces on anarcho-capitalism and libertarianism rather than a sustained argument like Rothbard's, but the style is more relaxed and conversational. For him too, private property is the central institution of a free society, as in this account of the meaning of anarcho-capitalism:

> I hold that there are *no* proper functions of government. In that sense I am an anarchist. All things that governments do can be divided into two categories – those we could do away with today and those we hope to be able to do away with tomorrow. Most of the things our government does are in the first category. The system of institutions I would like to eventually see achieved would be entirely private – what is sometimes called anarcho-capitalism or libertarian anarchy. Such institutions would be, in some respects, radically different from those we now have.[18] … An anarchist is not, except in the propaganda of his enemies, one who desires

> chaos. Anarchists, like other people, wish to be protected from thieves and murders. They wish to have some peaceful way of settling disagreements. They wish, perhaps even more than other people, to be able to protect themselves from foreign invasion. What, after all, is the point of abolishing your own government if it is immediately replaced by someone else's? What anarchists do not want is to have these services – the services provided by the police, courts, and national defence – provided by the kind of institution that now provides them: government.[19]

The task is thus seen to be one of devising how private institutions can take over the functions of government. Both Rothbard and Friedman cover an extensive range of such government functions, including State services that are not in Britain seen by most people as proper targets for privatisation, such as roads and streets, the police and courts, and welfare services. Laws against victimless crimes and any actions by consenting adults, including prostitution and pornography, are condemned: there is no puritan conservatism to be found here. There is imaginative thinking behind these proposals that might well have attractions to non-capitalist anarchists, such as alternative systems of policing, private rights enforcement and arbitration agencies to replace courts. Does this sound absurd?

Consider what Herbert Read said in *The Philosophy of Anarchism* (1940),[20] in which he approaches this issue from an unusual angle:

> There are principles of justice which are superior to these man-made laws – principles of equality and fairness inherent in the natural order of the universe … I do claim that [anarchism] has its basis in the *law* of nature rather than in the *state* of nature … *The object of anarchism … is to extend the principle of equity until it altogether supersedes statutory law* … Admittedly a system of equity, no less than a system of law, implies a machinery for determining and administering its principles. I can imagine no society which does not embody some method of arbitration. But just as the judge in equity is supposed to appeal to universal principles of reason, and to ignore statutory law when it comes into conflict with these principles, so the arbiter in an anarchist community will appeal to these same principles, as determined by philosophy or common sense; and will do so unimpeded by all those legal and economic prejudices which the present organisation of society entails.[21]

The anarcho-capitalists' analysis is based on the American experience and is not easily transposed to contemporary British or wider European contexts. How their diagnosis and proffered solutions would fit into our context is far from clear. Moreover, it is one thing to argue that government consists largely of various forms of legalised theft, but quite another to give assurances that their replacements would not leave existing inequalities undisturbed, or even exacerbate the growing gap between the very rich and poor. How would the anarcho-capitalists deal with, for example, the UK record of privatised railways or privatised utilities of water, gas and electricity?

Friedman favours high levels of self-employment in a society of completely voluntary associations and is especially wary of large firms and corporations, which he sees as inimical to the common good. He acknowledges the problems of the poor resulting from laissez-faire economic policies, but is unduly optimistic that abolition of the State will go far to remedy the problem of the poor: 'Almost surely, the poor would be better off if both the benefits that they now receive and the taxes, direct and indirect, that they now pay were abolished.'[22] The *almost surely* is hardly reassuring, is it? There is some truth in the argument that the tax system sometimes takes money from the poor to subsidise the not-poor and that some government programmes take from the poor, rather than the rich, to give to the even poorer, but this is insufficient assurance that the laissez-faire form of capitalism the anarcho-capitalists advocate would not increase inequality, perhaps substantially.

Peter Marshall reasonably concludes that from the anarcho-capitalist writings

> there is little reason to believe that the rich and powerful will not continue to exploit and oppress the powerless and poor as they do at present

but then adds that

> anarcho-capitalism is merely a free-for-all in which only the rich and cunning would benefit. It is tailor-made for "rugged individualists" who do not care about the damage to others or to the environment which they leave in their wake.[23]

This assertion strikes me as only partially justified and as too hasty a dismissal of some of their very interesting ideas for alternatives to the State from which all might benefit. Indeed, both Goodman and Ward had very broad interests in social policy, and we are now in a position to judge just how much the different brands of anarchism have to offer for the development of social policy; all the good ideas do not hang from any one branch of the anarchist tree.

For me the most telling weakness of the anarcho-capitalists is their excessive reliance on the individualist strand of anarchism at the expense of the communitarian strand, which would be essential in avoiding the dangers that rightly concern Marshall. Disparities in wealth are often the outcome of voluntary actions rather than deceptive exploitation or monopolies, as when football and pop music stars become rich because followers willingly pay at the necessary level to reward them. The commitment to the individual strand of anarchism means that the anarcho-capitalists shy away from the sense of mutual obligation that is of vital importance to communalist versions of anarchism, which explains why they approve of Stirner as well as the native Spooner and Tucker,[24] and neglect the equally home-grown, and perhaps the most important American anarchist,

Murray Bookchin (1921–2006), who argued that it is through community that individual freedom is possible. By refusing to confront the individualist–communalist tensions, the anarcho-capitalists never adequately explore solutions to the communal damage that inevitably arises from extreme individualism.

Schooling is precisely one area where anarcho-capitalists and anarchists might engage in dialogue about desirable practices that might be agreed in spite of philosophical differences. Rothbard's educational ideas are set out in the short *Education Free and Compulsory* (1979), originally written in the same year as *Deschooling Society*, and in *For a New Liberty* (1973). As expected, he sees State control of schooling as usurpation by the State of parental responsibility for, and control over, the development of the child. School cannot possibly cope with the huge diversity among children in ability and interest, since they lack the resources to meet individual needs. He thus rejects compulsion and cites with approval Thomas Jefferson's view:

> It is better to tolerate the rare instance of a parent refusing to let his child be educated, than to shock the common feelings and ideas by the forcible transportation and education of the infant against the will of the father.[25]

His brief history of schooling in many countries, especially Europe as well as the USA, covers conventional ground, such as the school acting as an agent of social control designed to mould obedience and conformity, suppressing individuality in the interest of equality and uniformity. He is aware of the work of Edwin G. West and of course Paul Goodman, but makes little use of them, which is surprising given that he notes the remarkable agreement between them, despite some differences.

However, his history of the schooling in the USA has some interesting parallels with Phil Gardner's account of the English experience. Rothbard argues that

> from the beginning of American history, the desire to mould, instruct, and render obedient the mass of the population was the major impetus behind the drive toward public schooling. In colonial days, public schooling was used as a device to suppress religious dissent, as well as to imbue unruly servants with the virtues of obedience to the State.[26]

By 1830 there was a concerted effort by reformers to gain control over the state boards of education – for schooling to this day is controlled at state, not federal, level and most teachers are civil servants – school superintendents and teacher training institutions. The reformers founded a spate of educational journals, including the *Common School Journal*, and sought the key positions in state school systems. Horace Mann, Archibald Murphy and Robert Dale Owen (son of the English Robert Owen) were major sources of influence. Mann did not advocate compulsory schooling, but advanced the cause of the common public school, following in Owen's footsteps and the campaign for compulsory schooling. As one reformer, Charles Mercer, had put it:

> The equality on which our institutions are founded cannot be too intimately interwoven in the habits of thinking among our youth; and it is obvious that it would be greatly promoted by their continuance together, for the longest possible period; in the same schools of juvenile instruction; to sit upon the same forms; engage in same competitions; partake of the same recreations and amusements, and pursue the same studies, in connection with each other; under the same discipline, and in obedience to the same authority.[27]

One can imagine the horror with which Godwin would have greeted such a proposition. One of the reasons for State control was the suppression, in the name of assimilation, of ethnic, linguistic and cultural minorities among immigrants, which was at a high level in New England, from where the drive to State control of schooling was led.

Rothbard argues that in a fundamental sense we are all self-educated, and parental teaching in the home is crucial: he is a friend of home schooling, though he accepts that most parents lack the means to hire home tutors with specialist expertise in areas outside the parents' range. He is sympathetic to the idea of school vouchers, which moves the financing of school from the State to the parents, but acknowledges that they make no sense unless the choice is a real and positive option for the vast majority of parents. This means that schools have to be encouraged to forge different identities based on different educational philosophies and different organisational and pedagogic practices. This is sound argument in that it invites educators to be innovators and then be subject to market forces on the basis of what they have to offer. He quotes with approval the British anarchist Herbert Read's view that

> Mankind is naturally differentiated into many types, and to press all these types into the same mould must inevitably lead to distortions and repressions. Schools should be of many kinds, following different methods and catering for different dispositions.[28]

There is little in the way of original thinking about alternatives to schooling: Rothbard favours a switch to private schooling rather than unschooling, which should delight James Tooley, who curiously seemed quite unaware of the anarcho-capitalists in his early books.[29]

David Friedman claims conventional State schooling is based on two assumptions. The first is that there is an agreed body of knowledge that all children should learn or at least be exposed to – our own National Curriculum has shown how difficult it is to achieve such agreement. The second is to transmit this through the authority of a teacher with textbooks. He rejects both assumptions as mistaken and indefensible. He favours a way to reduce State control of schooling by transferring the costs of State schooling from the schools and those authorities, central or local, who currently hold the purse strings, directly to parents as consumers. Thus he turns to Milton Friedman (his father) and his scheme of school vouchers, suggested ten years earlier, with the reservation that this would still leave the State with the prerogative of deciding the kinds of schooling on which the vouchers might be spent.

One of my own objections to vouchers is that in England and Wales the assessment regime and Ofsted, which relies so heavily for its judgements of school quality on test and examination results, mean that State schools, more than private schools, are so heavily constrained by these very narrow criteria that schools become progressively more and more alike. In such circumstances parental choice is limited and will focus on the schools that score most highly by examination and Ofsted criteria, leading to massive oversubscription of a minority of schools, which then requires State intervention. Real diversity of schools is surely a prerequisite of any serious voucher scheme.

Neither home schooling nor vouchers are Friedman's preferred option, which is *unschooling*. He comes to this from his and his wife's experience of schooling. 'Both of us had a good few teachers and classes, but what we most remembered was being bored most of the time.'[30] This, incidentally, was my experience too and it was by chance that I suddenly became more hooked on one of my subjects at the very point when I was on the edge of leaving school at 16. The Friedmans therefore started with a form of home schooling – 'no classes, just books, conversation, unlimited internet access'. Unschooling was simply 'throwing books at kids and seeing which ones stick', because this is consonant with his belief that 'People learn things much more easily and remember them longer if they are things they want to learn',[31] exactly the point on which Godwin insisted. It is, of course, also the lesson that every teacher learns at the beginning of a professional career: discovering or inducing this internal motivation is the teacher's most difficult task, but potentially the most rewarding of all. Is it possible that this is more likely to be achieved in the kind of schools advocated by Jonathan Kozol and George Dennison, who appear to be unknown to Rothbard and Friedman?

The price Friedman and his wife paid was finding the patience and time without limit to spend and talk with their children. He admits to nagging their children to master the multiplication tables, which his adult daughter now thinks was a mistake. There were parts of what is in a school curriculum that were missed out, but they ended up learning a great deal about what is not in the school curriculum. However, the long-term outcome of their approach is that their children have the confidence to set about learning anything they now find necessary but was omitted during their childhood. They have learned how to learn.

Friedman does not deny that some children would learn more in a conventional school and that some parents would be unwilling or unable to behave as they did. Like Rothbard, Friedman is sympathetic to home schooling, but he worries that it can easily become just 'schooling at home' rather than unschooling. So he proposes a variation on school vouchers, by which a group of parents who do not like any of the schools on offer might simply pool their voucher resources and set up their own school – a more radical version of England's 'free schools', which of course are funded by the State not by parents, and they are still schools. Friedman leans towards abandoning the conception of schools as specialised buildings, but does not go far enough for many anarchists. Instead of talking about *school choice* we should perhaps think of *education choice*, that is, a choice among different kinds of opportunities, and different kinds of locations, of how to become educated. School is just one among these diverse opportunities and locations. There is here potential agreement with the approaches taken by Goodman, Ward and Bentley in previous chapters.

The educational views and preferences of Rothbard and Friedman are far more progressive than those advocated by mainstream Conservative Party policies, both in the heady 1970s as well as post-1988 England. Indeed, to the horror of many Conservatives today, they are evidently much more at home with William Godwin's pedagogical philosophy:

> In a word, the first lesson of a judicious education is, Learn to think. To discriminate, to remember, and to enquire.[32]

Given that there are similarities, some unexpected, between Rothbard/Friedman and Godwin on the diagnosis of the ills of schooling, it is rather surprising that many contemporary anarchists simply ignore or reject out of hand the anarcho-capitalists, though they in turn are somewhat picky about which anarchists they admit to their fold. The significant differences between them cannot be denied, but given that they share some common ground, more exchange of ideas between the two might be very productive. If only there could be a debate, on the scale of Bakunin versus Marx, to command the attention of a wider public, but perhaps neither side today has a living fighter of sufficient stature.

All the writers we have discussed thus far are open to the claim that they are utopian. Usually the term is pejorative, implying that a proposal for change and for the future of society is unrealistic, a naïve and foolish pipedream, mere fantasy or fairy story, that is, impossible to realise. This is how Popper responded to Plato and Marx, but also how Marxists referred to socialists who did not believe in the need for revolution, though of course the Marxist vision of a post-revolutionary classless society as the State withers away is utopian too. Utopianism is the allegation commonly made against the various forms of anarchism. Many thinkers and writers become sensitive to the allegation, for it is taken to be a dismissive insult. Is this a risk that any writer about the future must take, or is the charge warranted only for those who draft blueprints lacking feasibility, or those who believe in the perfectibility of human beings and the possibility of a heaven on earth? David Friedman touches on the subject in a way that suggests it is a sensitive point:

> There are Utopias and Utopias. A Utopia that will work only if populated by saints is a perilous vision; there are not enough saints. Such a vision – liberalism,

> socialism, call it what you will – we have followed; it has led us where we are now. I have not tried to construct a Utopia in that sense. I have tried … to describe plausible institutions under which human beings not very different from ourselves could live. Those institutions must evolve over a period of time, as did the institutions under which we presently live; they cannot be instantly conjured up from the dreams of an enthusiastic writer. The objective is distant but not necessarily unreachable. It is well to know where one is going before taking even the first step.[33]

Friedman's utopia in the second sense is usually termed 'gradualism': he is close to Colin Ward in favouring the progressive evolution of new institutions towards the longer-term goal of a better society. For Friedman school vouchers could never be more than a temporary measure, since the true goal is a Stateless society with no taxes and therefore no vouchers, which from the perspective of the Stateless destination were just one intermediary step. Both accept the need to persuade the public and so follow William Godwin's strategy:

> We shall have many reforms, but no revolutions. As it is only in the gradual manner that the public can be instructed, a violent explosion in the community is by no means the most likely to happen as the result of instruction.[34]

Is Godwin's reliance on the power of reason utopian? Peter Marshall, our greatest expert on Godwin as on many other aspects of anarchism, concludes, with delightful ambiguity, that 'Godwin's gradualism demonstrates that he is no naïve utopian.'[35] This could mean that he is a utopian but not a naïve one, but also that he is no utopian because utopians are by definition naïve. After nearly 800 pages of *Political Justice*, Godwin concludes that

> Whatever be the object towards which mind irresistibly advances, it is of no mean importance to us to have a distinct view of that object. Our advance will thus become accelerated. It is a well known principle of morality "that he who proposes perfection to himself, *though he will inevitably fall short of that which he pursues*, will make a more rapid progress than he who is contented to aim only at what is imperfect".[36]

With this wonderful anticipatory sideswipe at Popper's excessive reliance on the removal of current evils, Godwin emerges as a *gradualist utopian*, like Friedman and Ward, with an optimistic ideal as the goal, but with an acknowledgement that it can never be entirely realised. The State cannot easily be murdered, though it might be slowly asphyxiated or starved to death, especially if some aspects of State control, such as schooling, can be wrenched from its hands. They do not want to murder the school: they want a far greater diversity of schools that can be supplemented or substituted by other means of education.

This raises, for the anarcho-capitalists, the possibility of a somewhat less ambitious goal, namely one of limited government, on either an intermediate or permanent basis (i.e. minarchism and 'the watchman State'), since clearly not every element of a State can be removed at a stroke, and perhaps not ever. Interestingly, however, the possibility of a strictly limited government has been rejected as a 'truly Utopian idea' by another anarcho-capitalist,[37] since there is every reason to think that a reduced State, as it changed political hands, would soon creep towards a resumption of its previous powers as a way of dealing with any transitional problems.

For all anarchists the abolition of the State would mean that much of what the State now does has to be undertaken directly by the community. Even for the anarcho-capitalists, much of the advocated private provision would be provided not merely to individuals or families, but to commissioning communities, and so be rooted in and made accountable to the community. Moreover many of the alternatives to State schooling, including the little private schools that have operated in such vastly different conditions, such as Phil Gardner's early-nineteenth-century England, the late-twentieth-century Boston of Jonathan Kozol or New York of George Dennison, or James Tooley's twenty-first-century India, are all in a very real way rooted in working-class communities, and this fact seems to be crucial to their success.

Both the anarcho-capitalists and mainstream anarchists today seem mostly to have abandoned the early notion of a sudden revolution and opt for a gradualist process. As Nicholas Walter put it:

> I want a government that governs less, but I want the lessening process to be continuous, so that government always governs less and less, and the people look after themselves more and more until in the end there is a government that does not govern at all.[38]

Such a progressive decline of the State would inevitably place enormous pressures on the community as it moves to shoulder new responsibilities. Is the anarchist concept of the community robust enough for this?

Notes

1 Stirner (1842: 23, original emphasis).
2 Stirner (1842: 26, original emphasis).
3 Rothbard (1973: 27).
4 Rothbard (2009: 1).
5 Rothbard (2009: 49).
6 Rothbard (1973: 50).
7 Woodcock, p. xii in his 1979 translation of *What Is Property?*
8 Godwin (1793: 721f).
9 Godwin (1793: 718).
10 Godwin (1793: 714).
11 Godwin (1793: 716).

12 Godwin (1793: 723).
13 Godwin (1793: 715).
14 The report of the two Select Committees (HC769), published 16 May 2018, made headlines in many national newspapers on this day.
15 Rothbard (1973: 63, original emphasis).
16 Hyams (1979: 46).
17 Rothbard (1979: 4–6).
18 Friedman (1973: 18).
19 Friedman (1973: 107).
20 In Read (1974).
21 Read (1974: 41ff, original emphasis).
22 Friedman (1973: 20).
23 Marshall (1992: 564–5).
24 For discussions on Stirner and Tucker, among others, for their influence on the USA, see Shone (2013).
25 Rothbard (1979: 41).
26 Rothbard (1973: 150).
27 Quoted in Rothbard (1979: 50).
28 Rothbard (1973: 159).
29 This can no longer be true, since he is an Adjunct Scholar at the Cato Institute in Washington DC, of which Rothbard was a founding member.
30 Friedman (1973: 312).
31 Friedman (1973: 311).
32 Marshall (1986: 132).
33 Friedman (1973: 143).
34 Friedman (1973: 252).
35 Marshall (2017).
36 Godwin (1793: 794, emphasis added).
37 Rockwell (2014: 168).
38 Ward (1987: 17).

7

STATE SCHOOLING VERSUS COMMUNITY EDUCATION

> We are the State, and we will be the State as long as we … have not yet created the institutions necessary for a true community and a true society of human beings.
>
> Gustav Landauer, 1911

> There is an inverse correlation between the two: the strength of the one is the weakness of the other. If we want to strengthen society, we must weaken the state.
>
> Colin Ward, 1973: 20

Do you remember the Big Society? It was David Cameron's big idea. In the 2010 Conservative Party manifesto this is how it was announced:

> Despite Labour's massive expansion of the State, many people's quality of life is getting worse. The number of people living in poverty has risen in the last three years, and inequality is at a record high … This terrible record of failure … is the result of a political approach that addresses the symptoms, rather than the underlying causes, of social breakdown; one that relies on top-down government intervention and bureaucratic micro-management. So we need a new approach: social responsibility, not state control; the big society, not big government … So we will redistribute power from the central state to individuals, families and local communities … Our approach is absolutely in line with the spirit of the age: the post-bureaucratic age.

At first sight, a proposal for decentralisation that brings joy to anarchist ears. But sceptical experience urges caution. Ignore the opening rhetoric about Labour. Assume the idea of the Big Society is not party political at all, but an idea that people in general might welcome. So enquire: how would such a commendable goal be achieved?

> We will use the state to help stimulate social action, helping social enterprises to deliver public services and training new community organisers to help achieve our ambition of every adult citizen being a member of an active neighbourhood group.

It sounds promising, doesn't it? Has the David Cameron team been listening to the American anarcho-capitalists? The aim is to use the State to strengthen existing community provision and stimulate new community provision, for this would transform the poverty and inequality they said their government had inherited. Colin Ward would surely have been delighted – if cautiously – by such steps towards his gradualist strategy.

But wait: what is their record eight years later? In undisputed fact, poverty and inequality have both increased. Many local services have steeply deteriorated, as libraries and swimming pools close, and social care is in crisis. Plainly, communities have been weakened, not strengthened. Where communities have responded positively to this idea – such as volunteers cooperating to keep public libraries open – it is a product of local commitment, in spite of the State, not because of it.

I am not making a party political point, for we have been here before. Do you remember this from the previous government? Here is an extract from *Working Together*, a 2009 government paper introduced by Gordon Brown:

> To get the best out of public services, it is essential that they are [*sic*] joined up locally around the citizen, are responsive to local circumstances and, crucially, harness the capacities of communities to identify and solve their own problems. In this way we will make public policy more sensitive to "place" – not only to recognise that places are different and need different solutions, but also to unlock the energy and creativity of people on the front line. To do this we need greater devolution and decentralisation not just to local councils, but crucially to individuals, families, community groups, and professionals working in local public services … But this devolution to Local Authorities and their partners is not enough. We also need to see devolution from Local Authorities and their partners to communities themselves … Empowering local people is particularly important during difficult economic times – engaging them in the difficult decisions which need to be taken. Local people will be given more opportunities in the coming year to get things done for themselves.

Was David Cameron engaging in policy theft? How confident are you that, had the Labour Government remained in office for a longer period, this rhetoric would have been turned into practical action? My own experience is that both ministers and senior civil servants may sincerely recognise the limits on what can be done from Whitehall, but when it comes to making decisions that might involve decentralisation *by them*, they are extremely reluctant to let go of their control. A related 2010 report by an independent body suggests this is not a party political issue and it expresses its view in language that is more diplomatic than mine:

> Government has traditionally found it difficult to support genuine local solutions while achieving national impact and scale ... Policymakers increasingly recognise that this kind of community participation is crucial in responding to many social challenges that drive escalating demand for public services. Centrally driven initiatives have struggled to make an impact on many of the complex issues confronting us today ... But despite support from across the political spectrum, genuine localism is something governments find difficult to achieve.

Undeterred by this admission, the report makes many powerful recommendations about decentralisation and local empowerment:

> Mass localism is an alternative approach to combining local action and national scale. Instead of assuming that the best solutions need to be determined, prescribed, driven or 'authorised' in some manner from the centre, policymakers should create more opportunities for communities to develop and deliver their own solutions. It is not enough to assume that scaling back government bureaucracy and control will allow local innovation to flourish. Mass localism depends on a different kind of support from government and a different approach to scale.[1]

From an anarchist perspective, this report and others of a similar character are always unlikely to be implemented, even when accepted in principle, because it is the nature of the State to cling to power. In this sense, the State is always likely to be the enemy of community empowerment.

This means that anarchists must have confidence that a community has the latent, and perhaps hitherto unused, capacity to assume enhanced responsibility. This is no mean task, for our current dependence on the State means that when the State fails, the common initial response is often not to fall back on the resources of the community, but merely to complain helplessly about State inaction. Is anarchism's confidence in the community warranted?

In a chapter with this title, Peter Kropotkin (1842–1921) finds a special place, for his contribution on the communalist side to anarchism is impressive. He should properly be thought of as an anarcho-communist, since he thought the two inextricably linked: 'Anarchy leads to Communism, and Communism to Anarchy'.[2] Though he supported the Russian revolution, he soon lost any faith in the Bolsheviks when they became unacceptably authoritarian and made use of hostages in support of their cause.[3] His letters of protest to Lenin remained unanswered; not a surprise. On the individualist–communalist tension within anarchism, he adopts the line taken by other founding fathers, but stresses their co-evolution over time, for anarchism

> seeks the most complete development of individuality combined with the highest development of voluntary association in all its aspects, in all possible degrees, for all imaginable aims; ever changing, ever modified associations which carry in themselves the elements of their durability and constantly assume new forms which answer best to the multiple aspirations of all.[4]

He favours the abolition of the State, of course, but opens his opposition by pointing out that for most of human history we have managed, often perfectly well, without the State, whose origin he dates to the sixteenth century. Before the introduction of State law, communities ordered their social lives through customary law, and an anarchist society develops these to fit modern circumstances:

> Without social feelings and usages, life in common would have been absolutely impossible. It is not law, which has established them; they are anterior to all law.[5]

Today, by contrast, he argued that we are subject to

> a race of law-makers legislating without knowing what their laws are about; today voting a law on the sanitation of towns, without the faintest notion of hygiene; tomorrow making regulations for the armament of troops, without so much as understanding a gun; making laws about teaching and education without ever having given a lesson of any sort, or even an honest education to their own children; legislating at random in all directions, but never forgetting the penalties …[6]

The State built law on the foundations of customary law, but then interwove it with the new State laws, so that the whole system seemed to be a product of the State. Like Godwin before him, he bewails the fact that once the State establishes laws, people faced with a problem become habituated to expecting the State to solve the problem by recourse to a new law. The price we pay for turning to the State in this way is the damage it does to self-help and creative problem-solving:

> We are so perverted by an education which from infancy seeks to kill in us the spirit of revolt, and to develop that of submission to authority; we are so perverted by this existence under the ferrule of a law, which regulates every event in life … that if this state continues, we shall lose all

> initiative, all habit of thinking for ourselves. Our society seems no longer able to understand that it is possible to exist otherwise than under the reign of law.[7]

He takes a distinctive line on the consequences of this, when he explores the justification for law-making. He says there are three main categories of law: protection of the property, of persons, and of government. The last of these, constitutional law, takes up about a third portion, and has 'no other end but to maintain, patch up and develop the administrative machine' of the State. Protection of the person, he says, 'occupies an imperceptible space … The major portion have but one object – to protect private property, i.e., wealth acquired by the exploitation of man by man.'[8]

Kropotkin parts company from some other anarchists in arguing, like a good communist, for the expropriation of private property, rejecting the arguments of Godwin and Proudhon that private property is a safeguard of individual liberty. One can see why Kropotkin might believe this when his background is considered, for he was a prince, belonging to an immensely rich family of the highest rank in Russian aristocracy. There are excellent biographies of Kropotkin,[9] but his autobiography, which covers his life up to the age of 47, is an absorbing and at times a thrilling book. He explains life at home during his childhood:

> Wealth was measured in those times by the number of "souls" that a landed proprietor owned. So many "souls" meant so many male serfs: women did not count. My father, who owned nearly twelve hundred souls, in three different provinces, and who had, in addition to his peasants' holdings, large tracts of land which were cultivated by these peasants, was accounted a rich man. He lived up to his reputation, which meant that his house was open to any number of visitors and that he kept a very large household. We were a family of eight, occasionally of ten or twelve; but fifty servants at Moscow, and half as many more in the country, were considered not one too many. Four coachmen to attend a dozen horses, three cooks for the masters and two more for the servants, a dozen men to wait upon us at dinner-time (one man, plate in hand, standing behind each person seated at the table), and girls innumerable in the maid-servants' room – how could any one do with less than this?[10]

One day, his somewhat irascible father, in a state of rage and frustration that strikes terror throughout the household, eventually picks on one of his assembled servants, a hapless sub-butler and piano-tuner, who has dropped some plates, and who is then sent to the police station with the instruction that he be given a punishment of 100 lashes of the birch. When the man returns, pale and with a distorted face, young Peter runs to him and tries to kiss his hand. The man tears it away and says, 'Let me alone. You too, when you are grown up, will you not be just the same?'

This may not have been a Damascene moment, but it seems to have been a milestone on his path to becoming an anarchist:

> Having been brought up in a serf-owner's family, I entered active life, like all young men of my time, with a great deal of confidence in the necessity of commanding, ordering, scolding, punishing, and the like. But when, at an early stage, I had to manage serious enterprises and to deal with men, and when each mistake would lead at once to heavy consequences, I began to appreciate the difference between acting on the principle of command and discipline and acting on the principle of common understanding. The former works admirably in a military parade, but it is worth nothing where real life is concerned, and the aim can be achieved only through the severe effort of many converging wills … I may say now that I lost in Siberia whatever faith in State discipline I had cherished before. I was prepared to become an anarchist.[11]

It was later, after a visit to the Jura Federation in Switzerland, when he observed what immediately impressed him as the right relationships between workers, that the moment of conversion arrived:

> The very organisation of the watch trade, which permits men to know one another thoroughly and to work in their own houses, where they are free to talk, explains why the level of intellectual development in this population is higher than that of workers who spend all their life from early childhood in the factories. There is more independence and more originality among the petty trades' workers … Here I saw that the workers were not a mass that was being led and made subservient to the political ends of a few men; their leaders were simply their more active comrades – initiators rather than leaders … and after a week's stay with the watchmakers, my views upon socialism were settled. I was an anarchist.[12]

Kropotkin was a geographer, a field in which he did original investigations that earned him a distinguished reputation. He believed passionately in the natural sciences and his most famous book, *Mutual Aid: A Factor in Evolution* (1902, but published earlier as articles) was central to his basic thesis about the social life acclaimed by anarchists. He greatly admired Darwin, but was incensed at the distortion of the theory of evolution in the suggestion that the natural state of human beings was the struggle for 'the survival of the fittest' – the term coined by Herbert Spencer but often mistakenly attributed to Darwin. The culprit here was T. H. Huxley, who was later President of the Royal Society and who was popularly known as Darwin's Bulldog. Huxley's *Struggle for Existence and its Bearing upon Man* emphasised the role of competition in evolution and seemed in line with Hobbes's dictum of the human condition as 'the war of each against all'. Kropotkin believed that this was an excessive emphasis on competition at the expense of cooperation, which is also found in nature, and in this way sought to widen the understanding of how evolution operates.

Kropotkin took exception to Huxley's 'manifesto', which he viewed as 'a very incorrect representation of the facts of Nature, as one sees them in the bush and forest' – in this Kropotkin was relying on his own direct experience of field work in Siberia and Mongolia – where there were ample examples of how relationships *within a species* were often characterised by mutual aid, and became competitive only in particular circumstances. So he felt the need to respond to 'a number of evolutionists who may not refuse to admit the importance of mutual aid among animals, but who, like Herbert Spencer, will refuse to admit it for Man'.[13] In reply, Kropotkin asserts 'the immense importance which the mutual-support instincts, inherited by mankind from its extremely long evolution, play even now in our modern society'.[14]

After detailed studies of mutual aid in insects, birds and animals – examples of which today are commonplace in David Attenborough's *Planet* television series – Kropotkin concludes that competition

> is limited among animals to exceptional periods, and natural selection finds better fields for its activity. Better conditions are created by the *elimination of competition* by means of mutual aid and mutual support. In the great struggle for life – for the greatest possible fullness and intensity of life with the least waste of energy – natural selection continually seeks out the ways precisely for avoiding competition as much as possible.[15]

He then turns to mankind, starting with the pre-historical period or, using the normal terminology of the period, 'the savages', to find examples of mutual aid. Of course, he is particularly attracted to examples that exemplify his own ideological position:

> Eskimo life is based upon communism. What is obtained by hunting and fishing belongs to the clan. But in several tribes, under the influence of the Danes, private property penetrates into their institutions. However, they have an original means for obviating the inconveniences arising from a personal accumulation of wealth which would soon destroy their tribal unity. When a man has grown rich, he convokes the folk of his clan to a great festival, and, after much eating, distributes among them all his fortune.[16]

In moving to the later historical period – 'the barbarians' – he says we should look underneath the official records of wars and conflicts to discover what everyday life is like for most people most of the time, where the stream of mutual aid constantly flows. It is this current that he then traces through the glories of the mediaeval city to his own day, where it flows despite the growth of the State:

> All these associations, societies, brotherhoods, alliances, institutes, and so on, which must be counted by the ten thousand in Europe alone, and each of which represents an immense amount of voluntary, unambitious, and unpaid or underpaid work – what are they but so many manifestations, under an infinite variety of aspects, of the same ever-living tendency of man towards mutual aid and support?[17]

Here he writes as a precursor to Robert Putnam's widely acclaimed and much-read *Bowling Alone: The Collapse and Revival of American Community* (2001), which chartered in the USA the steep decline in 'social capital', the new jargon term (coined in 1916) for something very close to Kropotkin's mutual aid. Yet Kropotkin never ignores the old anarchist tension, for

> mutual aid, even though it may represent one of the factors of evolution, covers nevertheless one aspect only of human relations; that by the side of this current, powerful though it may be, there always is, and always has been, the other current – the self-assertion of the individual.

He is in awe of mutual aid, but he never lets his fascination lure him into a romanticisation of it; and even then he acknowledges that individuality not only is necessary to resist community pressures to conformity, but also releases the creativity that serves to advance the human path of progress. He considers the relative strengths of these two factors, but can do no more than point out how history tends to underestimate the importance of mutual aid as a progressive force. Despite 'the opposition of a number of contrary agencies', mutual aid flows from the animal kingdom in an uninterrupted evolution to present-day mankind. He concludes on the ethical note that would be the subject of his incomplete final book:

> In the practice of mutual aid, which we can retrace to the earliest beginnings of evolution, we can thus find the positive and undoubted origin of our ethical conceptions; and we can affirm that in the ethical progress of man, mutual support – not mutual struggle – has had the leading part.[18]

Kropotkin's ethical stance shows itself in all his work, as in his attitude to prison, of which he had considerable personal experience, after being imprisoned first in the notorious St Peter and St Paul Fortress in St Petersburg and later in France:

> Every one knows that the absence of education, dislike of regular work, physical incapability of sustained effort, misdirected love of adventure, gambling propensities, absence of energy, an untrained will, and carelessness about the happiness of others are the causes which bring this class of people before the courts. Now I was deeply impressed during my imprisonment by the fact that it is exactly these defects of human nature – each one of them – which the prison breeds in its inmates; and it is bound to breed them because it is a prison, and

> will breed them so long as it exists. Incarceration in a prison of necessity entirely destroys the energy of a man and annihilates his will … he is more embittered against society, and he finds a more solid justification for being in revolt against its laws and customs; necessarily, unavoidably, he is bound to sink deeper and deeper into the anti-social acts which first brought him before a law court … prisons are "universities of crime, maintained by the state".[19]

A century earlier, William Godwin, who had never been in prison, showed that prison reform was a deep anarchist principle, not just a personal bias of Kropotkin's:

> The most common method pursued in depriving the offender of the liberty he has abused is to erect a public jail, in which offenders of every description are thrust together and left to form among themselves what species of society they can … Jails are … seminaries of vice; and he must be … a man of sublime virtue, who does not come out of them a much worse man that he entered.[20]

Are our prisons, whose population is greater than ever, any better today, and are we any nearer finding a solution? For anarchists, the solution is not to be found in reforms of what goes on in prisons, but rather in finding ways in which most (but not all) criminals can be rehabilitated and reintegrated into the community. This, of course, presupposes a certain kind of community and one that is willing to undertake such a re-education. Clearly this would need to be a community committed to mutual aid, or one with high levels of social capital – a bigger and better society.

Where did David Cameron's push for the 'Big Society' notion go wrong? The whole idea came over as a political gimmick. Evidently it was not properly thought through as a concept, especially in its sociological basis; and the government failed to anticipate a public reaction that interpreted the idea, not as building on past achievements and finding additional resources to strengthen them, but as a cover for cutting public services and dumping social problems on the community. The cynical reaction appeared to be confirmed by George Osborne's reign of austerity at the Treasury. In fact, the evidence suggests there was already a strong fund of social capital in the UK on which it could have been launched. Peter Hall has shown that in the UK, in contrast to what Putnam found in the USA, social capital has remained relatively robust over the last fifty years. The kinds of association here may have changed, but membership has not seriously declined:

> Since the beginning of the twentieth century, British governments have made substantial efforts to cultivate the voluntary sector, notably using it to deliver social services to a degree that seems striking in cross-cultural terms. Successive governments have devoted substantial resources to this objective.[21]

Civic involvement increases substantially with age, and women tend to be more involved than men. Education is very important here: every additional year of education increases the propensity to involvement, as Hall argues, so the growing number of women now in higher education augurs well for the future. There is also a social class effect, leaving an image of 'a nation divided between a well-connected group of citizens with prosperous lives and high levels of civic engagement and other groups whose networks, associational life, and involvement in politics are very limited'. And he adds that 'the two groups who face marginalisation from civil society are the working class and the young',[22] which is surely a matter of considerable concern, since it points to British society becoming ever more divided.

Had Cameron convincingly presented the Big Society as a means of strengthening social capital and integrating this with other radical changes, such as rethinking penal policy and the rehabilitation of offenders in the community to reduce the high rates of recidivism, especially among the young, there might have been a less cynical reaction. But such a genuinely bold policy would have needed careful public education, trained community champions, and sustained support from central government, including some initial finance, to make it a reality, the very thing that central governments are not good at.

How did Kropotkin conceive of the place of communities in a future society, one that at the end of the nineteenth century was unlike our own? The key lies in the process of decentralisation, which will draw back power from the State and restore it to, and reinvigorate it in, the communities that make up society – yes, shades of Cameron's Big Society theme. In this regard he had been persuaded, in documenting the evidence for *Mutual Aid*, by the character of the mediaeval city, which achieved new heights of mutual aid that were subsequently lost with the development of the larger, centralised State:

> No period of history could better illustrate the constructive powers of the popular masses than the tenth and eleventh centuries, when the fortified villages and market-places, representing so many "oases amidst the feudal forest", began to free themselves from their lord's yoke, and slowly elaborated the future city organisation … The city organised itself as a federation of both small village communities and guilds.[23]

The guilds were models of the kind of self-management that he had witnessed among the watch-makers:

> Self-jurisdiction was the essential point, and self-jurisdiction meant self-administration … To guarantee liberty, self-administration, and peace, was the chief aim of the city; and labour … [in the form of] the craft guilds, was its chief foundation.[24]

The change made by these cities was immense. Before that, the towns of Europe consisted mainly of miserable huts and clumsily built churches, and the crafts of weaving and forging were in their infancy. Three hundred and fifty years later, the new cities were embellished with fine architecture of 'a purity of form and a boldness of imagination which we now strive vainly to attain'. The arts and crafts flourished and had 'risen to a degree of perfection which we can hardly boast of having superseded';[25] learning and science made rapid progress. Yet the federations between cities gave way over the following centuries to the centralised State. Nevertheless, Kropotkin insisted, the current of mutual aid never ran completely dry.

> It flows still even now, and it seeks its way to find out a new expression which would not be the State, nor the mediaeval city, nor the village community of the barbarians, nor the savage clan, but would proceed from all of them, and yet be superior to them in its wider a more deeply humane conceptions.[26]

It was in his *Fields, Factories and Workshops*, first published as a series of articles in 1888–1890, that Kropotkin set out his optimistic superior conception. In support of his case, the subsequent book of 1898 was, as usual, packed with evidence, much of which is now badly out of date. In 1974 Colin Ward stripped out much of the old evidence and substituted contemporary evidence (it is perhaps time to update it yet again) to support the core argument, which of course was left untouched. Kropotkin at once sets out his stall:

> We proclaim *integration*; and we maintain that the ideal society – that is, the state towards which society is already marching – is a society of integrated, combined labour. A society where each individual is a producer of both manual and intellectual work; where each able-bodied human being is a worker, and where each worker works both in the field and the industrial workshop; where each aggregation of individuals, large enough to dispose of a certain variety of natural resources – it may be a nation or rather a region – produces and itself consumes most of its own agricultural and manufactured produce … [for] the present industrial system, based upon a permanent specialisation of functions, already bears in itself the germs of its proper ruin.[27]

Kropotkin's enthusiasm for self-governing communes, with their more balanced individual life, pushes him to a very small mono-cultural commune with limited ambitions, one that is not at all attractive to those of us who value pluralism and diversity. Do his self-sufficient communities remind you of the delightfully entertaining TV series *The Good Life* with Richard Briers and Felicity Kendal tending their smallholding as Penelope Keith's superior Margot looks on piteously but charitably? Is his whole scheme of community impossibly utopian? Colin Ward would hail the book as 'one of those great prophetic works of the nineteenth century whose hour is yet to come'[28] – and, perhaps anticipating an allegation of utopianism, with cautious optimism he tagged the word *Tomorrow* onto Kropotkin's original book title.

Nearly fifty years after Ward's revision, we can acknowledge the book's underlying and more enduring themes. Of these, the one of particular interest to us is his final chapter, which is devoted to education and illustrates how, for anarchists, education is linked in a reciprocal way to their conception of the community. From his autobiography we learn what was important for him in his own education, where the impact of the individual teacher and the way of teaching matters, for this needs a touch of magic for 'the bewitching power of all studies … that continually open us to new, unsuspected horizons, not yet understood, which entice us to proceed further and further'.[29] This is not achieved by a curriculum of tightly framed separate subjects without applications. The good teacher, he says, teaches not merely a single subject but also the link between subjects. The teacher of literature is best placed to do this, and for the sciences perhaps most readily a teacher of geography, a field that is inherently multi-disciplinary. He argues not for a curriculum relevant to the current life of pupils, but rather active learning with practical application:

> [C]hildren and youths long for the application of what they learn at school, and how stupid are the educators who are unable to see what a powerful aid they could find in this direction for helping their pupils to grasp the real sense of the things they learn … all this longing of children and youths for *real* work is wasted, simply because our idea of the school is still the mediaeval scholasticism, this mediaeval monastery![30]

So he opens the education chapter in *Fields, Factories and Workshops* by drawing the reader's attention to this fact in the lives of our greatest scientists. Newton learned how to manage tools in his boyhood so that for his later researches into optics he could grind his own lenses; Linnaeus became a botanist through helping his father, a gardener. 'We have changed all that', Kropotkin protests, because 'we have sharply separated the brain worker from the manual worker'. An education of this kind cannot provide a preparation for the society that Kropotkin has in mind – the small, self-sufficient communities of labour-intensive agriculture and small industrial workshops:

> We fully recognise the necessity of specialisation of knowledge, but we maintain that specialisation must follow general education, and that general education must be given in science and handicraft alike. To the division of society into brain workers and manual workers we oppose the combination of both kinds of activities; and instead of "technical education", which means the maintenance of the present division between brain work and manual work, we advocate *éducation intégrale*, or complete education, which means the disappearance of that pernicious distinction.[31]

A distinction that still perniciously blights English education, from school through to much of higher education, separating 'academic' from 'vocational' learning to the detriment of both. Just as the separation of science from handicraft leads to the decay of both, so too does the separation of art from handicraft.

These passages were immensely influential on me, for as I first read them I had become chairman of a committee of enquiry set up by the Inner London Education Authority to consider under-achievement in secondary schools. As we considered what should be in the curriculum – and this was five years before the advent of the National Curriculum – we had to recognise that the individual subjects were firmly embedded in secondary education and in the 16-plus examinations. Could bridges be found between the separate subjects to provide better curriculum coherence, I wondered? It was Kropotkin who led me to look very carefully at a subject about which I knew very little – CDT or craft, design, technology, which in many schools had a low or marginal status, for it was not an 'academic' subject. On investigation into the best exemplars of how the subject was being taught in the London schools I visited, I concluded that Kropotkin was right. When well taught, CDT was indeed a bridge both to science and to art, as well as to post-school vocational and technical education. Subsequently, to the surprise of many, we recommended that CDT should be part of the core curriculum in the secondary school and even so persuaded Sir Keith Joseph, the then Education Secretary. Many years later, sadly the *C* in CDT slipped away and the subject became just D&T. Government curriculum policy has continued to marginalise the subject and examination entries have been in decline for some years.[32] Kropotkin would, I think, have been the first to commiserate.

The teaching of mathematics as a way of getting pupils merely to commit parts of the subject to memory arouses Kropotkin's condemnation, for the result is that most of it is forgotten two years after leaving school, because 'they have never been taught to discover the proofs by themselves'. What should happen is that the knowledge should be presented to the pupils as a problem, to which the solution is not provided beforehand, in order to induce pupils to find the solution for themselves, which then also helps pupils to acquire confidence in their own reasoning. He is fully aware of what today we would call meta-cognition:

> [W]e kill independent thought in the bud; and very seldom we succeed in conveying a real knowledge of what we are teaching. Superficiality, parrot-like repetition, slavishness, and inertia of mind are the results of our method of education. We do not teach our children how to learn.[33]

Still today the pressure from central government on test performance discourages the problem-solving approach in favour of memorisation, when teachers know that problem-solving is a better motivator and also supports memorisation, for we remember best what we find interesting and useful.

Kropotkin does understand that the transition from his own society to the kind of society he envisages is a huge undertaking. He wonders whether the two great pioneers of great industry, Britain and France, might take 'a new initiative and do something new again' using their 'creative genius' for taking a new direction, 'namely the utilisation of both the land and the industrial powers of man for securing well-being to the whole nation instead of to the few'.[34] Today France and Britain may well be moving in opposite directions, with France, under President Macron, looking to the closer integration of the European Union, and a post-Brexit Britain desperately searching for a holistic new vision for itself, one that self-evidently has yet to be made beyond the platitudes of Theresa May and the Brexiteers.

Lest you think the whole of Kropotkin's vision of a future society and of education is too utopian ever to be realised, we should look more closely at his ideas both of the State and of the social revolution that leads to its abolition. In his short monograph *The State: Its Historic Role* (1897) Kropotkin offers a clarification:

> [I]t seems to me that the State and government are two concepts of a different order. The State idea means something quite different from the idea of government. It not only includes the existence of a power situated above society, but also of a *territorial concentration* as well as the concentration *in the hands of a few of many functions of the life of societies*. It implies some new relationships between members of society which did not exist before the formation of the State. A whole mechanism of legislation and policing had to be developed in order to subject some classes to the domination of others.[35]

Is politics necessarily linked to the idea of the State? I think not. I have always admired Michael Oakeshott's definition:

> Politics I take to be the activity of attending to the general arrangements of a set of people whom chance or choice have brought together … the activity is one in which every member of the group who is neither a child nor a lunatic has some part and some responsibility. With us it is, at one level or another, a universal activity.[36]

As Murray Bookchin insists:

> It is important to distinguish the social in humanity from the political, and, still further, the political from the State. We have created a terrible muddle by confusing the three and thereby legitimating one by mingling it with the other. This confusion has serious consequences for the present and the future. We have lost our sense of what it means to be political by assigning political functions and prerogatives to "politicians," actually to a select, often elite, group of people who practice a form of institutional manipulation called statecraft.[37]

So 'every institutionalised association that constitutes a system for handling public affairs – with or without the presence of a State – is necessarily a government'.[38] And you will have noticed that anarchist praise for self-government makes no sense if they object to all government.

In his discussion of the mediaeval city, Kropotkin elaborates and notes the importance of its self-jurisdiction and self-administration:

> But the commune was not simply an "autonomous" part of the State – such ambiguous words had not yet been invented by that time – it was a State in itself. It had the right of war and peace, of federation and alliance with its neighbours. It was sovereign in its own affairs, and mixed with no others ... The secret of this seeming anomaly lies in the fact that a mediaeval city was not a centralised State. During the first centuries of its existence, the city could hardly be named a State as regards its interior organisation, because the Middle Ages knew no more of the present centralisation of functions than of the present territorial centralisation.[39]

The city was divided into several sub-units or districts, some of which might be linked to particular trades, but all of which had a mix of inhabitants:

> The mediaeval city thus appears as a *double federation*: of all the householders united in small territorial unions – the street, the parish, the section – and of individuals united by oath into guilds according to their professions; the former being a produce of the village-community origin of the city, while the second is a subsequent growth called to life by new conditions.[40]

This double federation makes the city a more complex organism than a village, but nevertheless the city in this period was able to manage its overall affairs, to govern itself, without a centralised power.

This distinction between State and government is, I believe, of some importance. Many anarchists treat the State and government as essentially synonymous; anarchy is then defined by the wish to abolish State-and-government. If this is the case, then it is difficult to see how a complex social system could operate at all after the abolition of the State. If the definition of the State is restricted to a centralised system in the hands of a small number who resort to (the threat of) coercion through legislation and the police to enforce their will, then the government falls firmly within State control and is an expression of the State.

The abolition of the State, however, does not necessarily entail the abolition of *all* forms of government, at least some of whose functions can be operated in a different way: the exercise of power is not confined to a ruling and dominating minority; law can be replaced by customary law, the courts by systems of arbitration, the police by other means of maintaining social order. When anarchists claim to seek the abolition of the State-and-government, without any further elaboration, the critic can reasonably argue that anarchy necessarily entails disorder in the sense of chaos. The counter-claim that anarchy means order necessarily entails a specification of the alternative ways of managing social order without the ruling minority and the usual legal system and police force. It is through a regrettable lack of clarity about government-by-State and self-government that anarchists have invited the criticism that anarchism must mean chaos, for it is the fact of the relatively stable condition of the self-government of the smaller commune that anarchists can make the powerful argument that their philosophy of self-regulation is more likely to achieve social order than can the State.

Introductions to anarchism can in this way easily and unintentionally mislead. Just four lines from the beginning of his famous and oft-reprinted pamphlet *About Anarchism*, the notable Nicholas Walter writes that

> from the 1840s anarchists were people who accepted the name as a sign to show that they wanted anarchy in the sense of absence of government … For more than a century, anarchists have been people who believe not only that absence of government need not mean chaos and confusion, but that a society without government will actually be better than the society we live in now … It is the anarchists, and the anarchists alone, who want to get rid of government …[41]

Here the word 'government' means control by a ruling minority with the power of coercion over the rest. He clarifies his position later on in the pamphlet:

> This does not mean that anarchists reject organisation, though here is one of the strongest prejudices against anarchism. People can accept that anarchy may not mean just chaos and confusion, and that anarchists want not disorder but order without government, but they are sure that anarchy means order which arises spontaneously and that anarchists do not want organisation. This is the reverse of the truth. Anarchists actually want much more organisation, though organisation without authority.[42]

This is difficult terrain because in the popular mind government and the State are indeed often treated as synonymous. To my mind it would be more helpful for a newcomer to anarchism to be provided with Kropotkin's distinction, by which it becomes less confusing to say that indeed anarchists want order not so much *without government*, as order *without the State*, a condition in which a form of government without the State will necessarily involve some complex forms of organisation and administration. In Kropotkin's definition, the State is a particular form of government, which could vary from an absolute despot to a form of elected representative government; but both would involve a centralisation of power and control that are exercised and maintained through systems of law-making and law enforcement.

Kropotkin's vision is central to anarchist thought, a system that Nicholas Walter rightly described as 'co-ordination by free association' and 'extreme decentralisation on federalist lines' of organisations such as 'councils or co-operatives or collectives or communes or committees or unions or syndicates or soviets, or anything else – their title would be irrelevant, the important thing would be their function'.[43] For an anarchist society to function, the co-ordination to which Walter refers has to be managed and led in some way. This is a form of government, though it doesn't really matter what name you give to it. The important thing is to keep in mind the contrast between the authoritarian *versus* the libertarian, and between the centralist *versus* the federalist. Kropotkin is very clear that

> it is self-evident that this new form [of political organisation] will have to be *more popular, more decentralised, and nearer to the folk-mote self-government* than representative government can ever be.[44]

He acknowledges that differences and conflicts inevitably arise between these various units in society and, with characteristic optimism, he assumes they can be sorted out by goodwill lubricated with mutual aid. For me, it is Murray Bookchin (*confederalism*) and Pierre-Joseph Proudhon (*Le principe fédératif*), as well as anarcho-capitalists such as Rothbard, who have in this regard advanced better arguments than Kropotkin, but this is not the place to explore them.[45]

The philosopher, theologian and anthropologist Martin Buber (1878–1965), a key influence on Colin Ward, suspected that a State-free society is inherently unstable, both *within* each of its constituent communities and then also *between* them. He faced head-on the problem that Kropotkin side-stepped:

> Society cannot, however, quell the conflicts between the different groups; it is powerless to unite the divergent and clashing groups; it can develop what they have in common, but cannot force it upon them. The State alone can do that.[46]

In other words, the machinery that a small community can use to resolve conflicts cannot be trusted to work at a more macro level, and political rather than social means have to come into play – which opens the way to the rebirth of an embryonic State. There is no simple answer to this problem, though in my view it is reasonable to argue that should a society succeed in abolishing or reducing the State, its members would be highly cognizant of the need to be sensitive towards even the slightest indication of any drift in a centralising direction, and, once detected, to resist it as well as to identify less dangerous ways of coping with such challenges. Conflict resolution would be a highly prized skill.

Indeed, I think it important to remember that the slow and difficult process of getting to Kropotkin's *social revolution*, which means rejecting the *political revolution* by seizing power through force, would actually educate the members of society in both the construction of the new building blocks of such a society and in the concurrent destruction of those elements which are alien to an anarchist society. It is in outlining the process of social revolution that Kropotkin makes a distinctive contribution, and goes beyond the simplistic notion that a social revolution will somehow arise spontaneously:

> To wait therefore for a *social* revolution to come as a birthday present, without a whole series of protests on the part of the individual conscience, and without hundreds of preliminary revolts by which the very nature of the revolution is determined is to say the least, absurd ...[47] The life of society itself we understand, not as something complete and rigid, but as something never perfect – something ever striving for new forms, and ever changing these forms in accordance with the needs of the time. This is what *life* is in nature.[48]

Martin Buber sums up Kropotkin's position thus:

> [H]e believes rather that we must create here and now the space *now* possible for the thing for which we are striving, so that it may come to fulfilment *then*; he does not believe in the post-revolutionary leap, but he does believe in revolutionary continuity. To put it more precisely: he believes in a continuity within which revolution is only the accomplishment, the setting free and extension of a reality that has already grown to its true possibilities.[49]

What we do today not merely prefigures or foreshadows the future: *pre*figuration[50] is a precondition of the *trans*figuration and the path to its realisation. And it is a path to the future in which the means of getting there are consistent with the end – in sharp contrast with the Marxist view of the means–end relationship. Prefiguration means enacting the future in the present, but also investigating the past for valued practices that have been lost or forgotten but are rich in potential for the future, as Lewis Mumford points out:

> The workings of the natural environment and human history provide even the poorest community with a rich compost, far more favourable to life than the most rational ideal schemes would be if they lacked such a soil to grow in ... [E]very community possesses, in addition to its going institutions, a reservoir of potentialities, partly rooted in its past, still alive though hidden, and partly budding forth from new crossings and mutations, which open the way to further development ...[51]

Kropotkin understood that there is, during this process, a need to re-educate the many who are not actively striving for the new society and who may have sound reasons to resist:

> [N]o revolution, whether peaceful or violent, had ever taken place without the new ideals having deeply penetrated into the very class whose economical and political privileges were to be assailed.[52]

Martin Buber takes the same line, that the way forward must also formulate and implement its own educational strategy to counter the State's capacity to protect itself by disseminating defensive political propaganda:

> Social education … seeks to arouse and to develop in the minds of its pupils the spontaneity of fellowship which is innate in all unravaged human souls and which harmonises very well with the development of personal existence and personal thought. This can be accomplished only by the complete overthrow of the political trend which nowadays dominates education throughout the world. True education for citizenship in a State is education for the effectuation of Society.[53]

Kropotkin, as we have seen, believed that the young needed to be educated to fit the emerging society he envisaged. It is commonplace for both educators and politicians to insist that education entails socialisation into society in a variety of ways, such as learning about and enjoying the cultural heritage, acquiring the skills and qualities required in the world of work, being prepared for the challenges of a rapidly changing society, and more recently coming to espouse 'British values'. An acceptance of the State is, of course, very much part of all this, and this poses a problem for anarchists and others in what constitutes political education in schools.

Of the five great classical exponents of anarchism, Peter Kropotkin is my favourite: for his renunciation of his elevated social position and great wealth; for his warm, generous and constantly optimistic personality; and for the sheer breadth of his developing vision, one that he sought to support with an evidence base. His arguments for an evolutionary approach both to society and to anarchism itself played a vital role in the emergence of the so-called 'new anarchism' of the 1960s and 1970s that gave the English brand of anarchism a distinctive flavour. He is an inspirational figure for anarchists, but his influence, both direct and indirect, on those at the edge of or even outside anarchist circles is also huge, because he knew that at any one point making the journey to the future based on the best of the present is more important than defining the destination in an overly precise way.

This did not prevent him from offering quite a detailed sketch of his preferred future in *Fields, Factories and Workshops*. What matters more than his particular vision is his insight that educational development and community development are interdependent, an insight that only a few educationists, such as Henry Morris (of whom more later) have acted on. The anarchist social revolution is inherently both a community and an educational revolution. Kropotkin understood that a State is always more fragile than it seems, and thus possible alternatives to it are never erased. As Ruth Kinna puts it:

> Just as it was possible to imagine the further growth of the state, it was also possible to envisage its dismemberment through the stimulation of multiple processes of federation. Kropotkin's account of the European state's development was designed to expose the impermanence of statist institutions.[54]

Where, you may ask, does this leave us? Since the period of the classical anarchists as well as the new anarchists, State control over schooling has increased, whilst in some respects community may have declined. It will therefore be more difficult than it was to reduce State control and return education and schooling to communities in dialogue with professional teachers. Is there a danger that, in pessimistic frustration at the size of this task, we fall back on Popper's piecemeal social engineering? I accept Herbert Read's rejection of Popper:

> The trouble about the piecemeal methods of science is that they are myopic: they are not inspired by a sense of direction, by a view of horizons. Such horizons are discovered by the inspiration of genius, by the divine madness of the poet, by the holy enthusiasm of the hero. Such horizons reveal the sun in its revolutionary splendour.[55]

We clearly need to strengthen our ideals about community and of how education and schooling might prosper without heavy State control. But is this not to risk falling into the trap of utopianism? Do we need some sort of ultimate end-state for all our efforts if we are to inspire anyone to make the journey at all? If so, is the charge of utopianism against anarchism thereby justified? The charge has been made often enough, not least by the Marxists, who thus damned the anarchists and the socialists who would not accept their 'scientific' version – and the anarchists returned the insult on the grounds that the Marxist notion of the State just withering away after the violent seizure of power was also a fantasy. Should the concept now be abandoned, or can it serve some useful purposes?

Notes

1 Bunt and Harris (2010).
2 Kropotkin (1892: 32).
3 Miller (1976: 241).
4 Kropotkin (1927: 123f).
5 Kropotkin (1927: 202).
6 Kropotkin (1927: 200f).
7 Kropotkin (1927: 197).
8 Kropotkin (1927: 220).
9 Miller (1976), Morris (2007), Kinna (2016), Laughlin (2016).
10 Kropotkin (1899: 28).
11 Kropotkin (1899: 216f).

12 Kropotkin (1899: 286f).
13 Kropotkin (1902: xv).
14 Kropotkin (1902: xv).
15 Kropotkin (1902: 74, original emphasis).
16 Kropotkin (1902: 97).
17 Kropotkin (1902: 282).
18 Kropotkin (1902: 300).
19 Kropotkin (1899: 466–8).
20 Godwin (1793: 676).
21 Hall in Putnam (2002: 40).
22 Hall in Putnam (2002: 53).
23 Kropotkin (1902: 166, 176, 208).
24 Kropotkin (1902: 178, 181).
25 Kropotkin (1902: 209).
26 Kropotkin (1902: 222).
27 Kropotkin (1898/1974 edition: 26).
28 Kropotkin (1898: 9).
29 Kropotkin (1899: 87).
30 Kropotkin (1899: 125, original emphasis).
31 Kropotkin (1898: 176).
32 Design Technology entries at GCSE declined by 43 per cent between 2010 and 2017 as noted by culturallearningalliance.org.uk. See also the fuller report by Paul Woodward, *Times Education Supplement* 21 October 2016, available online.
33 Kropotkin (1898: 176).
34 Kropotkin (1898: 32).
35 Kropotkin (1897: 10, original emphasis).
36 Fuller (1989: 146f).
37 Bookchin (1992: 226f).
38 Bookchin (2007: 95).
39 Kropotkin (1902: 178f).
40 Kropotkin (1902: 181, original emphasis).
41 Walter (1969: 2).
42 Walter (1969: 7).
43 Walter (1969: 20).
44 Kropotkin (1927: 184, original emphasis).
45 It is with regret that I have not found space for Murray Bookchin, the anarchist and libertarian socialist with so much to say about community and, of course, about social ecology. This chapter devotes some length to Kropotkin, who fits better to my storyline, and is closer to Colin Ward and to educational issues. I hope to write more about Bookchin and a linked book, *The Impossible Community* by John P. Clark (2013), in my next publication on community.
46 Buber (1999: 173).
47 Kropotkin (1927: 191, original emphasis).
48 Kropotkin (1927: 184, original emphasis).
49 Buber (1949: 13, original emphasis).
50 See Franks in Franks et al. (2018) for a critical review of the concept.
51 Mumford (1922: 2f, 7).
52 Kropotkin (1899: 290).
53 Buber (1999: 176).
54 Kinna (2016: 198).
55 Read (1974: 26).

8

UTOPIA AND THE REMAKING OF SOCIAL AND EDUCATIONAL SYSTEMS

> We travel through utopia only in order to get beyond utopia.
>
> Lewis Mumford, 1922

> Before utopias became contaminated by the "realist" spirit of our time, they flourished with a variety and richness which may well make us doubt the validity of our claim to have achieved some measure of social progress.
>
> Marie Louise Berneri, 1950

When the Marxists and anarchists used 'utopian' in mutual exchanges of insults – which masked the serious differences between the two sides on the concept[1] – they seemed to accept the derogatory connotations of the word by denying that they themselves were guilty of utopianism. The 'new anarchists' of the 1960s were distinctly cool towards the concept, believing that it distracted attention from constructive action in the present. As suggested by an anonymous contributor to a 1967 issue of the anarchist organ *Anarchy* – it might have been Colin Ward, for it seems to reflect his views:

> We will always see revolutionary changes as a future ideal … Therefore our basic goal must be continuing evolution. All "classical" anarchist ideals must be borne in mind, even if they do at present seem utopian, but these should not prevent us from making piecemeal changes right now. The argument for piecemeal social engineering has been stated too conservatively by Karl Popper … but it is probably the best we can hope for … Rebellion must be a permanent feature of anarchist thought and action, but rebellion is not at variance with making small changes today which are themselves preconditions for wider changes.[2]

This may be seen, as Saul Newman has put it, as 'a kind of enacted utopia – an attempt to realise utopia in the current moment, rather than waiting for a revolution'.[3] Some anarchists dislike the term because it implies fantasy and a lack of realism. Others accept that an ideology or political philosophy usually contains some conception of a better society, though they might vary in how much detail to include. The conclusion I reach is that it is best to stop worrying about both the disparaging insults and the fear of being treated as fantasists, and instead critically examine different conceptions of society, either in the abstract or as a model for the future, both within or outside anarchism as to their potential value for developing one's thinking.

When I first thought of writing this book I felt I should clarify my mind over the concept of utopia and so investigated the literature. I was familiar with a few of the famous utopias – the pioneer of the modern genre, Sir Thomas More's *Utopia* (1516 in Latin, 1551 in English); Edward Bellamy's *Looking Backward* (1888); William Morris's *News from Nowhere* (1890); as well as the forerunners such as Plato's *Republic*, and of course Aldous Huxley's *Brave New World* (1932) and George Orwell's *Nineteen Eighty-Four*, or *1984* (1949), both usually called dystopias (as, for me, is Plato). Other thinkers, such as Robert Owen or Charles Fourier, were names I had come across in secondary sources. I was astonished, however, to find so many more published utopias, with a substantial and growing literature about them, and even a multi-disciplinary specialism of utopian studies.

My interest here is narrower. Is the concept useful to an analysis of anarchism and its relationship with education? This is not a simple question, because anarchists have conceptions of their ideal society and of an ideal education within such a society. An anarchist education would obviously seek to prepare learners for an anarchist society, but since most of us do not live in such a society, to what degree must an anarchist education prepare the young for a society that is quite unlike the society to which they aspire? This problem is not unique to anarchists, of course, and the answer obviously entails doing something of both: preparing the young to thrive in existing society but also fostering in them the qualities and capacities to change that society.

Various scholars have sought ways of determining the boundaries of the concept – for example, what distinguishes utopia from ideology or from science fiction – as well as ways of classifying utopias. One of the finest scholars of utopian studies, the sociologist Ruth Levitas, could find no satisfactory system. Seeking what all had in common, she concluded that 'The essence of utopia seems to be desire – the desire for a different, better way of being.'[4] As such, a utopia is an imaginary work that to this end looks back to a past or forward to a reconstituted future, or to no particular time. This variability in time frame often has a matching spatial one: it might be an imaginary land, or our own country, or a different planet or solar system, or nowhere at all.

I believe that the concept is useful in that the inhabitants of every utopia live in a different and better social imaginary – or, in the case of dystopias, a different but worse social imaginary. The author's chosen social imaginary cannot be completely different from ours, for then we would not be able to understand it. Rather it is different in carefully selected ways so that we readers share enough with inhabitants of the utopia to be able to recognise and understand the differences, whilst nevertheless having enough in common with them not to feel that we are in an incomprehensible alien world. Fortunately, the utopia's inhabitants usually speak our language, or have some means of inter-cultural communication; some device, often a sort of Intourist guide,[5] to explain the unfamiliar social imaginary to a visitor from our world.

From this point of view the most valuable feature of a utopia is that it allows us to be playful within and around the fragilities and flexibilities of our own social imaginary, both of society as a whole and in our case also that particular part, the system of education and schooling. We can play the anthropological game of projecting ourselves into a very different social imaginary that throws into sharp relief some features of our own social imaginary, both of society as a whole and of the schooling system in particular; it is a novel way, a different tool, by which to question the things we routinely treat as unquestioned and unquestionable. The most valuable utopias are those in which the author, with subtle skill, forces readers, at least temporarily, out of their normal social imaginary into an alternative one, which then works reflexively to make readers rethink their current social imaginary. This second element is crucial. In this regard Lewis Mumford's distinction between a *utopia of escape* and a *utopia of reconstruction* is helpful: the first leaves the readers' existing social imaginary undisturbed; the second forces a rethink of it – 'outward into the world … a new set of habits, a fresh scale of values, a different net of institutions'.[6] The popularity of science fiction demonstrates that many people enjoy such an experience, even though very often it is a utopia of escape rather than reconstruction.

Thus a utopia can serve several useful functions:

1. Utopia as an ideal. This is the most obvious function. We commonly express our ideas, even trivial ones, with the opening word 'Ideally …' In the case of a utopian ideal it must by definition be radically different from, as well as better than, the status quo. 'With the aid of ideals, a community may select, among a multitude of possibilities, those which are consonant with its own nature of that promise to further human development.'[7] A utopian ideal may be a means of consciousness-raising or a call to action to inspire followers.
2. Utopia as a goal. This could be very specific, describing a desired end-state in detail. It might be portrayed as a perfect society, and one that is stable and free of conflict. It is this version of utopia that is most open to criticism as unrealistic or fantasy: its conception of human nature as perfectible is unconvincing. Such a society is to me always dystopian, since I find a degree of instability and conflict in life to be one of its most appealing and

productive features. It is for these reasons that I am repelled by conceptions of Heaven. Utopias that describe an end-state typically assume a sudden revolution or some catastrophic event that ushers in the deep change; rarely is the journey to it described as fully as the destination. A utopia may be a model that sets out the desiderata of a better society, providing criteria, milestones or measures against which progress may be judged.

3. Utopia as critique. Here a future or timeless society serves as a critique of the present, drawing attention to its failings. For this function the utopia may not necessarily imply something to emulate, but simply something that exposes current shortcomings. A utopia or dystopia may function as a stimulus to imaginative playfulness by triggering some lateral thinking. Like scenario planning, it provokes new ends and means of attaining them. Dystopias can be particularly helpful in this regard and when they take the form of a satire on the present may function as a warning.

These three functions, singly or in combination, can stimulate the imagination to create and interrogate an alternative conception of a desirable society and so help to provide a motivating vision. This is important for anarchism, which is often much clearer about what its thinkers are against than what they are for, and we are all increasingly suspicious of politicians who tell us what they are for only in platitudinous slogans.

Ruth Levitas argues that utopia is a form of speculative sociology:

> For the Imaginary Reconstitution of Society intrinsically necessitates thinking about the connections between economic, social and political processes, our ways of life, and what is necessary to human flourishing … literary utopias are always intended – and predominantly read – as a criticism of the present, and thus also embed a sociology of the originating society. They represent and explain the institutions and practices of the society from which they arise, offering accounts of how its substantive irrationalities produce negative outcomes. They contain narratives of the place in history of both originating and alternative societies, of how we got *here*, and how we might get *there* … Sociology foregrounds what utopia backgrounds, while utopia foregrounds what sociology represses.[8]

From this point of view we could readily dispense with the term 'utopia' and replace it with 'Imaginary Reconstitution of Society' or even 'New Social Imaginary'. The labels do not really matter: more important is the recognition that within all the main anarchist positions, there is embedded some such vision of a future society and community, though there are variations in the form taken by the vision of society and its associated education system. We can then ask: does the vision provide, within its descriptions, the tools to aid us in reflecting on, and talking about, the future of society and education and their relation to the present? – which does indeed demand some sociological imagination by both author and reader. Levitas assists such an endeavour by proposing utopia as a *method*, one of particular value to sociologists, but one also available for use whenever we consider, in some fundamental way, what the future might bring and the choices we might make to shape it. Utopia as method has three modes:

- an archaeological mode: the images of the good society embedded in political programmes and policies
- an ontological mode: the kind of people, with their capabilities and values, that a particular society develops and encourages
- an architectural mode: the imagination of alternative scenarios for the future

The archaeological mode is of crucial significance for anarchists, and we could use it to interrogate what Kropotkin attempted in *Mutual Aid* in looking back at early human society:

> [E]very community possesses, in addition to its going institutions, a reservoir of potentialities, partly rooted in its past, still alive, though hidden, and partly budding forth from new crossings and mutations, which open the way to further developments. This points to the pragmatic function of ideals: for no society is fully awake either to its inherent nature or to its natural prospects, if it ignores the fact that there are many alternatives to the path that it is actually following, and many conceivable and possible goals besides those which are immediately visible.[9]

George Woodcock makes much the same point from a specifically anarchist position:

> [T]he anarchist does not seek to destroy the present political order so that it may be replaced by a better system of organisation … rather he proposes to clear the existing structure of coercive institutions away so that the natural society which has survived in a largely subterranean way from earlier freer and more originative periods can be liberated to flow again in a different future.[10]

The archaeological mode excavates 'what has survived in a largely subterranean way' and then, in anarchist style, we decide how to build on it to make society more anarchistic.

Erik Ohlin Wright in *Envisioning Real Utopias* (2010) uses the concept of utopia for sociological purposes, much like Levitas, of whom he seems sadly ignorant, because it embraces a tension between dreams and practice:

> It is grounded in the belief that what is pragmatically possible is not fixed independently of our imaginations, but is shaped by our visions … A vital

> belief in a utopian ideal may be necessary to motivate people to set off on the journey from the status quo in the first place, even though the likely actual destination may fall short of the utopian ideal.[11]

Like Levitas's Imaginary Reconstitution of Society, Wright's Emancipatory Social Science is concerned with social and political justice, but adopts a hard-headed stance that is designed to persuade sceptics. For any coherent and credible theory of alternatives to existing institutions, it must, if it is to be realistic, meet three criteria: desirability, viability and achievability.

We may use the suggestions of Levitas and Wright to construct an evaluative template with which to interrogate any utopia of interest:

1. Would the things I most value in my present society survive in the new society?
2. Would those things I most dislike in my present society be absent in the new society?
3. Are there elements of the new society to which I would strongly object?
4. On balance, would the new society be a better place to live in than my present one?
5. Is such a society achievable?

Can we find a society, inspired by utopian thinking, which gets through such an interrogation at least reasonably well? For me, Peter Kropotkin's vision of society as outlined in *Fields, Factories and Workshops Tomorrow* is not convincing by these five criteria, even though I can see some of the benefits, including a better integration of the schooling system with social reconstruction of working and living. Whilst quality of life would generally be good, it is unclear what might be lost from older forms of community and there are concerns about small-town conservatism and pressures to conformity.

If Kropotkin's utopia was already becoming obsolescent for larger towns and cities, were utopias better fitted to the twentieth century already in the making? Happily, in this same year of 1898, Ebenezer Howard, borrowing £50 from his brother-in-law, published his *Tomorrow: A Peaceful Path to Real Reform*. Does the name or the book title ring any bells with you? If not, the book was retitled four years later to make the content more explicit – *Garden Cities of Tomorrow*, a work, it is said, that has 'done more than any other single book to guide the modern town planning movement and to alter its objectives'.[12] Howard (1850–1928) is the man who invented – his word – the garden cities of Letchworth and Welwyn.

Born in London, he left school at 14. He had no training in architecture or town planning: he was a self-taught outsider. The result was astonishing. He came up with some original ideas, supported by detailed practical plans, ones advanced to fruition by entrepreneurial and networking skills among the rich and powerful, such as the Lever and Cadbury families. He was a doer, not just a thinker. His Damascene-type moment came when he read, in a single sitting, the best-selling utopian novel, Bellamy's *Looking Backward* (1888), in which a young American falls asleep and awakens in 2000 to find himself in a post-revolutionary socialist world. Production and distribution are managed by a highly centralised state – the nation is the sole employer and capitalist. Those with the worst jobs are the best paid and everybody retires at 45. Nevertheless I found it a very unattractive world, with uncomfortable shades of *Brave New World* and *1984*, and certainly much less fun than William Morris's *News from Nowhere*, written in reaction to Bellamy two years later. But it thrilled Ebenezer Howard:

> I went into some of the crowded parts of London, and as I passed through the narrow dark streets, saw the wretched dwellings in which the majority of the people lived, observed on every hand the manifestations of a self-seeking order of society and reflected on the absolute unsoundness of our economic system. There came to me an overpowering sense of the temporary nature of all I sought, and of its entire unsuitability for the working life of the new order – the order of justice, unity and friendliness.[13]

Howard abhorred the centralised and authoritarian State in Bellamy's novel, for his inclinations were more anarchist or libertarian socialist than Marxist.[14] He certainly wanted a different distribution of wealth and of property, but his idea was a cooperative commonwealth, with a balance between communal solidarity and individual liberty and initiative. In a decentralised society, each garden city of some 30,000 people would be a carefully designed mix of farming and industry so that the inhabitants could work part-time both in the small factories, offices or shops and on the farms, as sought by Kropotkin, whom Howard admired. All the land would be owned by, and for the benefit of, the community. The symmetry of the garden city would be the symbol and product of a harmonious community. A central park is the civic centre, with town hall, museum, library, concert hall and hospital. The residential areas around the centre are in geometric boulevards, and housing is designed along the lines of Howard's admired fourteenth-century village, with sufficient proximity between houses to encourage neighbourliness but enough independence to permit privacy. Surrounding all this are the farms and factories, but with ample green space to promote healthy living and leisure.

Getting his model garden city off the drawing board took time and energy and Howard was forced to make many compromises on the way to the implementation of his design. Some of the radical edge, as well its organic heart, was lost as the garden city concept gave way to the somewhat debased version of 'satellite towns' created after the Second World War. Even Letchworth never became the true garden city that Howard imagined, but more accurately a garden suburb.[15] Robert Fishman sums up Howard's achievement:

> Howard's experience at Letchworth and Welwyn led his followers to abandon his methods and make their peace with the welfare state [which] has

> since disappointed those who expected order and justice from it. In comparison, Howard's original goal of a genuinely multi-centred society seems surprisingly fresh and exciting. In an age of centralised bureaucratic planning, we can better appreciate the wisdom of Howard's modesty, his understanding of the limitations of outside control, his concern to leave the final development of a city to the citizens themselves, and his careful balance of co-operation and individualism … In Howard's thought the transformation of the environment became the central act in the creation of a new civilisation. To the planner – the man of imagination and justice – he assigned the task of designing homes and cities that would make co-operation among men and contact with nature the basis of daily life. The planner thus became the real founder of the new society. The responsibilities of this role were too great for Howard's successors who sought to redefine themselves as technicians for the welfare state.[16]

Today the solution of our housing crisis is left mainly in the hands of large private firms, whose chiefs have rightly been censored for using the advantages of help-to-buy schemes merely to enrich themselves from the public purse and have sold off leaseholds, leaving many new homeowners unable to sell their property.[17] At the time the State in fact did very little to support Ebenezer Howard; it is now party to the destruction of what is left of his heritage.

Sadly Howard does not provide any detailed thoughts about education and schooling, though one suspects that he would have been at home with Kropotkin's educational views, since both believed that education should prepare the young for adult life at work and in the community they envision. The opportunity to conceptualise a more explicit relationship between town and schooling was sadly forgone. This matters, for Howard's achievements in town planning were hugely influential and could have had more impact on the associated planning of education and schooling. Today the two have become deeply separated. When a new town or suburb is created, one or more standard schools are added simply to match the size of population, with little explicit thought about the link between the school and the community in which it will be embedded.

Moving from the big city to the small garden city, in Howard's time as well as much later, involved gains and losses. Later studies, such as Young and Willmott's *Family and Kinship in East London* (1957), which investigated the transition of working-class people from Bethnal Green to Essex, revealed some distinct losses as well as gains. Moreover the worries about small-town conformity in a garden city are as strong as with Kropotkin's plan. At the same time Howard made a major effort to treat his residents as co-constructors and co-owners of the garden city; they were not to be passive consumers of his design. If this were Howard's permanent legacy to town planning, it would be a huge achievement, because it would mean that town planners would always start with an assumption that both parents and teachers would be active models of how to participate in the design of a community and in its continuing maintenance. In effect, both planners and community members would have to adopt something like my evaluative template in working from their ideals to a real place. Is this what happened?

Howard's contemporary Patrick Geddes (1854–1932) sought to build on Howard's strengths. A proud Scot, Geddes was (like Kropotkin) a scientist, a biologist and botanist, and his vision was rooted in evolutionary science, but he soon branched out to become a remarkable polymath in sociology and town planning. He worked very closely with two other men of the time: the sociologist Victor Branford (1863–1930), born English but for most of his life an adopted Scot, whom Geddes first met as a student at Edinburgh University, and with whom he founded the Sociological Society in 1903; and the American urbanist, philosopher of technology and literary critic Lewis Mumford (1895–1990), who became Geddes's fervent admirer. They made a formidable and influential trio.

Geddes was a charismatic, larger-than-life figure, a powerful and passionate propagandist for his views. He was immensely energetic, bursting with ideas and projects, dashing around the world with his schemes. His character shows in his writing, which is often prolix and bombastic, replete with digressions as he meanders tortuously from topic to topic. As far as academic colleagues, rather than followers, were concerned, he paid the price of being dangerously multidisciplinary and suspiciously obsessed with synthesis in his wide interests, which included devising a Third Way (almost a century before Anthony Giddens's *The Third Way* for Tony Blair), which won him few political friends. Even admirers had their reservations about him:

> His appearance, perhaps deliberately cultivated, was that of the eccentric professor. In lectures and conversation alike he spoke in a continuous and rapid flow that not infrequently became an indistinct mumble as his disquisition turned into active thought and reflection.[18]

Colin Ward – who greatly admired Geddes for his firm belief that urban planning meant the development of a local life and that the city was the prime educator of citizens[19] – admitted, 'If I were wandering down the street, I would probably cross the road to avoid being button-holed by him and hectored for half an hour about what we should do with our inheritance.'[20] Nevertheless, there was a time when Geddes and Branford seemed destined to be leading lights in the developing field of sociology, but Geddes was too close to being a globe-trotting dilettante, and Branford was insufficiently gifted as a sociologist, for their partnership to achieve the enduring great fame to which they once seemed to be heading.

They were not anarchists, but they had sympathetic links to anarchists, especially Geddes's close friend Élisée Reclus (1830–1905) – the French geographer and anarchist, who showed how the ecology of a region affected people's lives – and Peter Kropotkin, both of whom taught in Geddes's Summer Schools in

Edinburgh. Perhaps this influence is best revealed in Branford's *Whitherward? Hell or Eutopia* (1921), with some extracts from an introductory section under the heading 'What to do':

> Have faith in moral Renewal, Re-education, and therewith Reconstruction. For fulfilment there must be a Resorption of Government into the body of the community. How? By cultivating the habit of directly constructive action instead of merely waiting upon representative agencies. Hence these social imperatives … Eschew the despotic habit of regimentation, whether by Governments, Trusts, Companies, tyrants, pedants or police; try the better and older way of co-ordination expanding from local centres through city, region, nation, and beyond; so may the spirit of fellowship express itself … Resist the political temptation to centralise all things in one metropolitan city; seek to renew the ancient tradition of Federation between free cities, regions, dominions … Let cities, towns, villages, groups, associations, work out their own regional salvation; for that they must have freedom, ideas, vision to plan, and means to carry out … Stimulate sympathetic understanding between all sections of the community by co-operation in local initiative … Along this road lies the way to Eutopia.[21]

What anarchist would have objected to this? A Kropotkinesque exhortation on education was included:

> In general, aim at making individuals more socialised and communities more individualised. To that end, let schools subordinate books to outdoor observation and handicrafts; let teachers draw the matter and the method of education from the life and tradition of their pupils' own region, as well as from the history and culture of mankind at large.

Geddes's reputation is based mainly on his most famous book, *Cities in Evolution: An Introduction to the Town Planning Movement and to the Study of Civics* (1915). His mission is social reconstruction, a civic awakening to make a better world. To this end he makes a distinction between *Eu*topia (good) and *Kako*topia (bad), for 'Eutopia lies in the city around us; and it must be planned and realised … by us as its citizens – each a citizen of both the actual and the ideal city increasingly seen as one.'[22] Like Kropotkin and Howard, he admired the mediaeval city, but he recognised that the emerging technologies had potentially transformative consequences. The city of the initial phase of the industrial revolution, which he called *paleotechnic*, was to be replaced by the new or *neotechnic* city and region, which would become

> Eutopia, each a place of effective health and well-being, even of glorious and in its way unprecedented beauty, renewing and rivaling the best achievements

> of the past, and all this beginning, here, there and everywhere – even where our paleotechnic disorder seems to have done its worst.[23]

The basic philosophy is close to that of Kropotkin and Howard, as well as Reclus, with a deep suspicion of government, that needs to be taken back into the hands of the community ('Resorption') to unleash popular control and creativity. The young have been deprived of any rustic experience and the city parks, taken over from the mansion houses of the rich, are now guarded by officials who keep them orderly and prettified, denying children their right to play and 'natural activities of wigwam-building, cave-digging, stream-damning, and so on' – words that must have thrilled Colin Ward. There are suggestions to please David Cameron and his 'Big Society':

> The upkeep of all this needs no costly increase in civic functionarism. It should be naturally undertaken by the regenerating schools and continuation classes, and by private associations too without number. What better training in citizenship as well as opportunity of health, can be offered any of us than in sharing in the upkeep of our parks and gardens? Instead of paying increasing park and school rates for these, we should be entering upon one of the methods of ancient and of coming citizenship, and with this of the keeping down of taxes, by paying at least this one of our social obligations increasingly in time and in service rather than in money. Thus too we shall be experimentally opening our eyes towards that substantial Resorption of Government, which is the natural and approaching reaction from the present multiplication of officialism, always so costly at best.[24]

Schools, 'hitherto so bookish and enfeebling' would become mostly open-air at the margins of open spaces, allotments and gardens 'connected up with hedgerows, open to birds and lovers'.

So far, so much aligned with Kropotkin and Howard, but there is a major advance involved. For Kropotkin and Howard simply thought up their ideas as imaginative ideals or utopias; Geddes, by contrast, recognised that the design of the new city or region had to be based on a far better scientific understanding of the personal and social context in which they would be built. To this end, he believed in the power of the survey. In this he adapted a triad of the French engineer and sociologist of the family, Frédéric Le Play (1806–1882), to make 'Place – Work – People' the key to understanding how people, their occupations and their location all interacted in complex ways and could not be ignored in planning for their future. Only then, he argued, could citizens be expected to take pride in, and to maintain and further develop, a new town.

Thus was born the Town Study by its participants, in which children could play a critical role as a 'Know your City' activity, a complement to the accepted nature study. City betterment involving the young was integral to citizenship education. Lewis Mumford understood the book's originality:

> *Cities in Evolution* was not a contribution to scholarship; its essential subject was the education of the citizen toward his understanding of urban processes and his active assistance in urban development. Using his own self-education, through study and practical activity as a basis, Geddes sketched out the background the citizen needed in history and geography and travel, in economics, politics, architecture, sociology. Thus at that juncture in urban history, *Cities in Evolution* performed the most valuable service that any single book could have performed: it taught the reader, in simple terms, how to look at cities and how to evaluate their development. See for yourself; understand for yourself; act on your own initiative on behalf of the community of which you are a part. That summarised Geddes' message.[25]

This is a considerable advance on Kropotkin and Howard, with a more radical decentralisation to the citizen, including the young. Little wonder that Colin Ward listed Geddes as one of his ten greatest influences, and he may indeed be a background figure in *Utopia* (1974), Ward's invitation to young people to investigate their own ideal place. For Geddes' espousal of what he called 'conservative surgery' in town planning meant making sure that one does not trample over what people say they value in their existing community.

The psychology of the child accepted by Geddes and Branford was that of the then fashionable evolutionary approach, which prepared the way for, and was then displaced by, the superior developmental psychology of childhood. But it pushed them in the direction of a progressive philosophy that emphasised play, practical activities and creative self-expression. Close to their educational ideal were a high valuation of arts and crafts, nature study, local social studies and civic involvement, with no hard separation between work and leisure.[26] Both men were closely associated with two leading independent schools, Abbotsholme and Bedales, leading lights in progressive education that sadly did not have, and could not be expected to have, many flourishing equivalents in State schools. Their contribution to educational thought and practice is rightly assessed by John Scott and Ray Bromley (2013) in their timely reconsideration of their joint achievements.

Overall, then, Geddes scores well on our evaluative template of utopian schemes: his vision is in some respects closer to an anarchist philosophy than those of Kropotkin or Howard, and his educational philosophy is more profound. His longer-term impact on the UK, however, is probably weaker than Howard's. He probably had more impact in India than in Britain, for he went there for periods between 1914 and 1924 and was a prestigious consultant to various maharajahs in the design of cities, parks and campuses. He was Professor of Civics and Sociology at the University of Bombay; much of his work in India seems to have been lost, but there remains enough to evaluate his contribution there.[27] Geddes made several trips to the USA, but much of his influence there was through the advocacy of Lewis Mumford, who in the 1920s was involved in a bitter debate with Thomas Adams, who had been the secretary of

Ebenezer Howard's Garden City Association at Letchworth. This clash of philosophy of urban planning 'had huge significance not merely for New York, but for every other great metropolis in the world'.[28] If we want to understand many later developments in the UK we must travel to the New York of a hundred years ago.

The problem was that Manhattan had become the focus for commercial, not residential, development: skyscrapers were rising so fast in the drive to make money that access to light and air became a problem. This led to restrictions on heights and divisions into zones and then a decision to create a regional plan to cover commerce and industry, transport and residential provision. Thomas Adams took over the management of the project. He had no aspiration to decentralise a big city along the lines dear to Howard, whose blandishments were to no avail: re-centralisation was the order of the day, with economic development as the primary consideration. Resources would go to luxury apartments and improved commuting from 'satellite communities', not garden cities. In short, it 'was quintessentially a big business plan to make New York City a bigger and better place to do business in'.[29]

The most savage criticism came from Lewis Mumford and the Regional Planning Association of America, with its urban philosophy based on Howard and Geddes, and its desire for a 'utopian urban form' with a variety of communities set in a landscape of farms, parks and wilderness areas. In the Adams' plan, by contrast, it seemed to Mumford, 'property values and private enterprise are looked upon as sacred'. Adams struck back, suggesting Mumford was demanding the impossible – 'A Utopia can be achieved only on the basis of despotism' with a clear implication that Mumford and his friends were communists.[30] In the end, Mumford lost the battle. Would New York one day look back with regret at this defeat of Mumford, Geddes and Howard? Was this battle an indication of a deep and permanent change in the relationship between citizens and those in charge of urban designs? What would be the future of the Kropotkin and Geddes concerns to establish clear links between educational planning and town planning? Were these links destined to disappear?

If Jane Jacobs, writing about New York less than forty years later, is a trustworthy judge, the outlook is bleak. In the opening words of her wonderful book, *The Death and Life of Great American Cities* (1961), the best on this topic I have ever read, she goes straight for the jugular: 'This book is an attack on current city planning and rebuilding … [and] on the principles that have shaped it.' She is scathing in her comments on planners who have made such a mess of cities because they simply do not understand how cities work in real life, and argues that it is only on the basis of such knowledge, including what does *not* work, that sound, and very different, principles can be derived. For her, city planning is an equivalent of blood-letting: dogma based on nonsense, creating a pseudo-science. To ditch this, she plays the anthropologist: looking closely with as few preconceptions and expectations as possible. For there is an underlying order in cities that is easily ignored, and if it is ignored, as when planners think about how a city ought to look, disastrous mistakes are made. From this emerges her basic principle: *cities need an intricate and close-grained diversity of uses that give each other constant mutual support.*[31] Jacobs was a critic of planners, and not herself a planner, but she identified a principle that, if adopted, would improve planning and ensure that an urban design would score more highly on our evaluative template.

Yet whom did she have in mind for the target of her attack on planners? The worst influence, she claims, is none other than Ebenezer Howard. She notes his Damascene moment I described earlier, looking at the dreadful conditions of the poor in the London slums, but she interprets this as the dawning of a deep hatred of the city per se, giving birth to his solution of 'doing the city in' and its replacement by the garden cities he so assiduously planned. However, 'As in all Utopias, the right to have plans of any significance belonged only to the planners in charge.'[32] Jacobs' concern is not so much with Letchworth and Welwyn, or copies undertaken elsewhere, but with the extensive influence of Howard's 'powerful and city-destroying ideas':

> He conceived of planning … as essentially paternalistic, if not authoritarian. He was uninterested in the aspects of the city which could not be abstracted to serve his Utopia. In particular, he simply wrote off the intricate, many-faceted, cultural life of the metropolis. He was uninterested in such problems as the way great cities police themselves, or exchange ideas, or operate politically, or invent new economic arrangements, and he was oblivious to devising new ways to strengthen these functions because, after all, he was not designing for this kind of life in any case. Both in his preoccupations and in his omissions, Howard made sense in his own terms but none in terms of city planning. Yet virtually all modern city planning has been adapted from, and embroidered on, this silly substance.[33]

Geddes does not escape her indictment:

> Along the avenue of planning, Sir Patrick Geddes … saw the Garden City idea not as a fortuitous way to absorb population growth otherwise destined for a great city, but as the starting point of a much grander and more encompassing pattern. He thought of planning of cities in terms of the planning of whole regions.[34]

This indictment is not entirely fair to Howard or Geddes, both of whom wanted to involve people in the making and development of the city. They did not ride roughshod over the lives of the inhabitants in a way that Jacobs implies. In speaking of education and social betterment, Branford spoke for Geddes when in 1913 he writes from the National Arts Club of New York and insists

> with the strongest emphasis, on the elementary scientific axiom that diagnosis must precede treatment; that action must be based on adequate

> knowledge; that, in short, survey must anticipate service. It insists that in order to change environment in one direction, or to divert social tradition in another, we must make the most careful observation and study of the given environment and of tradition as they are, and of how they have come to be … The new social and civil politics has, to be sure, its own special perils. Action proceeding from faulty or inadequate diagnosis may be as mistaken, and as lastingly unfortunate in its effects, as no deliberate diagnosis at all. In face of this peril there is a particular need to remind organisers of social politics that the surveys and exhibits, reports and plans, of the incipient civic order will be free from the surviving *defects* or the passing political order just in proportion as they embody the surviving *qualities* of past and present orders.[35]

Part of the problem is that Geddes and Jacobs were trusting very different kinds of sociological knowledge – Geddes the survey and Jacobs ethnography. Jacobs' distortion of the position taken by Howard, Geddes and Mumford makes sense when we consider her real objective, which was the subsequent development of town planning when it later led to Le Corbusier (1887–1965, Swiss-French, real name Charles-Édouard Jeanneret). Jacobs' target was this drift from Howard to Le Corbusier, which seemed to her both inevitable but terrible. Le Corbusier was enthralled by the potential of the newer technologies and he believed that when combined with centralised planning the city of the future could be built to generate a new harmony. This would be a 'vertical city':

> Radiant city, glass-and-steel skyscrapers set in parks; it would be an efficient and beautiful centre for the great bureaucracies whose total administration of society would bring the order and harmony he sought … He was afraid above all of the disorder of great cities, that "cancer" which made both organisation and order impossible.[36]

Although Jacobs could legitimately belittle Howard and his creation of 'self-sufficient small towns, really very nice towns if you were docile and had no plans of your own and did not mind spending your life among others with no plans of their own',[37] this was small beer when compared with the horrors of tower blocks, sited amid arterial roads to cope with the traffic. But her objection was not just to Le Corbusier's planning of the physical environment:

> He was planning for a social Utopia too. Le Corbusier's Utopia was a condition of what he called maximum individual liberty, by which he seems to have meant not liberty to do anything much, but liberty from ordinary responsibility. In his Radiant City nobody, presumably, was going to have to be his brother's keeper any more. Nobody was going to have to struggle with plans of his own. Nobody was going to be tied down.[38]

Nobody on anarchism's communalist wing was going to be happy here, and perhaps not anybody on the individualist wing either. The Le Corbusier Utopia would banish concerns with both community and education to the margins of urban planning.

Having disposed of her historical adversaries, Jacobs then turns to her very different reading of life in the city. Her story is too rich to be reduced to a short summary; I can merely offer examples of her insights. She starts with the street – the very element of city life that disappears in the designs of both Howard and Le Corbusier – for it is here that the most distinctive and valuable part of city life is to be found. The street is the bedrock of a successful city district: it is where people move about, and thus must do so safely, especially children and strangers. This is achieved by the designs of blocks and by an intricate network of social controls and shared standards of conduct, enforced by people themselves. It is a matter of self-organisation that requires three preconditions. There must be a clear demarcation between what is public and what is private; it must have natural proprietors, who have constant eyes on what happens and who is about; it must be in continuous use by people. In the successful city, 'diversity [is] intricately mingled in mutual support'. The city works when there are the right proportions of high *density* and high *diversity* working in subtle interactions. Ahead of her time, she conceives of the city as 'organised complexity', multiple variables interacting to make an organic whole. She rightly sees that Ebenezer Howard approached the issue of town planning 'as if he were a nineteenth-century physical scientist analysing a two-variable problem of simplicity … The two were conceived of as simply and directly related to each other, in the form of relatively closed systems',[39] when biological, open systems were the more appropriate model.

It is on this basis that a web of public respect and trust is built. This cannot be institutionalised, but its absence spells disaster. It is necessary to support the delicate balance between ease of contact between people when they choose it, but also the indispensable protection of privacy when this is also needed. This balance is achieved by 'small, sensitively managed details, practised and accepted so casually that they are normally taken for granted'.[40] This is also crucial to the solidarity of the community in which people take a modicum of social responsibility for one another even when they have no ties of friendship and kinship.

Diversity is natural to big cities, Jacob writes, and for this reason they are natural generators of further diversity and become incubators of new enterprises of all kinds. Small towns or communities, of the kind advocated by classical anarchists Godwin and Kropotkin as well as Howard, tend to be conformist places with a low tolerance of difference. As Richard Florida showed later,[41] creative industries are attracted to big cities that also attract bohemians, artists and gay people, some of whom are among the people he calls the 'creative class'. Whereas the old industries were often located close to natural resources, the creative class members are mobile and go to where they feel at ease and can meet socially. This may help to explain why schools in creative cities such as London and Manchester have been more successful in improving schools than have towns with similar social deprivation in rural and coastal areas.

Jane Jacobs's analysis does not ignore the fragility of the successful and diversity-rich city, and its vitality has to be maintained if it is not to self-destruct: 'if density and diversity give life, the life they breed is disorderly', which is not a form of chaos but 'a highly developed and complex form of order' – a conclusion very close to the anarchist concept of self-regulated order. The main risk here is from those who want to design the city as a work of art, which means death to its life:

> Indirectly through the Utopian tradition, and directly through the more realistic doctrine of art by imposition, modern city planning has been burdened from its beginnings with the unsuitable aim of converting cities into disciplined works of art[42] ... Instead of attempting to substitute art for life, city designers should return to a strategy ennobling both to art and to life ... helping to illuminate, clarify and explain the order of cities ... To see complex systems of functional order as order, and not as chaos, takes understanding.[43]

In these ways Jane Jacobs made what is a potentially massive contribution to urban design, both in the reconstruction of established city districts and in the planning of new towns, and the development of community through diversity that has become characteristic of so many of our cities. She brings people back in: they enliven her pages and enrich her vision with what Ruth Levitas termed the ontological mode that is lacking in earlier utopian designs, where people are more like puppets that merely act out the limited parts scripted for them by their designer.

For a significant advance on Jacobs we must turn to the last of our major thinkers, Richard Sennett and his *The Uses of Disorder: Personal Identity and City Life* (1996), where the very different starting point is the well-known notion of the adolescent 'identity crisis' in which young people often respond to their insecurities by various means of self-protection against their felt vulnerabilities – uncertainties which he observes are often made worse as adults push young people, at far too early an age, to choose a specialism at school and in higher education, with the consequential tracking towards a particular career. This adolescent search for security entails the careful avoidance of ambiguity and uncontrollable forces that threaten identity. For some young people, this self-protection extends into adult life, when what is perceived as potentially disruptive to the protected identity has to be resisted at all costs.

This situation is exacerbated by town planners, house builders and estate agents, who encourage the tendency for communities to become ever more homogenous – ones that people desire because they feel more comfortable and less vulnerable when they live alongside 'people like us'. House builders in the UK now actively resist diversity by the tactic of avoiding the inclusion of affordable properties in new developments, fearing the resentment of potential buyers who seek the homogeneity of 'people like us'.[44] Such relatively affluent communities, Sennett argues, are in fact not beacons of communal solidarity but believers in a myth of shared identity and experience, and when the members are not poor, there is less need to rely on mutual aid to survive. The myth of solidarity strengthens the resistance to the possible intrusion of people who are 'different'. This contrasts with Jane Jacobs's contention that it is diversity, not homogeneity, that gives the city its special vitality: it is the very lack of diversity that makes such communities dull places in which to live, as people protect themselves from challenge, like frightened adolescents who resist the painful but necessary ingredients of growing up.

There are clear implications for a local school, which often draws mainly and even almost exclusively from local families, since this reinforces the myth of local solidarity and strengthens in the young the belief that any normal community consists in 'people like us'. In my experience of working in London, in neighbourhoods characterised by high diversity in terms of family income, the rich mainly opted for private schools so that their offspring could escape the dreaded social contamination from local schools. On the other hand, where the neighbourhood was highly diverse in terms of ethnicity, religion or home language, the local school gained from this mix from non-rich families and thereby could make a vital contribution to wider social solidarity.

In the second part of Sennett's book, called 'A new anarchism', he argues that to prosper we need social situations that weaken rather than strengthen the desire for self-protective control. In place of the fear of being manipulated by external and hostile forces, people need to become self-confident agents with the will and capacities to manipulate the world for its improvement. This means learning how to accept the inevitability and desirability of a degree of instability, and so how also to create and manage a new context of such diversity, complexity and disorder. To this end, he builds on Jane Jacobs's belief in high population density and a housing design that brings inhabitants into the possibility, even probability, of high levels of social contact. This inevitably creates a situation that is higher in its potential for tension and conflict than the pattern of suburban estates with their safe, widely spaced houses in a dead-end close rather than busy streets. These diverse communities do not arise spontaneously, Sennett insists: they need to be created and urged into being by a change in strategy from town planners and local officialdom, as well as house builders.

Some of Sennett's proposals, such as greater decentralisation of resources to local groups for them to make spending decisions in line with their priorities and local knowledge, build on Jane Jacobs's analysis and are welcome to anarchists:

> For example, police control of much civil disorder ought to be sharply curbed; the responsibility for making peace in neighbourhood affairs ought to fall to the people themselves ... Until they learn through experience that the handling of conflict is something they have to deal with, something that cannot be passed on to the police, this polarisation and escalation of conflict into violence will be the only end they can frame for themselves.[45]

Sennett's view is that if we are to lead fulfilled lives we have to learn to avoid too much order and too much coherence:

> Extricating the city from preplanned control, men will become more in control of themselves and more aware of each other. That is the promise, and the justification of disorder.[46]

This is a finer conception of 'taking back control' than the version currently on offer as a lure to Brexit that invests all the control in the hands of State politicians. Sennett argued that once citizens feel empowered to take greater responsibility for their communal affairs, political leaders who have captured the centralised bureaucracies would be

> forced back into a more modest, less dictating mould: uncharismatic, sensing that their power lies in how well they distribute the goods of the state. City politicians would become "middlemen" rather than beautiful leaders: they would be successful to the extent that they channel the revenues and coercive powers of the state down to the level where it could be used as materials for communities engaged in formulating the rules of their own survival. This may seem utopian, but it is much less dangerous than the utopia invoked now every election day, when one is told to vote for the cleansing saviour, the charismatic leader who will restore order and decency.[47]

This involves a significant reduction in the power of political leaders and their associated central bureaucracies, and a redistribution of power – and the responsibility for its use – to citizens, a proposal that is bread-and-butter anarchism. But this has not happened; these battles have still to be won. We need to learn from the story of Grenfell Tower before and after its disastrous fire so that residents take back control from the planners and builders and local politicians.

The writers discussed in this chapter recognised the challenge of how young people are to be prepared for the changing role of citizens who are more active in shaping and managing their lives and communities. The school should play a role here, and one with more vigour than it currently obtains in the 2013 National Curriculum guidance on citizenship in Key Stage 4 (14 to 16-year-olds). There is the usual material on 'civics' such a parliamentary democracy and electoral systems, which in my experience pupils find rather dull, but which would become more relevant if they could look forward to exercising the vote at 16. Yet there is far too little about active citizenship, where the main focus is:

> the different ways in which a citizen can contribute to the improvement of their community, to include the opportunity to participate actively in community volunteering, as well as other forms of responsible activity.

This is written in the style of a timorous Sunday School teacher of the 1950s rather than an educator who wants to inspire the next generation with the courage and resolution to fight against the abuses of power that have been all too common in England in recent years. In place of this travesty of what active citizenship should involve, there should be a clear statement that if citizens do not constantly hold politicians, both local and national, to account, then their rights and aspirations will at best be overlooked and at worst trampled on with disdain. Case studies of Jane Jacobs in New York and those of the Hillsborough disaster and of the Grenfell Tower residents (when the full story is known) would make far better material than conventional 'civics' in portraying what active citizenship means. Another good teaching aid is *Design Your Own Utopia* by Chaz Bufe and Libby Hubbard,[48] which would bring to light similarities and differences in the way students think about their ideal society. It would almost certainly expose the flaw common to many utopian designs, namely the excessive emphasis on the desirability of harmony and peace. There can, of course, be too little, as in parts of cities bedevilled by high levels of criminality and drug addiction, but the search for harmony can go too far by suppressing the diversity on which healthy communities thrive.

For me, the design of the city sought by both Jacobs and Sennett is close to an anarchist philosophy and thus to meeting the criteria suggested in my evaluation template. Is it so for you? I feel confident that it is very attractive to many young people, who will be the ones to make it work, for it means developing conceptions of community that fit our age, not ideals from the past. How we apply this approach to communities outside the big cities is not yet clear to me, but it is precisely the young who, one hopes, will discover the way.[49] I am convinced of two important tasks: that of grappling with the heavily loaded distribution of power into the hands of the State, at both national and local levels, and their relationships with the large building firms; and that of thinking through how younger people can be better educated to play yet more active roles in the development and protection of the community than Howard and Geddes conceived.

The notion of utopia plays a useful function in helping us to develop and sustain ideals of a better society, but it also harbours dangers when in the hands of those determined to bend society into conformity with their conception of utopia in defiance of those natural forces of disorderly order in which humans thrive. This danger is at its greatest when the utopian has great power and those who are to be inhabitants of the planned utopia have little power to shape or resist the grand design, as we must now demonstrate.

Notes

1 Kinna in Davis and Kinna (2009) provides the best discussion of this.
2 Quoted by David Stafford in Apter and Joll (1971: 93).
3 Saul Newman in Davis and Kinna (2009: 217).
4 Levitas (1990: 181).
5 Northrop Frye in Manuel (1973: 973).
6 Mumford (1922: 21).

7 Mumford in Manuel (1973: 7).
8 Levitas (2013: xv, 75, 84, original emphasis).
9 Mumford (1922: 8).
10 Quoted by Colin Ward in Goodway (2012: 317).
11 Wright (2010: 6).
12 Lewis Mumford quoted in Fishman (1982: 23).
13 Howard quoted in Fishman (1982: 33).
14 Fishman (1982: 35).
15 Hall (1998: 704).
16 Fishman (1982: 87).
17 House of Commons Briefing Paper 03668 *Extending Home Ownership: Government Initiatives*, 28 December 2017, as well as Patrick Collinson, 'Help to buy has mostly helped housebuilders boost profits', *Guardian* 21 October 2017.
18 Scott and Bromley (2013: 25).
19 Ward (1989: 15).
20 Ward (1991: 105).
21 Branford (1921: xiv).
22 Geddes (1915: Preface).
23 Geddes (1915: 73).
24 Geddes (1915: 101).
25 Mumford (1955: 105f).
26 Scott and Bromley (2013: 145ff).
27 See Tyrwhitt (1947).
28 Hall (1998: 783).
29 Hall (1998: 788).
30 Hall (1998: 791).
31 Jacobs (1961: 14).
32 Jacobs (1961: 17).
33 Jacobs (1961: 19).
34 Jacobs (1961: 19).
35 Branford (1914: 77, 361).
36 Fishman (1982: 164, 260).
37 Jacobs (1961: 17).
38 Jacobs (1961: 22).
39 Jacobs (1961: 435).
40 Jacobs (1961: 59).
41 Richard Florida (2002, 2008).
42 Jacobs clearly has Lewis Mumford in mind. Cf. Mumford (1938: 484).
43 Jacobs (1961: 375).
44 Sennett (1996: 160).
45 Sennett (1996: 16).
46 Sennett (1996: 198).
47 Sennett (1996: 168).
48 Available online: www.seesharppress.com/utopia.html.
49 I had hoped that Sennett would develop his ideas further, not least in relation to the growing diversity in urban areas in terms of race, religion and gender and the new 'politics of identity', but in this regard his latest book, *Building and Dwelling: Ethics for the City* (2018), the last of his trilogy, disappoints. He writes in a way that is reminiscent of Patrick Geddes: he is wonderfully well-read, he has been a sociological researcher, planning practitioner and consultant throughout the world, and he writes engagingly. It is a big book, long and wide-ranging, but whilst it makes some very good points, it does not make the significant advance I hoped for.

9

POWER AND RESISTANCE IN SOCIETY AND IN EDUCATION

> The government and society have a burning desire to educate the people and, in spite of all the force, the cunning devices and the obstinacy of governments and educated classes, the common people constantly declare that they are not content with the education offered to them and, step by step, give in only to force. In this, as in any conflict, we have to answer the question: which is the more justifiable, the resistance or the pressure itself? Should we break down the resistance or change the pressure?
>
> Leo Tolstoy, 1862, quoted in Pinch & Armstrong (1982)

> Everyone carries within himself the germs of this lust for power ... No one should be entrusted with power, as anyone invested with authority must, through the force of an immutable social law, become an oppressor and exploiter of society.
>
> Michael Bakunin, 1871, quoted in Maximoff (1953)

The battles fought by Jane Jacobs, only partially reported in her book,[1] were on a David versus Goliath scale. Goliath was Robert Moses, who shaped the planning and design of New York over a forty-four-year period. He skilfully built himself a vast empire and was untouchable by those to whom in theory he was accountable, he instilled fear in everyone he dealt with and those who tried to cross him were never forgotten or forgiven. He became America's greatest builder, endlessly honoured for his achievements. Yet to construct his highways he dispossessed 250,000 people of their homes. He had very grand ideas, but unlike Howard and Geddes he discounted the views of those affected by his schemes:

> Corruption before Moses had been unorganised, based on a multitude of selfish, private ends. Moses's genius for organising it and focusing it at a central source gave it a new force, a force so powerful that it bent the entire city

> government off the democratic bias. He had used the power of money to undermine the democratic processes of the largest city in the world, to plan and build its parks, bridges, highways and housing projects on the basis of his whim alone. In the beginning – and for decades of his career – the power Robert Moses amassed was the servant of his dreams, amassed for their sake, so that his gigantic city-shaping visions could become reality. But power is not an instrument that its possessor can use with impunity. It is a drug that creates in the user a need for larger and larger doses. And Moses was a user ... But little by little there came a change. Slowly but inexorably, he began to seek power for its own sake. More and more, the criterion by which Moses selected which city-shaping public works would be built came to be not the needs of the city's people but the increment of power a project could give him. Increasingly, the projects became not ends but means – the means of obtaining more and more power.[2]

How did the Moses case come about? The anthropologist James C. Scott (1998) suggests the combination of conditions under which such utopian social engineering schemes flourish. The first condition he calls 'high modernism', the conviction among planners, technocrats, high-level administrators, scientists and visionaries of the need to impose order as a tool of improvement. The second is the concentration and unrestrained use of power to execute such designs. The third condition is a prostrate civil society lacking the capacity to resist.[3] Scott uses these ideas to make sense of what Jane Jacobs achieved in New York by courageously adopting a favourite anarchist resistance tactic, direct action, to mobilise the resistance that neutralised this third condition. Curiously, however, the target of his attack is Le Corbusier with his vertical city, tower-block designs, not Robert Moses, who is accorded just a tiny footnote. The evidence clearly shows that Moses was the problem, not Le Corbusier, whose ideas would never get off the ground without the people with real power, the city planners, both political and professional. It is they who had to be resisted, not Le Corbusier directly.

Scott's second condition is of particular relevance to the anarchist objection to State power, for he describes in fascinating detail the ways in which States assemble their power to achieve control. For in the absence of a State, there is enormous local variety in the way people organise themselves, but such local practices are *illegible* to outsiders and so cannot be monitored or recorded. To make them legible, the State steps in to simplify in conformity with imposed standards. Just as States seek to reduce linguistic diversity to impose the dominant version spoken by the State's elite, so also they devise ways to homogenise other local diversity relevant to State control. For instance, the use of surnames arose so that we could be distinguished as unique individuals that can be recorded and counted, a necessary step for the collection of taxes. Measures of many different kinds have to be standardised – weights and volumes, as well as distances and areas through State mapping – a process of simplification without which State control would be very limited. Remember the etymology of the word 'statistics': from Latin to Italian *statista* = statesman.

> If we imagine a State that has no reliable means of enumerating and locating its population, gauging its wealth, and mapping its land, resources and settlements, we are imagining a State whose interventions in that society are necessarily crude. A society that is relatively opaque to the State is thereby insulated from some forms of finely tuned State interventions ... An illegible society, then, is a hindrance to any effective intervention by the State.[4]

Apply Scott's last point to current educational standardisation by our State and you get this result:

> Imposing standardised forms of assessment of pupil performance by means of State tests and examinations renders what schools do more legible and so permits the State to make finely tuned interventions at the level of individual schools, especially through Ofsted inspections. Headteachers and, through them, teachers also then become obsessed by the same State-demanded measures, for it is the only way in which they can hope to exercise any influence over State interventions in their school. As teachers become "data-driven", with official approval, this affects how they classify pupils, decide which ones to focus on (e.g. those at the C/D borderline in secondary schools), who in turn become data-driven in terms of how they manage their learning and the typifications they use to forge their self-identities. Successful school leadership is shaped by the leaders' capacity to manipulate and "game" this system.

In this way the State acquires the means for the surveillance and control, not merely over the *outcomes* of schooling but also, and more menacingly, over the internal *practices* of both teachers and pupils in what was once the professionally protected sphere of the classroom. Quite simply, every teacher and every pupil is now potentially legible by the State. For anarchists, for me, and perhaps for you, this penetration of the tentacles of the State into the lives of individuals is of a dystopian *1984* scale.

How might teachers and parents oppose such moves? By acts of anarchist-style resistance.[5] Some parents keep their primary-school children at home during the week of the SATs and a few head teachers have refused to enter the pupils for the tests, putting their jobs at risk.[6] Boycotts are not always low-risk and need large numbers to achieve success. At present too few parents or head teachers resist, so cannot effect a poll-tax style success.

For classroom teachers, however, no such resistance is available. They now live in a world of performativity. Stephen Ball summarises it brilliantly:

> The essential point about performativity is that we must make ourselves calculable rather than memorable. In regimes of performativity, experience

> is nothing, productivity is everything. Last year's efforts are a benchmark for improvement ... We must keep up; strive to achieve the new and ever more diverse targets which we set for ourselves in appraisal meetings; confess and confront our weaknesses; undertake appropriate and value-enhancing professional development ... Performativity is enacted through indicators and targets against which we are expected to position ourselves but often in ways that also produce uncertainties about how we should organise ourselves within our work ... Increasingly, as we adapt ourselves to the challenges of reporting and recording our practice, interpersonal social structures and social relations are replaced by informational structures and performance indicators ... Performativity then, is a "new" moral system that subverts and re-orients us to its truths and ends. It makes us responsible for our performance and for the performance of others. We are burdened with the responsibility to perform, and if we do not we are in danger of being seen as irresponsible.[7]

When we compare this with the condition of schooling fifty years ago the change has resulted in a dramatic, but not irreversible, shift in the educational imaginary. Some aspects of performativity have today become the taken-for-granted common-sense way of doing things in schools. Pupils have too little experience to imagine anything very different, but teachers are far from being duped by the shifting imaginary. They want to do their best for their pupils and have to work with the grain for them. But at the same time, they often feel a moral disgust and outrage at this invasion of their professional integrity. As a result many lead a double life, in part playing the game by the rules they resent but cannot reject or alter, but also in part continuing to be a teacher by their own very different set of rules whenever they can – the relative privacy of the classroom leaves space for doing some teaching differently and even subversively. But this causes stress, frustration and ambivalence for classroom teachers that are often hidden from the public. Many young teachers take flight to other professions, but neither this nor moving to a school with better leadership are easy options for older teachers.

Anarchism provides a telling diagnosis of, as well as radical responses to, what is happening in schools, because of their long-standing critique of power. The absence of serious dialogue about power and the State between anarchists and those on the political left means that the latter too often recoil from making any serious challenge to the State. A good example is Frank Coffield and Bill Williamson's *From Exam Factories to Communities of Discovery: The Democratic Route* (2011). They offer a compelling critique of the policies that have shaped recent history of schooling in England, and are sceptical of conventional approaches to school reform. They rightly focus on the

> alarming growth in the power of ministers and civil servants ... [which] has been replicated in schools, colleges and universities up and down the

> country, where a yawning gap has opened up between those who manage and those who teach.[8]

Their solution is democratic renewal in education as part of a wider programme of reform in political institutions and processes. Moreover they recognise that this will entail looking not at mainstream schools but at the periphery where exciting, innovative practice flourishes because it is here that the State has little interest in exerting control. Yet they flinch from asking the fundamental questions about the State to which their analysis surely points. In such an inspirational book, this is a pity since they acknowledge that the issue behind their discussion is *power* and their alternative 'communities of discovery', self-regulated and moderated by peers, where 'power is openly, widely and more equally shared among members of those communities'[9] resonate with anarchist ideals. In these, however, power cannot be redistributed without challenging the State itself.

Yet anarchists are in part at fault here, for they use many terms to describe what they are against – State, government, authority, hierarchy, domination – concepts variously interpreted and debated by anarchists and sometimes used interchangeably and in confusingly loose ways when what is now needed is greater clarity as well as openness to ways of interrogating the concept of power. For anarchists, the greatest of all abusers is the State and its agents, such as Robert Moses. Anarchists target any abuse of power by an unreasonable, unnecessary or unfair distribution of it, or by an oppressive deployment of that power to infringe, undermine and negate the qualities they value – freedom, liberty, autonomy, independence. Power pervades all human relationships where it assumes many forms, as Proudhon so memorably captured:

> To be governed is to be kept in sight, inspected, spied on, directed, law-driven, numbered, regulated, enrolled, indoctrinated, preached at, controlled, estimated, valued, censured, commanded, by creatures who have neither the right, nor the wisdom, nor the virtue to do so. To be governed is to be at every operation, at every transaction, noted, registered, enrolled, taxed, stamped, measured, numbered, assessed, licensed, authorised, admonished, forbidden, reformed, corrected, punished. It is, under pretext of public utility, and in the name of the general interest, to be placed under contribution, trained, ransomed, exploited, monopolised, extorted, squeezed, hoaxed, robbed; then, at the slightest resistance, the first word of complaint, to be repressed, fined, despised, harassed, tracked, abused, clubbed, disarmed, choked, imprisoned, judged, condemned, shot, deported, sacrificed, sold, betrayed; and, to crown all, mocked, ridiculed, outraged, dishonoured. That is government; that is its justice; that is its morality.[10]

Teachers today read Proudhon with a sense of recognition that would have seemed unreal to teachers in the 1960s and 1970s; the performativity to which the State has led us was excoriated by Proudhon almost a hundred years ago.

Schools and education systems are power-rich social institutions. Educators do not, however, use the word 'power' much in their talking and writing,[11] preferring power-related words such as 'discipline', 'classroom management', 'orderliness'. 'Power' is perhaps too raw, too brutal a word for comfortable talk among professionals. In fact, the head teachers, and to a lesser degree governing bodies, have immense power over staff and students. Apart from parents, no adults other than teachers exercise so much power over children and young people for so sustained a period and in such privacy, probably for the rest of their lives. And students have power over one another, much of it again hidden from view.

In a State, the government has power over schools, whether they are accountable directly to ministers or indirectly to local authorities, or are purportedly 'independent' of the State. Moreover, account needs to be taken of the power of parents and how that relates to the power of the school as well as of local or national authorities and their agents. The way power is distributed between these various parties is complex and in constant and often confusing flux, as noted in Chapter 1. An anarchist perspective on education and schooling is particularly sensitive to the distribution and exercise of power. We turn first to the sociological literature to clarify our terms,[12] and then examine how power and government operate at the macro level of the State as well as at the more micro level of social and institutional relationships.

Power, then, is not so much a possession as a relationship between two or more persons, or between some sort of body or institution and persons: it is a transactional concept. At its simplest, A has power over B if A can get B to comply with A's demand or request. There are different ways this can be achieved and for different reasons. The basic form relates to A's ability to reward or punish B for compliance. With *reward power* A offers B a reward – something that B must value – to gain compliance; and with *coercive power* B complies to avoid A's threatened punishment for non-compliance. It is coercive power that anarchists seem principally to have in mind: the State gets people to comply by imposing penalties, and ultimately with force, for non-compliance. But then, as every parent and teacher knows, withholding a reward is often more effective than a threat of punishment to ensure conformity.

Anarchists often treat the terms 'power' and 'authority' as synonyms, but in everyday use we make distinctions, for we judge whether or not a power is judged to be rightfully or justifiably used. When A is seen, by both A and B, to have a right to exercise the power, it is a case of *legitimate power*, which may include both reward and coercive power. But of course B may consider A's power to be illegitimate or even illegal; in such a case A is alleged to be exceeding or abusing his or her power, an allegation that A may reject. If A's power is perceived to be illegitimate, even if legal, it may provoke *resistance*, a favoured anarchist word. Power is often distributed unequally and this creates a *hierarchy* of power, and this can become *domination*, which may or may not be desired by one or both parties. These variations around the concept show that the distribution and/or exercise of power, and responses to them, are negotiated, accepted or resisted in transactions between the parties.

When power is legitimate, it is often perceived as *authority*, as when people query 'Do you have the authority for that?' or 'Should we report that to the authorities?' (= 'the powers that be'). There are other meanings of 'authority'. To say A is an authority on the Second World War means that A is very knowledgeable about the topic and has *expert power*, which can be used to command respect and deference. This is the power base of professionals, such as doctors, teachers and scientists. Then there is the case of what is sometimes called *referent power*, where B complies with A because B admires or identifies with A. In both expert and referent power A's power takes the form of *influence* rather than *control*, and is more subtle, taking various forms such as persuasion, advice, imitation, inspiration, incitement and so on. Influence is often more effective than the crude exercise of reward or coercive power. Moreover influence is usually more easily resisted than reward of coercive power. One common distinction in types of power is that between *bureaucratic* and *charismatic* power: the former rests on the office a person holds and so is a type of official power, whereas the latter derives from a person's personal and magnetic qualities. Bureaucratic leaders rely on reward and coercive power, whereas charismatic leaders use influence. People who enjoy disproportionate amounts of power and influence over others are sometimes exercising *leadership*, which may or may not be legally based or perceived as legitimate.

In practice, an individual may combine several types of power and authority, thus strengthening his/her power base, and thus increasing the probability of compliance – or requiring more effort to resist. Teachers in schools combine three types of power; that of an adult; that of the legal holder of an office with designated powers; and the expert power of being a trained teacher. In the case of secondary schools especially, the teacher's subject, based on a university degree, is a critical source of power and authority. The subject forms part of the teacher's identity: I am not just a teacher, but a *maths* teacher.

Anarchists keenly scrutinise power wherever it may be found. Kropotkin rightly suggested that mutual aid was practised by early human beings and was essential to their survival and evolution. In their pre-State conditions, did humans have distinctive or better ways of handling power in their relationships? Were these lost with the growth of the State? If so, could they ever be recovered? Kropotkin knew that we have very little evidence of the lives of pre-literate, State-less humans, but there is evidence by anthropologists of contemporary human communities in remote places living in State-free circumstances. How do such people handle power and its distribution? How do they respond when power is abused? What happens when people from modern States arrive on their doorstep and attempt to exert power over them by incorporating them into a State? Can some aspects of pre-State society survive such contact with strangers from a State?

In *People Without Government: An Anthropology of Anarchism* (1982) Harold Barclay (North American, 1924–) demonstrates the wide range and complexities of social arrangements in archaic (formerly so-called 'primitive') societies and the extent to which they conform to what anarchists conceive as their preferred society.[13] The move from hunter-gatherer communities to settled agricultural societies in which the early states become established is well documented. It seems to be an inevitable trend, though it would be a mistake to see it, as have many in the nineteenth and twentieth centuries, as evolutionary progress. Here I want to examine how two surviving State-free societies in very different parts of the world handle power in their social and communal lives in ways that can reasonably be described as anarchistic – though this is not to claim they are typical of surviving State-free societies.

The most important study here is the ground-breaking *Society Against the State* (1974, English translation 1987) by the French anthropologist Pierre Clastres (1934–1977). He undertook fieldwork of archaic South American Indians for a period of ten years before his early death. He rejects the view that a society that does not display coercive power is thereby a society that is apolitical. He accepts, implicitly, Michael Oakeshott's definition of politics as 'the activity of attending to the general arrangements of a set of people whom chance or choice have brought together', which means that all societies, ancient and modern, are political and governmental. 'Political power as coercion … is not the *only* model of true power, but simply a *particular case*, a concrete realisation of political power in some cultures',[14] such as our own. Other societies, however, like his chosen Amerindians, do not engage in the coercive power that characterises the State. They are, in short, societies without the State, but not without government. So how is power exercised in these circumstances?

Clastres shows that the distinguishing feature of many anarchic societies in North and South America is the lack of social stratification that then limits the potential concentration of power. There are chiefs – but what defines the chief since he has such limited power? Throughout the two Americas there are three indispensable qualifications for a chief.

First, the chief is a peacemaker, the group's moderating agency, responsible for maintaining peace and harmony. He appeases quarrels and settles disputes, relying not on coercive power but on influence – his prestige, his fairness and his verbal powers of persuasion. He is not a judge passing sentence, but an arbiter seeking to reconcile. Exceptionally, when the group goes to war, another person, one more suited to the warrior role, then assumes power to command. But as soon as the war is over, he loses his position as chief, and any attempt to extend his status post-war is rejected.

Second, the chief must be generous with his possessions in response to requests from supplicants. In some tribes you can spot the chief as he has the fewest possessions or wears the shabbiest ornaments. It is the price he pays for his position: greed is incompatible with his role. He therefore has to be skilled in creating a supply of gifts he can offer to his people: he is often the person who works hardest within the tribe. It is industry, not idleness, that marks his superior social status.

Third, he must be eloquent: only a good orator can become chief. At dawn and sunset he must gratify people with an edifying discourse: he is a clever teacher and entertainer who commands attention. In some places, the chief is rewarded by an additional privilege: polygyny is his prerogative, which must come as a welcome consolation for the costs of holding office. These leaders are, in short, *servant leaders.* Do they in any way provide a model for the senior leaders in schools? I suspect few classroom teachers would define their current head teacher in these terms, especially in secondary schools. It is the strong, forceful leader who is more likely to be promoted, since in the age of performativity head teachers are defined and judged, like football managers, on their power to exert the pressure that gets results from staff performance in delivering test and examination grades.

In archaic society by contrast power could be very widely diffused, as, for example, in Madagascar where Peter J. Wilson (1933–2005) and his wife spent several years in the 1960s in fieldwork among the Tsimihety, reported in *Freedom by a Hair's Breadth* (1992). There is always a risk of becoming *ethnocentric* in our judgements, taking our own social arrangements as the proper or only standard by which to judge others. This, of course, is the attitude that characterises colonialists, whose tendency is to view archaic societies as something we have ceased to be, and then to assume that our society is what by natural evolution they are destined to become. Thus a State-free society is thought to lack something that it ought to have, indeed which it can have with a bit of 'civilising' help from outsiders. The anthropologist, of course, intentionally puts such a perspective on one side. The Tsimihety are remarkable because their supreme value was liberty and they took strong measures to protect their autonomy:

> Tsimihety freedom was freedom from the institutional instruments of constraints and power. This meant, in particular, freedom from any semblance of an all-inclusive hierarchy, be this externally imposed or internally generated, and from ritual, political and jural hierarchies in which may be vested the power to determine or interfere with any and all aspects of life.[15]

They were not seeking freedom for themselves as a polity managing its own affairs: there was no Tsimihety polity. They dispensed with the guidance and authority of leaders. It is this that makes Wilson's account so very fascinating, not least because the value given to autonomy made the Tsimihety extremely self-protective and suspicious of outsiders, not merely of other Malagasy peoples or the French, but also of anthropologists, however unthreateningly Wilson and his wife sought to conduct themselves. As a consequence, the Tsimihety rejected the French projects for them to convert to cash crops, which could then be sold at a profit and thereby generate the money to improve their standard of living. For this mode of production and consumption linked to money could, in the Tsimihety view, only lead to an unwanted dependence on outsiders and thus to a weakening of their autonomy. Not surprisingly the French authorities, locked in their colonialist social imaginary, found them difficult and incomprehensible. It is not that the Tsimihety declined to be appropriately deferential and obedient: instead of open resistance, they constantly stonewalled and blocked, making promises and appointments for meetings, which were never kept. This was much more effective than organised opposition, which could and would have been more easily defeated by the French. Flight, both mental and physical, often works better, or at least more safely, than fight. One wonders what would happen if England's head teachers were to adopt the Tsimihety line in resisting the State's pressure on them.

This would, however, entail a less hierarchical and more egalitarian attitude from head teachers to their staff. For much of Tsimihety life, such as norms of residence and land tenure, was operated as a means to a political end – the guardianship of their liberty and egalitarianism. This entailed much mutual aid and an equitable distribution of resources, producing no more than what was needed, with little in the way of surplus. Ownership was often more a matter of stewardship rather than permanent possession and there were safeguards against the accumulation of wealth, since there was no money and no means of turning anything one owned, such as cattle, into a convertible resource. The emergence of hierarchy is forestalled. All of this had a foundation in principle:

> The rejection by most Tsimihety of Christianity, Western education, commercial exchange, bureaucracy, and their insistence on remaining as free as possible to live the same sort of life as their ancestors was less a form of cussed nostalgia and more a means of expressing autonomy, which is to remain continually able to be part creators of their moral world.[16]

They were not naively imprisoned in their own social imaginary: they understood well enough the nature of the threat posed by the French.

Resistance to power by whole societies, including those that are far less anarchistic than the Tsimihety, is widespread. James C. Scott estimates over 100 million people in Southeast Asia from different ethnic groups and speaking many different languages deliberately withdraw from States to hide and live in the hills where they can escape the clutches of the State. Their fascinating story is told in *The Art of Not Being Governed: An Anarchist History of Upland Southeast Asia* (2009), which builds on his earlier book, *Weapons of the Weak: Everyday Forms of Peasant Resistance* (1985), in which he notes that much work on the peasantry is devoted disproportionately to their rebellions and revolutions that, if only momentarily, pose a threat to the State. This ignores their far more commonplace resistance, so he sets out to document

> the simple fact that most subordinate classes throughout most of history have rarely been afforded the luxury of open, organised, political activity. Or better stated, such activity was dangerous, if not suicidal. Even when the option did exist, it is not clear that the same objectives might not be pursued by other stratagems … Formal, organised political activity, even if clandestine and revolutionary, is typically the preserve of the middle class and intelligentsia … Here I have in mind the ordinary weapons of relatively powerless groups: for dragging, dissimulation, desertion, false compliance, pilfering, feigned ignorance, slander, sabotage, and so on.[17]

The weapons of resistance that Scott describes in his books are becoming familiar to classroom teachers in their response to the pressures of performativity. That these weapons are used so widely by other people in other places but for not dissimilar reasons should help to comfort teachers and relieve them of their guilt – for in my experience teachers are unusually susceptible to feelings of guilt when they do not play by the official rules. If the anthropological literature seems somewhat remote, they can find more familiar examples in Stan Cohen and Laurie Taylor's *Escape Attempts: The Theory and Practice of Resistance in Everyday Life* (1976):

> Every day's living constitutes a series of projects in which we either accept the arrangements that await us, or attempt to manipulate them, so that they will be more amenable, more compatible with the view that we hold of ourselves. In this book we talk about how people make out in their world, the whimsical, pathetic, desperate, outrageous ways in which they manipulate its demands.[18]

It is institutional forms of power that often arouse our resentment and resistance. The Canadian sociologist Erving Goffman (1922–1982) provided a highly influential analysis of institutional power. He earned his spurs as an ethnographer in the Shetland Islands by living in an hotel, where he learned how the staff had a 'backstage' unknown to the guests before whom they had to present a very different 'front' to conceal the reality of life below stairs. This led to his first book, *The Presentation of Self in Everyday Life* (1956), which elaborated the theatrical metaphor in how people manage their performances by controlling the impressions others have of them. It makes a good read for teachers, who know how what might seem to be designed in their interest – appraisal interview, personal and career development plans – become management tools for setting targets that managers want them to achieve, so manufacturing an impressive 'front' becomes a self-protective essential.

The subject of Goffman's second book, *Asylums: Essays on the Social Situation of Mental Patients and Other Inmates* (1961), comes closer to schools as he turns to institutions where these dramaturgical tactics are even more important because of a greater power differential between actor and audience. Goffman understood the demands of performativity before the word was invented. What he calls 'total institutions' have four features:

> First, all aspects of life are conducted in the same place and under the same single authority. Second, each phase of the members' daily activity is carried on in the immediate company of a large batch of others, all of who are treated alike and required to do the same thing together. Third, all phases of the day's activities are tightly scheduled, with one activity leading at a pre-arranged time into the next, the whole sequence of activities being imposed from above by a system of explicit formal rulings and a body of officials. Finally, the various enforced activities are brought

> together into a single rational plan purportedly designed to fulfil the official aims of the institution.[19]

Examples of total institutions are prisons, prisoner-of-war camps, secure mental hospitals, closed monasteries/convents, military academies. 'In our society, they are the forcing houses for changing persons; each is a natural experiment in what can be done to the self.'[20] Most of the book is devoted to his preferred institution, the mental hospital, perhaps because his wife had mental problems and committed suicide in 1964. Only the boarding school meets all four criteria: ordinary schools do not qualify as fully total institutions – though you might think that some get worryingly close.

Goffman's somewhat hair-raising account of the inmate's induction into a total institution describes the various means of mortification, and the way these disrupt the normal processes by which we convince ourselves and others that we are able to have control, autonomy and freedom of action. The recruit experiences a severe loss of self-determination achieved by various techniques employed by the staff, who justify them on the grounds of their necessity in managing the inmates. Conformity is achieved by punishments and privileges, the latter often being a withdrawal of the former, and they are unlike what happens to adults in the normal world. Like the Tsimihety, inmates often avoid direct challenges to the staff by using techniques to achieve forbidden satisfactions – learning 'the angles'. Some inmates adapt by 'colonisation', settling for the maximum satisfactions that can be procured from the institution, or even take the further step of 'conversion', becoming the model inmate by accepting the staff's view of the self.

In Goffman's analysis it is easy to see reflections of life in schools, albeit in an attenuated version. Just how close are schools to total institutions? At first sight it looks as if one of the greatest and earliest sociological accounts of life in school, that by Willard Waller in *The Sociology of Teaching* (1932) – a neglected masterpiece, now very difficult to obtain in the UK – treats schools in very similar terms, since he insists in his opening pages that schools have a 'despotic political structure'. But he qualifies this assertion:

> It is not enough to point out that the school is a despotism. It is a despotism in a state of perilous equilibrium. It is a despotism threatened from within and exposed to regulation and interference from without. It is a despotism capable of being overturned in a moment, exposed to the instant loss of its stability and prestige.[21]

This is quite unlike a fully-fledged total institution. The authority of the school executive and of the teachers, he says, is constantly threatened and in unremitting danger from various parties – the students, parents, the school board, one another, hangers-on, alumni. It is significant that he puts students at the head of his list. His school has some of the marks of a despotism in its distribution of power, but it is far too fragile to qualify as a total institution. He has several brilliant chapters, including one on 'Social distance: buffer phrases', with which the teacher keeps a necessary distance from the students to prevent an erosion of teacher authority by an unwelcome familiarity that is 'not compatible with dominance and subordination' – even though this risks making the teacher 'relatively meaningless as a person'.[22]

The opening sentence of his chapter on 'The battle of the requirements' touches on one of the most important aspects of the anarchist view of teaching: 'It is only because teachers wish to *force* students to learn that any unpleasantness ever arises to mar their relationship.'[23] This line recalls Godwin's conviction that 'We mistake compulsion for persuasion and delude ourselves into the belief that despotism is the road to the heart.'[24]

And what is it that the students are forced to learn? Waller stands back and worries about the taken-for-granted assumption that knowledge can easily be pre-structured for learning:

> The division of knowledge into subjects, and the subdivision of subjects into courses, must seem arbitrary to anyone who is not involved in the schools; and the system of grades upon performance must often seem even to the most experienced teacher to rest upon nothing at all ... Teachers display an extravagant devotion to academic standards. The complex of attitudes centred around standards and the attempt to uphold them comes to be the dominant trend in the teacher's personality. In the mental universe of teacherdom, academic learning is the supreme value, and life revolves around it. All persons are judged upon the basis of past or present achievement. No knowledge is of any account save that which can be built into a course and roofed over with an examination. The only effort worth the making is the struggle for the improvement of learning. It is this mania for classroom perfection which most deeply characterises the teacher ... The social life of a whole little world revolves about the issue of tests and requirements.[25]

This was written in 1932, long before *Black Paper* writer Brian Cox could complain about rebellious students. So, nearly eighty years later, are our own 'standards agenda' and 'performativity culture' as new as they sometimes seem?

No discussion of power can ignore the work of Michel Foucault (1926–1984), whose treatment advances our understanding in fundamental and startlingly original ways, ones that in this book I can deal with in only a partial and selective way.[26] His work is very complex and it developed in subtle ways over time, generating vast numbers of followers and commentators; it is easily distorted in selective and simplistic summaries. Some anarchists inevitably turn to Foucault as a source of ideas and insights[27] (though as far as I can see admirers of Foucault seem more reluctant to turn to anarchist thinkers and writers), yet his treatment of power is neglected in some important anarchist writing.[28] I first consider one of his books of major relevance to education, along with some reservations on his analysis – Foucault approached power and politics as a philosopher and historian, and I am neither. I then discuss Foucault's later and richer views on power and how these set challenges for anarchist approaches to education and schooling.

Fifteen years after Goffman's *Asylums*, Foucault published *Discipline and Punish: The Birth of the Prison* (1975, English translation 1977). This is a work of obvious interest to anarchists, especially if one considers the original French title, *Surveiller et Punir*, since *surveiller* means to keep under observation, to monitor, to keep an eye on,[29] which recalls Proudhon's famous 'To be governed is to be kept in sight, inspected, spied on', etc., quoted earlier. There is also an obvious link to Goffman's book since Foucault covers a range of very similar institutions: Goffman chooses to focus particularly on the mental hospital, Foucault on the prison. 'Is it surprising,' asks Foucault, 'that prisons resemble factories, school barracks, hospitals, which all resemble prisons?'[30] Foucault is apparently unaware of Goffman's book, but his scope is vastly greater than Goffman's and with far deeper and more controversial implications. For Foucault is interested in these institutions not merely as ones of a similar kind, but as exemplars of deeper and widespread forces that make a *collective* impact on society and on people: they are not truly the source of this impact, but expressions and outcomes of it.

Discipline and Punish concerns the fundamental relationships between power, knowledge and subjectivity/identity. Penal history is the vehicle for a deeper and broader analysis of developments in Europe from the period of absolute monarchy to modern times, with a particular interest in the years 1760–1840, a time he calls 'a great transformation' – a profound shift in social imaginary that proceeded unevenly but steadily. I shall draw on a few aspects of the book that are of particular relevance to this chapter, with the hope that you will read *Discipline and Punish* for yourself.[31]

Foucault charts the transition of power from the monarch and the aristocracy to the middle classes that is linked to the change from punishment to the body (torture) to incarceration, where the punishment then works in a very different way, because it 'acts in depth on the heart, the thoughts, the will, the inclinations'. To interpret this change in how an offence is understood and handled simply as an increase in humanistic treatment of offenders is to be misled, for this ignores the increase in power displayed in more subtle forms at the hands of those who punish in a variety of circumstances:

> It is no longer "Who committed it?" But: "How can we assign the causal process that produced it? Where did it originate in the author himself? Instinct, unconscious, environment, heredity?" It is no longer simply: "What law punishes this offence?" But: "What would be the most appropriate measures to take? How do we see the future development of the offender? What would be the best way of rehabilitating him?"[32]

The offence does not merely have to be detected: its causes have to be diagnosed and the prognosis of any possible punishment taken into account. It is a different way of making sense of, and so treating, the offence and the offender. It is a switch from a technology of power over the body to a technology of the 'soul',[33] entailing a different kind of investigation and different considerations when deciding on treatment, all drawing on a different kind of language, the emergent social science vocabulary, especially psychology. Power and language are entangled inextricably; neither can exist without the other; theirs is a co-evolution, which can be found in the history of prisons – and of schools. One must start from an analysis of power and then trace it through various institutions, because the power relations that 'are embedded and crystallised in institutions' have their source outside the institutions.[34]

This ubiquitous discipline Foucault defines as a relationship of docility–usefulness ('*un rapport de docilité-utilité*'), with its 'uninterrupted, constant coercion, supervising the processes of the activity' through the use of time, space and movement.[35] And true enough, in school pupil docility is indeed linked to productivity: teachers want pupils to be obedient so that they will get on with their learning, which so often is actually called work rather than learning – 'David, stop talking and get on with your work.' Doing well at school is held to make you a more useful and valued member of society. Foucault extends the notion, maintaining that discipline, in school and elsewhere, is a key aspect of capitalism, in which power renders the working classes both docile and productive. His new 'political anatomy' involves many different processes, often on a very small scale, with different origins and forms in different locations, overlapping and repeating, but gradually converging to produce 'the blueprint of a general method'. He says he cannot provide a history of the different disciplinary institutions; he will refer to them, including the school, for illustrative purposes (saving his detailed case-study of the prison for the end of the book). This 'new micro-physics' consists of the manifold, meticulous and often minute acts of cunning assuming subtle forms that are widely diffused in the entire social body:

> The meticulousness of the regulations, the fussiness of the inspections, the supervision of the smallest fragment of life and of the body will soon provide, in the context of the school, the barracks, the hospital or the workshop, a laicised content, an economic or technical rationality, for this mystical calculus of the infinitesimal and the infinite.[36]

It is not simply through the law, and therefore the police, that the State achieves its aims.[37]

In our age of advanced performativity, any teachers reading this will feel their condition is being recognised in the first twenty words, though what they will make of the rest of the sentence I cannot say. But note that the institutions he names are in a much looser category than those labelled by Goffman as 'total institutions': not just schools in general, but specifically boarding schools; not just any kind of hospital, but closed mental hospitals; not just barracks, but military academies. Goffman stresses the significant differences; Foucault, in his too broad generalisations, does not. Is there not a serious danger here, that in sliding from one of the most total of institutions, the prison, to just ordinary schools, he exaggerates the degree to which his interpretations are evidence-based, even in his preferred historical periods? Pupils may claim that school is like a prison, but happily they lack the experience to judge.

Sometimes schools are compared to factories. Are these places that also oppress like total institutions? Take the case of *docility*, one of Foucault's central concepts. It was well captured by Simone Weil's letter of June 1935:

> What working in a factory meant for me personally was as follows. It meant that all the external reasons (which I had previously thought internal) upon which my sense of personal dignity, my self-respect, was based were radically destroyed within two or three weeks by the daily experience of brutal constraint. And don't imagine that this provoked in me any rebellious reaction. Nor, on the contrary; it produced the last thing I expected from myself – docility. The resigned docility of a beast of burden. It seemed to me that I was born to wait for, and receive, and carry out orders – that I had never done and never would do anything else.[38]

Is today's school, as opposed to the Dotheboys Hall of Charles Dickens, really like this for some children? The anthropologist Jules Henry carefully observed docility in the school context, and then provokingly interpreted it, in his famous piece 'Docility, or giving the teacher what she wants', as long ago as 1955:

> When we say a human being is docile we mean that, without the use of external force, he performs relatively few acts as a function of personal choice as compared with the number of acts he performs as a function of the will of others. In a very real sense, we mean that he behaves mostly as others wish him to ... It is not based on authoritarian control, backed by fear of corporal punishment, but rather on fear of loss of love. More precisely, it rests on the need to bask in the sun of the teacher's acceptance. It is not fear of scolding or of physical pain that makes these children docile, but rather fear of finding oneself outside the warmth of the inner circle of teacher's sheltering acceptance. This kind of docility can be more lethal than the other, for it does not breed rebellion and independence, as struggle against authoritarian controls may, but rather a kind of cloying paralysis; a sweet imprisonment without pain.[39]

This account is very much in line with Foucault's later analysis: power is more effectively exercised when it forestalls the very possibility of rebellion rather than having to suppress it.

Anarchists are well versed in the issues of power and some of their finest writers experienced life in prison and have told their stories in the most vivid terms.[40] They would, I think, approach Foucault's account of power with an inbuilt degree of caution, because in *Discipline and Punish* he says very little about *resistance* to power. Its absence dilutes the strength of his argument about the overwhelming penetration of power into our lives, which he relentlessly piles on the reader. Yet the anthropological evidence about the range and variety of forms of resistance is considerable, especially in the books of James C. Scott. I think Foucault's lack of balance in not reporting the literature on the frequency and effectiveness of resistance confirms that his argument is overstated. Had he been more familiar with the sociological literature he would have been more aware of the problems that arise from overstatement, such as Dennis Wrong's telling indictment of sociology, in 1961, for indulging in an over-socialised conception of man. Foucault convincingly argues that power penetrates in far more numerous and subtle ways than earlier writers allowed; but resistance too can take subtle forms, with which teachers are only too familiar, and is well documented in the sociology of education literature.[41]

It is a weakness of sociological studies of schools that, as changing theoretical frameworks are used to interpret quite similar material, it becomes difficult to know in what sense our knowledge and understanding are being cumulatively advanced. In one of the earliest and most important, but now much neglected, contributions to the sociology of education, the leading theorist of the American functionalist school, Talcott Parsons (1902–1979) aimed to show how the classroom functions to internalise in pupils, from their earliest days in school, their commitment and capacities for their later adult roles and their place in the social and class structure. In school, unlike in the home or the community, children are now differentiated by their teachers on the basis of their achievement in schoolwork. Pupils are judged, in addition to this cognitive dimension, by a moral dimension, of how well they behave. And the two dimensions are fused. In secondary schools the pupils have the alternative attraction of the peer group as a source of prestige. He notes that the

> anti-school side of the ideology [of youth culture] is that it provides a means of protest against adults … Truancy and delinquency are ways of expressing this repudiation. Thus the very *improvement* of educational standards in the society at large may well be a major factor in the failure of the educational process for a growing number at the lower end of the status and ability distributions … The stratification of youth groups … has a selective function: it is the bridge between the achievement order and the adult stratification system of the community.[42]

Parsons concludes modestly that his short article is the 'merest outline' of the analysis needed:

> It is, however, hoped that it has been carried far enough to suggest a field of vital mutual interest for social scientists on the one hand and those concerned with the actual operation of the school on the other.[43]

A constant stream of work, under various theoretical formulations, has developed this field initiated by Parsons.[44] It is such processes that Foucault pinpoints with his notions of normalisation and individualisation, the pressures that schools exert to get pupils to conform to the 'good pupil' role – with its docility and industry – that is taken as the standard or normal one.[45] In accordance with such categorisations, pupils are launched on developmental pathways by organisational devices such as streaming, setting and tracking, between classes and within classes, all of which is well documented in the sociology literature. Indeed, how can the school avoid such organisational systems that segment pupils into smaller units by age, ability and/or achievement, conformity to school values? My own work with two colleagues (Hargreaves et al., 1975), an ethnographic study of deviant behaviour in two secondary schools, focused on how pupil identities were constructed in relation to their conformity or non-conformity with the basic rules that teachers impose on their classrooms to create order, rules that are often quite idiosyncratic. We were surprised to discover just how quickly, in the very first few meetings with new pupils, teachers matched the pupils' responses against an ideal of the 'good pupil' and how, once formed, these imputed identities became highly resistant to change, and often transferred to pupils' self-images. This is not a criticism of the teachers: it is something teachers can hardly avoid doing because it is a consequence of the existence of schools and classrooms in which they believe order has to be imposed on collectivities of pupils for the system to operate effectively and efficiently. But it was on such processes that the assessment regime introduced by the 1988 Education Reform Act would later build in shaping pupil identities with more devastating consequences.

Foucault developed his ideas on power further after *Discipline and Punish*, and he clarified the matter of resistance: 'There is no power without potential refusal or result',[46] and any subject of a power relationship has 'a whole field of responses, reactions, results, and possible interventions', though these remain unelaborated. This admission is no substitute for the detailed documentation of resistance that is largely absent from *Discipline and Punish*. Moreover it focuses on coercive power, with little discussion of referent power/influence, which arguably has become more important with the declining use of coercive power in schools and elsewhere.

Power, for Foucault as for anarchists, is always a question of 'government', what he calls 'the conduct of the conduct of others':

> To govern … is to structure the possible field of action of others … Power is exercised only over free subjects and insofar as they are "free". By this we mean individual or collective subjects who are faced with a field of possibilities in which several kinds of conduct, several ways of reacting and modes of behaviour are available.[47]

This, Proudhon and anarchists might well respond, is a statement of what we believe and have always believed: it is at the core of anarchism. But Foucault pursues a different line. He says his principal interest is not the phenomena of power, but rather the different ways in which persons are made subjects.[48] As the State develops, it begins to incorporate what was originally a feature of the Church, its pastoral concerns, the care of the shepherd looking after his flock, which involves knowing considerable detail about individual sheep.[49] The State needs to know much about individuals and their circumstances in order to maintain its very existence – how else could it levy taxes, as James Scott argued above? – but it also now proclaims a duty to look after citizens as well. The State becomes a modern matrix of individualisation, a new form of pastoral power.[50] In this sense 'it is clear that, right from the start, the State is both individualising and totalitarian',[51] by simultaneous processes and techniques. Can the same argument be transposed to the school: power is exercised to maintain itself as an institution, but part of the rationale for this is the care and well-being of the student?

For me, the most impressive application of Foucault to education is Ansgar Allen's *Benign Violence: Education in and beyond the Age of Reason* (2014). At the beginning of the book he draws a disturbing picture of the forms of examination and assessment in education in the nineteenth century, ones from which we would today firmly distance ourselves, but then continues the analysis into recent history where this tradition has been built up to new levels in our current assessment regime, which are even more distressing because these exercises of power and violence have become cloaked in teacher concern for the learner:

> Even those examining techniques that seek to listen to the child – techniques that are celebrated for their benign attention to the unique needs of the individual learner – are not innocent of power interests and their effects. They are tied within a system of moral coercion that operate through carefully devised modes of examination, based on relationships that are often warm and kindly in manner.[52]

Jules Henry first touched on this sensitive nerve in all of us teachers in his treatment of docility, quoted above, but Allen drills it so ruthlessly to its roots that one emerges from the book in a state of shock. If you are a teacher, at school, college or university, dare to read it to catch sight of yourself and your institution in Allen's mirror as you would never wish to be seen.

The school becomes one agent, a singularly important one, for a far wider process, claims Foucault:

> It is certain that, in contemporary societies, the State is not simply one of the forms of specific situations of the exercise of power – even if it is the most important – but that, in a certain way, all other forms of power relation must refer to it. But this is not because they are derived from it; rather, it is because power relations have come more and more under State control (although this State control has not taken the same form in pedagogical, judicial, economic, or family systems). Using here the restricted meaning of the word "government", one could say that power relations have been progressively governmentalised,

> that is to say, elaborated, rationalised, and centralised in the form of, or under the auspices of, State institutions.[53]

What matters, then, for our contemporary world is 'not so much statisisation of society, as the "governmentalisation" of the state'.[54] Thus Foucault gives birth to his neologism for this process: *governmentality*.[55] It is by means of the tactics of governmentality that the State survives and thrives. He insists that

> power relations have been governmentalised, that is to say, elaborated, rationalised, and centralised, in the form of, and under the auspices of, state institutions[56]

In the same 1982 essay he draws a somewhat elusive conclusion:

> Maybe the target nowadays is not to discover what we are but to refuse what we are. We have to imagine and to build up what we could be to get rid of this kind of political "double bind," which is the simultaneous individualisation and totalisation of modern power struggles. The conclusion would be that the political, ethical, social, philosophical problem of our days is not to try to liberate the individual from the State, and from the State's institutions, but to liberate us both from the State and from the type of individualisation linked to the State. We have to promote new forms of subjectivity through the refusal of this kind of individuality that has been imposed on us for several centuries.[57]

He does not suggest how to do this, though we should perhaps treasure this rare sanguine moment. If you accept the anarchist view that, as the State has expanded its reach, the vulnerable fragilities within it are inevitably exposed, then there is room for optimism. The notion of an emancipatory social science, as propounded by Erik Olin Wright in his masterly *Envisioning Real Utopias* (2010), requires a sociological theory of social reproduction, but it also examines the exposed cracks, contradictions and gaps. These open up spaces in which collective struggles for the new possibilities[58] mark the paths to the new social imaginary to which the classical anarchists aspired. We must now take them.

Notes

1 For the full thrilling account, see Lang and Wunsch (2009) and Flint (2011).
2 Caro (2015: 18f).
3 We should not forget the part played by corruption here. The shocking collapse of the Morandi bridge in Genoa in August 2018 drew attention to related disasters in the past and warnings of ones yet to come in a country riddled with civil corruption. In 1959 Vito Cianciminio, a mafia boss born in Corleone, became head of public works and later mayor in Palermo, where he master-minded a destruction of fine nineteenth-century buildings and green belt to replace them with dreary low-cost constructions using sub-standard materials.

4 Scott (1998: 77f).
5 I use 'acts of resistance' as a generic term to cover a wide range of tactics, including, for example, 'direct action' and 'civil disobedience'. Such terms are used in very different ways by different writers and so can be confusing. See Franks (2006) for the best review of anarchist strategies and tactics; Kinna (2005) offers shorter but helpful coverage.
6 A recent case is that of Jill Wood, who refused after consultation with parents and governors. *Times Educational Supplement* 19 May 2017.
7 Ball (2013: 136–9); see also Ball (1990, 2017).
8 Coffield and Williamson (2011: 63f).
9 Coffield and Williamson (2011: 12).
10 P.-J. Proudhon, *The General Idea of the Revolution in the Nineteenth Century*, trans. J. B. Robinson, London: Freedom Press (1923: 293–4) in McKay (2011).
11 Nyberg (1981), a significant exception, notes the aversion to the concept of famous educationists such as R. S. Peters.
12 Dahl (1970), Lukes (1974), Watt (1982), Starhawk (1990), De Jouvenel (1993), Wrong (1995), Martin (1977). See also Russell (1938).
13 Kinna (2005: 108ff) provides a summary of Barclay in comparison with some other writers on anthropology and anarchism.
14 Clastres (1987: 22).
15 Wilson (1992: 127).
16 Wilson (1992: 168).
17 Scott (1985: xv).
18 Cohen and Taylor (1976: 10).
19 Goffman (1961: 17).
20 Goffman (1961: 22).
21 Waller (1932: 10).
22 Waller (1932: 279).
23 Waller (1932: 355, emphasis added).
24 Godwin (1793: 110).
25 Waller (1932: 356ff).
26 For a considered treatment of Foucault on education, see Ball (1990) and Ball (2017).
27 See especially May (1994) and Deleuze (2006).
28 A good example would be Franks et al. (2018), which I think is an admirable and essential source on anarchism, but which surprisingly does not list power as one of anarchism's fundamental concepts, and perhaps for this reason makes very few references to Foucault.
29 In the Penguin version in English, Alan Sheridan reports that Foucault suggested *discipline* as the best translation of *surveiller*. Today, as opposed to 1976, I would argue that *surveiller* and the notion of 'keeping under surveillance' has become very more relevant to understanding the impact of official power, as when the State seeks the right to intercept private communications on the internet and our streets in so many places are subject to video-camera recordings.
30 Foucault (1977: 228).
31 If you do not find the book easy or have not already done so, I suggest you read Schwan and Shapiro (2011), which summarises the argument in plain English as well as offering a useful commentary. A short general introduction to Foucault is Gutting (2005).
32 Foucault (1977: 19, 1975: 27).
33 Foucault (1977: 30, 1975: 39). The French '*âme*' can also mean 'spirit' or 'character'.
34 Faubion (2002: 343).
35 Foucault (1977: 137).
36 Foucault (1977: 140).
37 Foucault (1978: 211).
38 Miles (1986: 26) and Weil (1951/2002: 59).

39 Henry (1955: 34 and 41), *Journal of Social Issues*, 11 (2) 33–41, reprinted in Beck et al. (1976).
40 Kropotkin (1899), Berkman (1912), Serge (1967).
41 Hargreaves (1967), Willis (1977), Youdell (2011).
42 Parsons (1959: 312f original emphasis, 315).
43 Parsons (1959: 318).
44 The most immediate follow-ups were by Cicourel and Kitsuse (1963) and Dreeben (1968).
45 Foucault (1975: 183).
46 Foucault (1979: 324).
47 Foucault (1982: 341f).
48 Foucault (1982: 327).
49 This is most fully developed in Foucault (1979).
50 Foucault (1982: 334).
51 Foucault (1979: 325).
52 Allen (2014: 26).
53 Foucault (1979: 345).
54 Foucault (1978: 220).
55 The essay on governmentality can be found in Faubion (2002) and Burchell et al. (1991). See also Dean (1999).
56 Foucault (1982: 345).
57 Foucault (1982: 336).
58 Wright (2010: 27).

10

TWO PATHS TO A NEW IMAGINARY FOR EDUCATION AND SCHOOLING

> It may help to clear up some old-fashioned confusions in this field if we remember there is another type of school very different from what we ordinarily understand by the term.
>
> Victor Branford, 1914

> Worthy work carries with it the hope of pleasure in rest, the hope of the pleasure in our using what it makes, and the hope of pleasure in our daily creative skill. All other work but this is worthless; it is slaves' work – mere toiling to live, that we may live to toil.
>
> William Morris, 'Useful work versus useless toil', 1884

Every education and schooling imaginary is embedded in a wider social imaginary that largely shapes it. It is true that a schooling system can in turn reshape society, often in ways that were neither intended nor anticipated, but I believe, to the disappointment of many past and present school reformers, that a radical change in the dominant educational imaginary is rarely possible without some significant change in the wider social imaginary.

In the State model of education and schooling, that is the dominant educational imaginary, there is a basic and unquestioned assumption. The institution of the school is the essential starting point: education for children and young people becomes in the public perception largely what takes place there. Teachers know better, of course, but for others it is easy to forget how much children learn outside school. But the popular perception of 'an education' means what can be fitted in at school, which is no easy matter, since there are many purposes and functions that the State would like to fit in when there is too little room (time, space, personnel, etc.) for all of them. Yet it is possible to invert such thinking by putting the problem differently in the form of three questions:

first, what are the aims of an education for children and young people? Then, and only then, a second question: what sort of provision is needed for the achievement of such aims? If the terms 'education' and 'provision' are interpreted broadly, as they should be and as they are in anarchist thinking, the answer would probably not be schools as we know them, though of course it might well include schools. The rub lies in the third question: what in the wider social imaginary will inhibit or facilitate the implementation of any very different provision that emerges as an answer to the second question?

There is some room to manoeuvre. As noted earlier, the law today still allows us to invert the order in which we think about education and schooling, for the 1944 Education Act insisted that education, not schooling, was compulsory. Certainly today schooling is what most parents want, but it remains an optional choice, even though by law they are free to choose 'education otherwise', which includes home schooling. At present there could hardly be a better basis for an anarchist conception of education. The classical anarchist writers lived at a time when there was not one of the State benefits we now take for granted and which most people want to retain. Within education there exist many options by which State control over schooling might be reduced and the State's tendency ever to extend its grip might be reversed. If most parents were to choose to educate their children, for the whole time or just some of the time, outside the State system, State schooling as we know it would be forced to retrench on a matching scale. This could happen only if the alternatives to State provision of schooling were attractive and widely available, and expensive private provision were not the only alternative. If the choice were a stark one between State and no State at all, the public would support the cautious politicians and opt for the State, and rightly so. An education system in which the State played a reduced role would have to be carefully constructed over time to give everybody confidence in it. If successful, education could be a forerunner for reducing other aspects of State provision. The State would, of course, be suspicious and instinctively resist. But just as the centralisation of education through the 'standards agenda' and performativity has slowly but steadily established itself over some fifty years, so constructing ways out of it all must be expected to be a relatively long haul, with the State always on the defensive, and perhaps aggressively so.

In this chapter I shall focus on just two of the many important pathways to an imaginary that prizes education over schooling. One pathway relates to a major change taking place in the wider society, which is expected to accelerate rapidly over coming decades. The other pathway lies within the existing school system and is one in which I have been heavily involved at national and local levels. What I propose developed slowly in my mind over a long period beginning with the arrival of New Labour in 1997. Like many, I hoped this would make a break with the direction charted by Kenneth Baker in the Education Reform Act of 1988. As noted in Chapter 1, David Blunkett, the new Education Secretary, was pushed further in the same centralising direction by having to use the inherited assessment regime ever more firmly as the instrument of school and teacher accountability for the continuing standards agenda. Blunkett appointed me to join his Standards Task Force, essentially a small advisory body. This experience gave me a taste for trying to influence policy more directly than by writing and researching from my base in Cambridge and when the opportunity arose in 2000, I left the safety of my professorship for the more turbulent waters of government service, in which I served in various capacities for the next few years.

For me, this period was one of extraordinary absorption and frustration. One of the greatest pleasures was working closely with Estelle Morris, when she was Schools Minister and later the Secretary of State. She had such a passionate interest in education combined with an acute sensitivity to how government policies affected life in schools and most of all in classrooms. She understood, as I had to learn to understand, the limitations on the freedom of action of those who occupy positions at the centre, whether as a politician or as a public servant working for and with a minister. Both are always to some extent prisoners of a policy environment controlled by a variety of others, which become a source of frustration that I found difficult to bear. When this rewarding phase of my life ended, I had no desire to retreat to academic life for the second time, so instead began working directly with schools and local authorities (LAs) and with two fine organisations, the Specialist Schools and Academies Trust (SSAT), which was an independent body with subscribing member schools, and the National College for School Leadership, a body created by government but enjoying a delicate semi-independent status, until it was seized by Michael Gove to be absorbed into his Department under his direct control. Both the Trust and the College acted as bridges between the State and the schools, though in different ways. With Sue Williamson and her colleagues at the Trust and later with Steve Munby and colleagues at the National College I was able to work with school leaders as well as undertaking some writing tasks.

In this dark tunnel of growing centralisation we all looked for rare chinks of light in the distance, and one appeared when in May 2004 Tony Blair suggested schools might learn from industry about the value of personalisation. Estelle Morris had become Education Secretary and David Miliband her Schools Minister, who would take the idea forward. Sue Williamson of the SSAT, John Dunford of the then Secondary Heads Association and I had been working on school-led innovation, which was being actively encouraged by Labour ministers, and we thought that personalisation would work best if treated as a strand of this school-led innovation. This appealed to Miliband and he was persuaded against yet another top-down 'national strategy', which we all knew would not be well received in schools. As a result of several conferences for school leaders, from 2004 the SSAT produced a series of pamphlets reporting interesting practice and new ideas. Later developments and the creation of research networks of schools led to a further set of pamphlets over the next two years.

By this stage we suspected that innovations in a few exceptional schools were paving the way to a new educational imaginary. The conditions seemed more favourable than they had been for some time: the perceived need for change was at a high level among school leaders, combined with a higher degree of perceived freedom to change fed by Estelle Morris and David Miliband. At this period schools were increasingly caught in a cleft stick. Some of the pressures upon them arising from the standards agenda, the national curriculum, the assessment regime and Ofsted were for the most part unrelenting, but nevertheless considerable creativity and innovation was taking place. Performativity was real enough, but in our experience it told only part of an increasingly complex story. Were these innovating schools, albeit a minority, simply idiosyncratic exceptions? Or was a more fundamental shift beginning to take shape at school level?

We concluded that underneath the system's surface some significant reconfigurations were indeed taking place, ones involving some rethinking that led to experimentation, which in turn undermined some of the long and largely undisturbed traditions reaching back to the nineteenth century. The important point is that these reconfigurations were taking place in State secondary schools under the leadership of outstanding head teachers. In recent years the opportunity for any radical alternatives within the State sector has been small, though of course there is more room in the private sector; and there have been important movements that span both sectors, such as human scale education.[1] The reconfigurations indicated that radical changes were now entering the mainstream of secondary education and included the following:

1. Collaborative partnerships between schools
2. Flatter, less hierarchical staff structures
3. Distributed leadership – more opportunities for leadership at lower levels
4. Greater staff participation in school decision making
5. More staff engagement in innovation projects
6. Smaller organisational units within the schools – 'mini-schools'
7. Flexible and permeable age-cohorts – 'stage not age' for student grouping
8. Vertical tutoring and pastoral systems that mix age groups
9. Flexible time schedules, usually longer lesson length, amid new designs for the school day, term and year
10. New designs for school buildings and learning spaces – often includes the abandonment of the standard classroom
11. Student voice and leadership, with co-construction of lessons
12. Pupils plan and manage their own work schedule with a tutor

This is a compilation from different schools. None simultaneously adopted all twelve, but all pursued several of them. Most schools had something in common: they had been 'grant-maintained' (GM) schools. The most welcome feature of Baker's 1988 Education Reform Act had been the devolution of financial responsibilities from the LAs to schools, but the motive had been to curtail LA powers as much as to trust head teachers. My impression at the time was that LAs were resentful, often bitterly so, for LAs were as tenacious of their power as any central government department. However, those head teachers who chose to 'opt out' for the new GM status[2] made a resounding success of their independence. Not surprisingly they reached high levels of student achievement by government criteria, which, combined with the freedom of their GM position, provided them with the licence to innovate. This innovation unleashed teacher creativity, which in turn enhanced teacher confidence and work satisfaction. These were exciting places to be, for both staff and students.

The driver for these reconfigurations was the imagination and energy of the leaders in these schools. Taken as a group, the reconfigurations seemed to us the green shoots of a school-led redesign of the school system. Potentially this would be a truly radical change – I avoid the word 'transformation', which has been so badly abused and over-used by educationists in recent years – but one that might justifiably be called a new social imaginary. For a school-led system redesign would inevitably shift the centre of gravity away from the State and back to the schools themselves. So from 2007 onwards the next eight pamphlets were accordingly issued under the titles *System Redesign* and *Leading System Redesign*.

It was essential to get beyond the dominant conceptions of school improvement, a theme that had been dominant since the mid-1980s. The 1988 Act had encouraged the concept of the self-managing school, especially those with GM status. Self-managing schools had the leadership capacity to be more effective at self-improvement, especially since LA effectiveness at school improvement was highly variable. The improvement agenda had increasingly been colonised by the State's Education Department and its agencies as a way of pushing its own priorities, hijacking many forms of developmental work for schools and teachers on the way, reducing them to instruments of control, sometimes overtly, sometimes covertly. The schools had to think of themselves as the heart of educational innovation and professional development, and the groundwork for this was already being laid by the outstanding head teachers who were at the heart of the SSAT's developmental work led by Sue Williamson and by Steve Munby at the National College for School Leadership.

Early in 2010 I wrote a 'think-piece' for the National College on the notion of a self-improving school system. This was the opportunity to offer a real alternative to conventional school improvement that still tended to focus on individual schools. Self-management is a basic principle of anarchism and a self-managing and self-improving *system* would be at the very heart of a decentralisation that would reduce the power of the State. Some of what I saw as the building blocks of such a system were already partially in place, particularly partnerships between schools, building on the recently formed federations of schools under an executive head teacher, some of whom had been among the pioneers of the new configurations discussed earlier, and on the recent development of inter-school networks, such as networked learning communities led by David Jackson.[3] Another building block was the emergence of outstanding schools leaders and system leaders, especially National Leaders of Education (NLEs), who would be well placed to lead the change. My model replaced insulated individual schools with clusters of schools taking collective responsibility for the improvement of all their members by working collaboratively on the task. The National College published my paper *Creating a Self-improving School System* in July 2010, to become the first of a series of four.[4]

You will not, I am sure, be surprised to learn that my paper did not use anarchism as a theoretical basis for the arguments (nor did the three later ones). This would have alarmed the National College and of course invited instant rejection from the incoming Conservative government with Michael Gove as Education Secretary. It was not rejected; on the contrary, in the White Paper, *The Importance of Teaching*, that appeared shortly afterwards in November 2010, the notion seemed to be pursued with enthusiasm, framed in a context of apparent government self-limitation by which centralisation would be rolled back:

> In this country, the ability of schools to decide their own ethos and chart their own destiny has been severely constrained by government guidance, Ministerial interference and too much bureaucracy. We want every school to be able to shape its own character, frame its own ethos and develop its own specialisms, free of either central or local bureaucratic constraint … We will increase freedom and autonomy for all schools, removing unnecessary burdens, and allowing all schools to choose for themselves how to develop.

To achieve this, some redesign of the school system would be needed:

> Over recent years, centralised approaches to improving schools have become the norm. Government has tended to lead, organise and systematise improvement activity seeking to ensure compliance with its priorities. And the attempt to secure automatic compliance with central government initiative reduced the capacity of the school system to improve itself. Our aim should be to support the school system to become more effectively self-improving. The primary responsibility for improvement rests with schools, and the wider system should be designed so that our best schools and leaders can take on greater responsibility, leading improvement across the system.

Of course, ministerial talk of ceding power to the frontline had been heard many times before, and it was tempting to be sceptical of the rather loose use of phrases such as the 'increased freedom and autonomy for schools', but perhaps every new Secretary of State should be given a chance, so this news was received with excitement by some school leaders. A key element in the redesign would be the identification of the schools that would lead improvement:

> We will create a new national network of Teaching Schools, on the model of teaching hospitals, giving outstanding schools the role of leading the training and professional development of teachers and headteachers.

Did Michael Gove really set about creating a self-improving school system (SISS)? Unfortunately not. It became clear that this notion had been little more than the usual rhetoric, a cover story and charm offensive for the real policies at the heart of the White Paper. All government White Papers contain a disparate set of proposed policies. So to reduce the possible interpretation of the document as a ragbag of ideas, some overarching narrative has to be provided to suggest coherence. This is true for all political parties. I recall a New Labour minister telling me how grateful they were to Michael Barber, who had this gift for devising just such a narrative for their education policies.

Michael Gove's White Paper seized on the concept of a SISS as its persuasive veneer. It was not itself a policy at all, in the sense of being a governmental goal with a linked set of actions designed to achieve that goal. There was never any detailed specification of what a SISS would be like, no action plan, no targets, no criteria by which progress or outcomes might be measured – all the usual backup we have come to expect of education policies. Instead the concept was used as the wrapping for what were indeed real policies, with goals and means for achieving them. These goals can be simply stated: they were to reduce further the control by local authorities over schools and to reduce further the control of higher education over teacher education and training. The means were turning schools into academies – academisation – offering 'freedom' from the LAs, getting them to work together in larger units such as federations and chains. The new teaching schools would be a new type of partnership designed to develop school-based teacher training and professional development, adding to previous moves to transfer initial teacher training from higher education into schools; and the teaching school alliances could in due course become chains of academies:

> It is our ambition, therefore, to help every school which wishes to enjoy greater freedom to achieve Academy status. Some schools will not want to acquire Academy status just yet, others do not yet have the capacity to enjoy full Academy freedoms without external support or sponsorship. But our direction of travel is towards schools as autonomous institutions collaborating with each other on terms set by teachers, not bureaucrats … It is our ambition that Academy status should be the norm for all state schools … We will … ensure that there is support for schools increasingly to collaborate through Academy chains and federations.[5]

In short, the true policy was one of extracting schools and teacher development from the LAs and to a degree also from universities in order to group them into clusters of autonomous schools, which would soon become known as multi-academy trusts (MATs) led by a chief executive. In effect, the schools would lose their short-lived autonomy – the autonomy championed in the White Paper was quickly forgotten – as they became subservient to the MATs, which in turn would be replacements for the LAs, and be directly accountable to the

Education Department, i.e. ministers. The whole purpose of the exercise was to ensure that most schools, under strong leaders either as exceptional head teachers or chief executives, could through closer collaboration be enabled to reach the government's criteria of high performance, that is, test and examination results, and do so faster and more effectively than the record of most LAs. In other words, the standards agenda was being imposed, but now by other means. Despite the luring words 'freedom' and 'autonomy' in the White Paper, the policy would inevitably mean an *exchange* of control rather than an *abolition* of it. Most head teachers would, as Foucault might have argued, by accepting the bribe of a new freedom apparently choose their new servitude of their own volition.[6]

My model of a SISS – based on small groups of schools genuinely choosing to work with one another on a voluntary basis and, whilst nevertheless retaining their autonomy, collaborating to create progressively deeper partnerships, by which they would share moral purpose in working for all the children in all the cluster's schools by innovating better teaching and learning, and by honing their capacity to evaluate and challenge one another based on trust – all this was a far cry from the government's direction of travel, and simply incompatible with it. The government continued to use the rhetoric of a school-led self-improving system as its continuing cover for academisation, though it would soon have to become more open and coercive in reaching this goal.

I contributed to the conferences of the newly-designated teaching schools held at the National College at which Michael Gove was the main speaker. The outstanding head teachers present were full of energy and enthusiasm for their new role, though very much aware of the costs in time and energy for their staff that this would involve. In the short term there were too few teaching schools for the plan to work adequately and they were unevenly distributed around the country. With time, though, it might work. I was also in demand as a speaker and workshop provider, most often at LA-organised events, but sometimes at head teacher groups. I covered much of the country, from the far north in Northumberland to Kent in the southeast and Devon in the southwest. The differences I met were astonishing: differences in size (small boroughs to large counties), in attitude to the White Paper (from a complacent 'carry on as usual' to 'this is the biggest ever challenge to the future of our LA'), in style of responding (from 'the LA will decide the structure and practice of inter-school partnerships' to 'a new partnership of joint decision making between LA officers and headteachers') and in reaction to it all at the level of the individual school (from excitement at the possibilities opening up to a very high level of anxiety and insecurity). I measured this last element by asking them to signify in a vote how they felt about the planned changes. In a few places the enthusiasts were in a majority; in others the anxious predominated; in most the vote was split. Never in a long professional life have I witnessed such a wide variety of responses by schools to government action.

One concern stood out above all the others – not an aspect of a SISS as such, but the plan for academisation, especially among primary school leaders, of whom over 90 per cent had declined the White Paper invitation voluntarily to choose to become one: they preferred to remain loyal to their LA, some of which were already involved in partnership schemes. Nor would minds be changed by the threat of compulsion targeted at those with a poor inspection report. Despite continuing pressure to convert, at the time of writing three-quarters of primary schools have stubbornly resisted.

This will change quickly. The 2016 White Paper[7] proposed that by 2020–2022 every LA school should become an academy. Although this plan was withdrawn after protests, the aim remains unchanged, but subject to a slower timetable. The period of grace is over: the days of schools being allowed, in the words of White Paper, to 'chart their own destiny' have gone, and primary schools will be coerced to make the choice they declined. The schools system's architecture will soon be dominated by MATs and teaching school alliances. The Department for Education (DfE) had to provide a regional structure for academies, mostly secondary, since the task had become too big for it to handle, and this regional structure will now expand. The government is finally reaching its goal of abolishing local control of schools, leaving LAs with some bits it does not want. It will be a challenge to make the new regional layers less bureaucratic and more participative for school leaders, but through them the DfE retains ultimate control. As Robert Hill notes in his fascinating blog, 'The DfE still essentially sees itself as a giant local authority responsible for all schools in the country.'[8] Despite the official talk of greater autonomy for schools and a school-led and self-improving system, centralised control is intact, holding the reins through the combined test/examination regime and Ofsted by which schools are judged and held accountable. Government-set goals for school are largely unchanged: schools are simply charged with the responsibility for meeting them. Indeed, in giving schools the *primary* responsibility for improvement, Michael Gove was handing head teachers a poisoned chalice, in that if their schools did not improve by government criteria, who else would now take the blame?

So the change has been profound and relatively rapid. The evolution of the academies is told in Andrew Adonis's *Education, Education, Education: Reforming England's Schools* (2012). Adonis, a man of exceptional ability, was in May 1998 appointed by Tony Blair to the Number 10 Policy Unit, where he played a key role in shaping education policy. He became head of the Unit in 2001 and a life peer and an education minister in 2005. He was the architect of the original academy concept. He believed that the comprehensive reforms had failed and many comprehensives were essentially a continuation of the previous defective tripartite system – secondary modern comprehensives, as he called them. Critical of local education authorities, many of which he considered incompetent, he produced schemes for their replacement, but he drew back and the idea was dropped. He then visited one of Kenneth Baker's City Technology Colleges (CTCs), was hugely impressed, and the radical idea of 'independent state schools' with 'chains' of linked schools was born. This soon morphed into the academies policy, greeted with less enthusiasm by David Blunkett than by Prime Minister Blair. The academy programme was launched in March 2000, with Adonis as the de facto chief executive. He ends his fascinating account by suggesting that 'English education is in transition from a low-achieving comprehensive system into a high-achieving academy system. It is a revolution which cannot come fast enough … So the best academy chains need to become larger and more numerous.'[9] This has now happened, though it is unclear whether they were indeed the best and by what criteria.

Just as the governments of Blair and Brown maintained substantial (though never complete) continuity with the Kenneth Baker educational agenda, Adonis had prepared the ground for continuity in policy for the incoming Conservative government and Michael Gove. So it is not surprising that in the same year as Adonis's book, James O'Shaughnessy, Director of Policy to David Cameron from 2010, and later a life peer, published *Competition Meets Collaboration: Helping School Chains Address England's Long Tail of Educational Failure* (2012), in which he urged much the same robust policy for school chains and cited the National Association of Head Teachers (NAHT), which allegedly had 'dropped its "one head, one school" policy and is in favour of schools coming together, and general secretary Russell Hobby believes the government should do more in trumpeting the benefits of federation if they want to drive chain formation'.[10] O'Shaughnessy concluded that 'it is the use that academies are making of this freedom to find new ways to collaborate, *within a competitive market*, which will provide the most significant impact on standards'.[11]

This is the rub. The system changes actually increased the competitive relationships between schools. There was no understanding that collaboration between schools is very difficult to achieve in a highly competitive market where the incentives for collaboration rapidly diminish. O'Shaughnessy emphasised the importance of collaboration within chains of schools, without realising that real collaboration requires the assiduous and inevitably slow cultivation of trust and social capital between schools, whilst the spirit of competition that had become so ingrained into the system, and especially among secondary schools, could not easily be removed from the relations between schools in a chain, especially a large one.

The 2016 decision that all schools should become academies will simplify the system. Most, and eventually all, schools will be pressured into clusters or partnerships of various kinds. Admittedly hastily arranged and shotgun marriages between schools can pay off, but my experience is that high-quality and long-lasting partnerships depend on high levels of trust and social capital among all the people involved, not just at school leader level. Without this, it becomes very difficult to achieve one of the most valuable benefits of partnerships between schools, which is the development of *collective moral purpose*, that is, a shared belief that the achievement and success of the pupils in partner schools matter as much as those of pupils in one's own school. Collective moral purpose, however, cannot be mandated: it has to be won slowly as trust grows.

The outcomes of the years post 2010 will be very variable. In my experience of working with a large number of LAs, some developed inter-school partnerships with great sensitivity, adopting a midwife role in supporting school leaders to make the necessary choices in their own way. Other LAs tried to impose partnerships, because they had some kind of overall plan for the area. As a result, they provoked resistance, conflict and ill-feeling: local officials were too impatient and too lacking in trust to let school leaders decide for themselves, carefully sounding out the situation and taking tentative steps before entering a more formal relationship. What will happen when all this LA history is replaced by successor MATs? The nature of the inter-school partnerships specified by the MATs is likely to be equally variable, reflecting the difference in philosophy and leadership style of the chief executives and trustees, and perhaps their size, as they vary from being very small to very large, some having over sixty member schools. Some schools will leave weak LAs to become members of strong MATs where there is the knowledge and skill to build high-quality inter-school partnerships; other schools will have the misfortune of leaving strong LAs for weak MATs where inter-school partnerships are shallow and superficial – all the result of central government hastily insisting on forced marriages between unwilling partners. What is the point of MATs as a replacement for LAs if they end up with the same wide variation in quality, effectively much the same architecture for schooling but under a different label?

What is the overall position today? The fact is nobody knows the full story and no agency exists to draw together all the relevant data and the experiences and views of the key people involved, let alone the thousands of classroom teachers who have been affected. Goodbye to any lingering hopes of evidence-informed policy. Is there any independent evidence to inform policy? Fortunately we have a major research report, *Hierarchy, Markets and Networks* by Toby Greany and Rob Higham (July 2018), for the current state of play, based on a limited sample of four LAs and a survey of 700 school leaders. Curiously the authors accept the government's position at face value, believing that the SISS is a genuine policy. Admitting that this is 'largely undefined in official texts' – their diplomatic version of what I consider to have been intentionally elusive – they then elect to call it a *policy agenda*, which rolls all the policies into a bundle with a SISS label, just as Gove intended. The real weakness of this is to make it look as if the schools' responses to this agenda are somehow to the concept of the SISS, when they are not: their responses are to the policies that bear down on them most heavily, namely the central one of academisation and the extraction of schools from the LAs. Greany and Higham rightly describe this as a move to hierarchical governance, not to the claimed increased autonomy but to what they call 'coercive autonomy' – which to an anarchist ear is distinctly oxymoronic – based on a false premise that the local authorities were a hindrance to school improvement. The result is what they call 'chaotic centralisation', noting the inevitable tensions arising between the various bureaucratic structures that oversee and regulate schools, and between the LAs and the regional structures for academies. Replacing conventional school improvement services in LAs by school clusters and teaching schools alliances in the transition to MATs is inevitably going to cause difficulties and resentments, not least because, as I found, so many of the best LAs had been active in promoting school clusters and in a way that was likely to ensure high-quality and enduring partnerships.

What the report does so well is to demonstrate how the very notion of a SISS is being damaged, where it is already in existence in embryonic forms, or simply hindered, where it has yet to grow, by the government's other policies that promote competition between schools and leave the role of Ofsted completely unchanged, both of which undermine the collaboration at the heart of a SISS. Competition in the secondary sector is acute, producing a corrosive rivalry between schools and a sense that there are winners and losers – 91 per cent said local schools compete for students and 85 per cent said that there was a clear local hierarchy of schools, fed by Ofsted inspection grades:

> In reality, then, our interpretation of the "self-improving system" agenda is that it is replete with, and is being layered on the top of, existing and contrasting systemic governing structures and incentives for schools ... As we have shown, this can lead central government to refine its policy objectives regularly and to increasingly coercive local change in order to try to "get things done", in the process moving ever further away from the ideal of a "self-improving" system based on lateral networks and towards "chaotic centralisation".[12]

The government might well be unhappy with the Greany and Higham analysis overall, but it might congratulate itself that its true policy of academisation and the weakening of the loyalty of most primary and some secondary schools to their LA is working, even if at some cost in terms of resentment and confusion in many quarters. It might dismiss this as unavoidable turbulence whilst the system is being radically reformed. That there is not much evidence of progress towards a SISS might not trouble the government, since there is no serious policy on this. I, by contrast, believed that a SISS was an important pathway to a new education imaginary and have to consider whether what is happening is inflicting permanent damage on the notion.

I conclude that the evidence shows that many features of a SISS are alive and well, partly because the foundations were created before the 2010 White Paper and partly out of self-protection measures being taken by school leaders. The majority of schools have regular interactions with one or two schools, and less frequently three or four schools.[13] This is exactly in line with what I recommended and found in practice, since it was evident that 'deep' partnerships cannot be developed and sustained in larger numbers. The potential to move to deep partnerships remains, but the competitive climate in the secondary sector will continue to be an inhibitor. Moreover almost half of school leaders reported that they had received a peer review in the last year, as had almost 60 per cent for secondary schools with a low Ofsted grade. Such peer review systems I argued in 2010 were absolutely crucial to securing a mechanism for evaluation and challenge that would make Ofsted redundant.

Some interesting questions arise over the MATs, which the government sees as the main form of cluster in the future. The Greany and Higham report interprets the MATs structure as not so much true partnerships as a case of 'mergers and acquisitions', that is, a take-over, sometimes hostile, leading to a loss of autonomy and agency for the target school:[14] the LA bureaucracy is 'replaced by another more complex and less accountable form of bureaucracy'.[15] Yes, some MATs might simply be a replacement for the LAs, and not necessarily good LAs either. Some MATs are likely to exercise stricter control over the day-to-day operation of their member schools than any LA would ever have dreamt of attempting. Moreover where a MAT's schools come from a range of geographically distant LAs, then the sustained inter-school interactions that characterise deep partnerships become almost impossible. I also have a concern that some small to medium-sized towns, and especially coastal towns with high social deprivation and unemployment, could end up with several or even all of their secondary schools in different MATs, which could terminate established local partnerships, especially between secondary and primary schools, and preclude the formation of new ones. It will be important that a majority of the MATs be formed from schools in one locality, one that is not necessarily coterminous with LA boundaries.

Yet what will happen is completely unknown. My impression at this relatively early stage is that MATs will vary in both quality and character. Some will have the good sense to encourage diversity within and between their schools. I am also confident that some will be models and leading exemplars of the partnership structures and cultures that will be at the heart of a SISS and thus the pioneers of the pathway to the new educational imaginary that I shall describe in the next chapter. Much will depend on the MATs' chief executives and whether they are as visionary as the head teachers who developed the original reconfigurations. It is they who will play the crucial role in fostering both greater collaboration, to ensure that any competition is of a healthy kind, and also robust peer review systems within and between school clusters, for that is the only way in which to ensure a reduced role for Ofsted.

From 2020 to 2030 the system's architecture will undergo a profound change, the greatest since 1870, and it will generate a confusing mix of optimistic excitement and dispiriting despondency. There will be a continuing struggle between schools and the State, but it is often out of such unsettling, unstable and unpredictable conditions that the best innovation springs, as our best school leaders have demonstrated repeatedly in recent years. For it is through such determined and imaginative innovation that the self-managing and self-improving school system will continue to develop, even if and when the State realises the implicit threat of a full SISS to its own control. It is innovation on an unprecedented scale that will be needed if schools, individually or collectively, are to respond effectively and creatively to find a better destination for a school system that puts education before schooling as a new imaginary begins to unfold. This will require a built-in flexibility to the emergent school system. It must be made much easier for a school to secede from a MAT than appears to be the case at present, or for its constituent schools to agree to a MAT's dissolution. Without such flexibilities MATs could become as immovable as bad LAs. A school-led SISS has to able to evolve in its own terms without any rigid framework that stifles the very possibility of unimpeded evolution.

The response of schools during the period will be affected by many factors interacting in complex ways, but among these there is, I believe, a second critical pathway to a new educational imaginary. The key catalyst for this structural revolution will, I believe, be the changing nature and extent of *work* or *employment*, for these will force changes in education that in turn will drive further changes in work. The simultaneous reciprocal shifts in work/employment and education/schooling within the broader social imaginary of the twenty-first century will be exhilarating (for those who pioneered the reconfigurations and the SISS) or frightening (for those who did not).

We are accustomed to speaking of work and its link to residual non-work as a work–leisure divide. This is an unhelpful concept, for as Bob Black notes, leisure is non-work for the sake of work,[16] that is, recovery time, often much needed. In our society the norm has been full-time paid employment, with leisure time plus holidays being the residue after taking account of the time consumed by employment, travel, domestic duties and sleep. As more people spend yet more time at work, we anxiously debate the 'work–life balance'. Has it always been so? We usually think of pre-literate societies as leading terrible lives of drudgery whilst they struggle against nature to achieve a minimal subsistence, without opportunity for what we call leisure. It is, in fact, untrue of many archaic societies. The anthropologist Pierre Clastres concluded that in primitive societies all the work necessary to support life could be completed in half a day or less:

> Thus we find ourselves at a far remove from the wretchedness that surrounds the idea of subsistence economy. Not only is man in primitive societies not bound to the animal existence that would derive from a continual search for the means of survival, but this result is even bought at the price of a remarkably short period of activity. This means that primitive societies have at their disposal, if they so desire, all the time necessary to increase the production of material goods. Common sense asks then: why the men living in those societies want to work and produce more, given that three or four hours of peaceful activity suffice to meet the needs of the group? What good would it do them? What purpose would be served by the surplus thus accumulated? What would it be used for? Men work more than their needs require only when forced to. And it is just that kind of force which is absent from the primitive world; the absence of that external force even defines the nature of primitive society.[17]

Anthropologist Marshall Sahlins (1930–) has called hunter-gatherers the original affluent society,[18] a claim that shocks us out of our preconceptions.

We know why some people work to create a surplus, especially in societies where grain can be stored for when it is in short supply, so that they can then sell it, make a profit, become rich, gain power and – sometimes but by no means always – get extra leisure. Here lie the origins of social stratification on which capitalism and the State are built,[19] with those who would never dream of working at the top, and the slaves and poor who have no choice but to suffer a life of drudgery at the bottom. This has been a central theme in anarchism, and at the end of the eighteenth century was a major concern for William Godwin, who with horror viewed his fellows 'condemned to slavery and sweat, incessant drudgery, unwholesome food, continual hardships, deplorable ignorance and brutal insensibility'.[20] They are still with us today and known to teachers feeding undernourished pupils whose parents are in badly-paid, insecure and unrewarding jobs or are unemployed. Godwin knew little or nothing about pre-literate communities, but he surmised that if work were better distributed and shared, and especially if all contributed half an hour a day to physical labour, and good use were made of the newly developing machines, then all could also enjoy the pleasures of work-free time:

> The commodities that substantially contribute to the subsistence of the human species form a very short catalogue. They demand from us a slender portion of industry … If the labour necessarily required to produce them were equitably divided among the poor, and still more if it were equitably divided among all, each man's share of labour would be light, and his portion of leisure would be ample … Those hours which are not required for the production of the necessaries of life may be devoted to the cultivation of the understanding, the enlarging our stock of knowledge, the refining our taste, and thus opening to us new and more exquisite forces of enjoyment.[21]

Kropotkin's calculations had a better scientific basis, but he came to remarkably similar conclusions:

> In short, the five or seven hours a day which each will have at his disposal, after having consecrated several hours to the production of necessities, will amply suffice to satisfy all longings for luxury however varied. Thousands of associations would undertake to supply them. What is now the privilege of an insignificant minority would be accessible to all … Every one would be the happier for it.[22]

With anarchists' characteristic celebration of diversity, opportunities for the use of free time must be sufficiently diverse to meet the full range of aspirations:

> Would life, with all its inevitable sorrows, be worth living if besides daily work man could never obtain a single pleasure according to his individual

> tastes? … Aims of life vary with each and every individual; and the more society is civilised, the more will individuality be developed, and the more will desires be varied.[23]

In allocating leisure time women are entitled to a fairer deal, for their domestic labour is discounted. Every woman 'should claim her share in the emancipation of humanity'.[24]

Today it is impossible to consider the work–life relationship without taking account of two problems. The first is that there are not enough jobs: some people are unwillingly forced into unemployment, and are often additionally stigmatised as lazy welfare scroungers. The second is that too many of the available jobs are not rewarding, usually in the double sense of low pay and lack of personal satisfaction: these are jobs very few people would freely choose. A minority of people enjoys – the right word – jobs that are highly paid and bring great personal satisfaction, though often they have to work unusually long hours, and risk serious levels of exhaustion and stress. As a consequence, free-from-work time cannot justly be called leisure time. There is a compensation for some of us, however, for our terms of employment offer substantial choice over exactly what to do, when and even where. Though all our duties have to be done if we expect to be paid, the flexibility is an incredible privilege. The gross inequalities in pay could be reduced by a redistribution of wealth, but could the same be done for the inequalities in the pleasures and privileges of work?

In 1972 the American oral historian Studs Terkel published his masterpiece *Working: People Talk About What They Do All Day and What They Feel About What They Do*, which vividly reported the way many people coped with the less attractive features of their jobs. It is Karl Marx, of course, who most famously treated the issue of alienation in work, and later writers have always been indebted to him. Most of us are ambivalent about work. We want it because a job and perhaps a career have been ingrained in us as the right and natural path for an adult and our very identity is often closely linked to our work; and in many ways we enjoy our jobs, especially where this puts us in contact with other people, as colleagues or clients. On the other hand, many would prefer less of it, to provide more time to do other enjoyable things, including family life. It was once held that automation would lead to the disappearance of the jobs that are boring, mind-numbing and degrading and it was with this hope that Godwin and Kropotkin welcomed technological invention. But it has not happened on the scale expected and when it does it is more likely to displace skilled rather than unskilled workers, including many white-collar jobs affected by advances in artificial intelligence (AI). The chief economist at the Bank of England estimates that up to 15 million jobs are at risk.[25] The IPPR think tank argues that 44 per cent of jobs in the UK economy could be automated through advances in robotics and AI.[26] Cities with weak economies in the north are particularly vulnerable, potentially losing 30 per cent of jobs within ten years.[27] Currently it is the retired, especially the early retired, who mostly enjoy greater leisure; how and when will the displaced workers claim their share? How will schools, so used to dangling the prospects of a decent job before less industrious pupils, respond?

In some respects the situation has worsened over the years, as disappearing skilled work is replaced by compensatory jobs that have no point at all, those that David Graeber describes in *Bullshit Jobs: A Theory* (2018). It's as if, he says, somebody is making up pointless jobs simply to keep us all working, when the opposite is supposed to happen. Bullshit jobs are those where even the holder of the post admits there is no good reason for it to exist, and Graeber suggests that up to four out of ten jobs fit this description. They are often well-paid jobs, especially in the finance, insurance and real estate sectors. Many people say they want a job in which they can make a difference; bullshit jobs are ones in which it is totally impossible to make any *worthwhile* difference at all, though they can cause other people in real jobs to engage in entirely worthless effort: they don't make people at all happy, but they do provide one with an income. The book offers many illustrations of bullshit jobs from across the world. Graeber suggests they are found everywhere and on a larger scale than one imagines, yet their existence remains officially unacknowledged as a problem. Politicians will do almost anything to be able to boast of low unemployment figures. Unofficially we all know the phenomenon is linked to the expansion of bureaucracy and middle managers and their self-justificatory 'make-work' practices, about which Graeber has written elsewhere.[28] On this teachers need no persuasion, for the absurd demands made by the assessment regime and by Ofsted must be among the most wasteful and singularly useless ever demanded of any profession.

So whilst bullshit jobs might indeed have proliferated, the picture of work drawn by Studs Terkel some fifty years ago has changed surprisingly little, as is shown in David Frayne's *The Refusal of Work: The Theory and Practice of Resistance to Work* (2015) in which he conducted similar interviews with his British subjects, with very interesting results. He was concerned with one core question: 'Might it be possible, in the future, for everybody to be able to work less and have more time for their own, autonomous self-development?'[29] In framing an answer, Frayne fully recognises his considerable debt to a truly original thinker in this field, André Gorz, for both his analysis and his solution. Graeber, by surprising contrast, barely acknowledges him, when his own evidence in my view simply confirms the growing importance of Gorz's contribution to both theory and policy application. Moreover, Graeber shies away from solutions on the unconvincing grounds that as an anarchist he prefers 'solutions to immediate problems that do not give more power to governments or corporations, but rather, give people the power to manage their own affairs'.[30]

André Gorz (1923–2007), born in Austria but naturalised French, was not an anarchist, more a libertarian socialist, but with an approach that is remarkably close to anarchists' thinking, despite their neglect of him.[31] A friend of both Sartre and Marcuse, he was deeply affected by the events in Paris in May 1968 and impressed by the work of Ivan Illich, whom he met in 1971 on the publication of the French translation of *Deschooling Society*. Later he prepared a summary in translation of Illich's *Tools for Conviviality* (1973).

> Realist and utopian, reformist and visionary, journalist, philosopher and social theorist, Gorz has made little attempt to ally himself with hallowed academic perspectives or established schools of thought. It is this intellectual autonomy … that makes him such an inspiring thinker to many.[32]

The flavour and tenor of Gorz's work has been well captured in a way that reveals his natural, though never acknowledged, affinity with anarchism:

> Underpinning the whole of Gorz's work is an unshakeable commitment to … the freedom of all individuals. It is thus a commitment to freedom, equality and justice … Everything that Gorz has written is dedicated, directly or indirectly, to identifying the obstacles to individual freedom and *what can be done* to create the social conditions which best serve the individual's choice of autonomy.[33]

His core argument was set out in *Farewell to the Working Class* (*Adieu au Proletariat*, 1980, English translation 1982), *Paths to Paradise* (1985) and *Critique of Economic Reason* (1989). The central theme is 'the liberation of time and the abolition of work'. By 'work' for most people he means paid employment as a heteronomous activity, work carried out for somebody else who sets the rules for the action in exchange for money. Such activity is neither an end in itself, nor self-determined or autonomous, and so is not freedom. Working less should not mean resting more, relaxing by watching endless TV, chasing new products created by the capitalist machine that invents new needs to boost profits. No, it should mean *living* more. Working less does not mean the end of making an effort, but using the effort to enjoy self-determined activities unrelated to any economic goals. This is Gorz's thesis.

The trend that has led to the disappearance of the old crafts cannot be reversed, and the standardised work of modern industry cannot be got rid of, so Godwin's and Kropotkin's preferences are no longer feasible. But as technology leads to increased productivity, a better balance between heteronomy and autonomy can be achieved. Communities should be able to produce *part* of their own goods and services to replace those provided by capitalist markets.

Gorz explains the way forward in terms very reminiscent of Colin Ward:

> No new liberties can be granted from above, by institutionalised power, *unless they have already been taken and put into practice by people* themselves-[34] … The State can only cease to be an apparatus of domination over society and become an instrument *enabling society to exercise power over itself with a view to its own restructuring, if society is already permeated by social struggles that open up areas of autonomy* keeping both the dominant class and the

> power of the State apparatus in check. The establishment of new types of social relations, new ways of producing, associating, working and consuming is the fundamental precondition of any political transformation. The dynamic of social struggles is the lever by which society can act upon itself and establish a range of freedoms, a new state and a new system of law.[35]

These new, prefiguring forms of association extricate society from the State in order to enlarge the sphere of autonomy, which is also the sphere of ethical relations.

The dual society notion accepts the need for the necessities of life to be organised through systems of planning, coordination and regulation, which cannot be done in societies consisting of small villages. Nor can it be achieved, Gorz argues, by the complete abolition of the State, for the State is the only known available means to do three things: to ensure that the production of necessities is not monopolised by a social class for the purposes of domination; to keep to a minimum some needed heteronomous labour; and to reduce progressively its own power and influence as autonomy increases,[36] though anarchists would be sceptical about the realism of this last point. So the heteronomous sphere continues to exist, *but only as a means of enlarging the sphere of autonomy.* The heteronomous sphere thus becomes subordinate to the autonomous sphere. Some of this work, most notably domestic work in the home, could and should be shared equitably throughout the community, for when properly shared the cost in time per person need not be very high.

Those who identify with their work and realise themselves through it – the highly skilled workers and professionals – also need more autonomous time, and Gorz suggests that they should work for no more than an average of four hours a day, which would be good for teachers and their teaching. This then opens space for more people to train for professional roles. In consequence, fewer people will engage in full-time heteronomous work and more people will have more skilled and rewarding work, with ample time left over for rewarding autonomous activities in their free time. So there must be complementary changes to the social environment with new cultural, educational and urban policies to help people to exercise free choice for more readily available activities of a fulfilling character.

Gorz identifies a stratum 'a non-class of non-workers' that includes those in unskilled, temporary, casual, seasonal and part-time employment, and today we would have to add those on zero-hours contracts and those who in response to online shopping become the so-called self-employed making deliveries from warehouse to homes – as well as the unemployed. But this neo-proletariat (or precariat) is not a class in the old sense of a class like the working class, one that could ever seize power, but rather a 'fragmented and composite movement' that cannot be turned into a political force. This is a strength and a weakness:

> It is its strength because a different kind of society, opening up new spaces of autonomy, can only emerge if individuals set out from the very

> beginning to invent and implement new relationships and forms of autonomy. Any change in society presupposes an extra-institutional process of cultural and ethical change. No new liberties can be granted from above, by institutionalised power, unless they have already been taken and put into practice by people themselves … It is its weakness, however, because spaces of autonomy captured for the existing social order will be marginalised, subordinated or ghettoised unless there is a full transformation and reconstruction of society, its institutions and its legal systems.[37]

Have the pros and cons of prefigurative practices ever been better expressed?

For Gorz, the future will not arise spontaneously through the growth of the 'non-class of non-workers': a society that is more 'diverse, complex, pluralistic and libertarian' is a possible choice, but one needing consciousness, action and will if it is to be realised. He confesses his ignorance of how this might come about:

> I have therefore deliberately left this question open and unresolved. In the present phase, we must dare to ask questions we cannot answer and to raise problems whose solution remains to be found.[38]

In his last book, *Reclaiming Work* (*Misères du présent: richesse du possible*, 1997, English translation, 1999), Gorz revises some ideas to take account of globalisation and transnational financial capitalism. Globalised capital 'being itself a power without society, it tends to engender societies without power'.[39] Under post-Fordist developments in the workplace, especially with Japanese influence, teams of workers are now given considerable amounts of autonomy over their work. Such self-management requires particular attitudes to flexible working practices and self-development, a readiness to question their own assumptions and to come up with their ideas for improvements. Is this liberation more apparent than real? Gorz argues that it is a new and more powerful form of subjugation in that the workers take over the responsibilities that were formerly those of management and they have to put the interests of the company above everything else. Control by management becomes self-control and self-policing: what was once imposed is now freely chosen. This is encouraged by the firm's emphasis on the workers as a family without need for a trade union. Recruits are young and career-oriented, carefully screened to ensure that they display the approved characteristics of intelligence and eagerness. Is this, asks Gorz, a new kind of feudalism with the worker becoming a proud vassal? He doubts it merits being called real autonomy:

> Autonomy in work is of little significance when it is not carried into the cultural, moral and political spheres; and cultural, moral and political autonomy does not arise from productive cooperation itself, but from activism, and from the culture of resistance, rebellion, fraternity, free debate, radical questioning and dissidence which that activism produces.[40]

As the years passed Gorz's earlier convictions strengthened. The right to an income, to full citizenship, to a sense of identity and fulfilment, 'can no longer be centred on and depend upon occupying a job. And society has to be changed to take account of that.'[41] The shift in social imaginary will be painful, and of course resisted by the forces of capital, which makes it crucial to explore '*how* that other life and society can be anticipated and prefigured right now'.[42] Vainly attempting to shore up a wage-based society, politicians lag behind shifting values in the population, and fail to face up to the challenges of the redistribution of both work and income as we move towards a society 'regulated not by the market and money but by reciprocity and mutuality'.[43]

From his earliest writing Gorz raised the notion of a guaranteed income for life as a necessary condition of sharing work as its availability declines. In his 1994 book he devoted a whole chapter to the theme of 'shorter hours, same pay' in a detailed counter-argument to the trades unions' claim that reducing hours of work necessarily meant reduced pay. His most extended treatment, however, is in *Reclaiming Work*, in which he sets out policies for making a break with a work-based society to open up the possibilities of the multi-activity life. This involves a deep psychological change in which we have to cast off unquestioned assumptions – what I interpret as the sloughing of our existing social imaginary – and think ourselves into a radically different society. This means having some notion of a future end-state so that the paths out of a work-based capitalism can be determined for the process of transition. Alternative social practices already exist, but more space for them is needed, for they are 'both the engine of the exodus and its final goal'[44] – an approach that is highly compatible with anarchist thinking. Three policies are necessary.

The first is the unconditional guarantee of a sufficient income for everybody. The political right has proposed a guarantee at less than subsistence level, as a tidying up of welfare benefits, like the current Universal Credit introduced by Iain Duncan Smith as minister for work and pensions.[45] This simply forces the poor to accept casual, often part-time, and low-paid jobs simply to survive – workfare – thereby subsidising employers and strengthening one of the worst features of capitalism. By contrast, a sufficient basic income enables people to refuse work of this kind. The aim is not to enable people not to work at all, but to enable people to take charge of their own lives, where there are options for different kinds of cooperative and self-providing ventures. Gorz accepts it cannot be implemented immediately, but the way for it can be prepared.

The second policy is to combine the redistribution of work with increased individual and collective control over time. It is not just a matter of a shorter working day or a shorter, four-day working week, now under discussion in a very promising development on the political left.[46] There must be further flexibilities to allow people to choose their own hours within 'a very wide range of forms of discontinuity'[47] in work, without forfeiting security of employment: a flexible workforce with intermittent work must no longer mean temporary or contract workers – all good news for women in particular. And the third policy involves 'encouraging new socialities to blossom and new modes of cooperation and exchange',[48] which is familiar terrain for anarchists' commitment to mutual aid. The book's epilogue offers a defence against charges of utopianism, by asserting the positive value of a utopia as the means of distancing ourselves from the existing state of affairs so that we can judge what we now do in the light of what we could or should do.

Nearly twenty years after Gorz's book, Nick Srnicek and Alex Williams in *Inventing the Future: Postcapitalism in a World Without Work* (revised edition, 2016) see a universal basic income (UBI) as central to a post-work imaginary in four inter-related ways:[49]

1. It is a demand for a political, not just an economic, transformation, because it overturns the current asymmetry of power between labour and capital.
2. It transforms unemployment and casual employment from insecurity to a state of voluntary flexibility.
3. It necessitates a rethinking of the values attributed to different kinds of work: currently low-paid work would require better pay and more rewarding conditions from employers if they cannot opt for automation.
4. It is in many respects a feminist proposal in its recognition of women's domestic labour – though care would have to be taken that UBI does not exclude women for gaining equality in employment. It should encourage experimentation in how we organise communities and families.

They understand that overcoming the deep-seated work ethic is crucial to building a post-work world, and this needs a counter-hegemonic strategy. Like Gorz, they believe that utopia has a role to play here, and that 'the left must release the utopian impulse from its neoliberal shackles',[50] for an alternative common sense can emerge from 'thinking big' about the future, a terrain that has to be reclaimed. A similar line is taken by Annie Lowrey's (2018) approach to UBI:

> Yet if rising productivity, yawning inequality and mass joblessness do come about, a UBI would not be enough … A broader change in our understanding of worth and compensation, of work and labour, would also be necessary. The neoliberal values of free markets, unfettered competition, and economic growth as the primary arbiters of human progress would need to change.[51]

In *Envisioning Real Utopias* (2010) Erik Ohlin Wright chooses UBI as one of four ideas that provide 'empirical and theoretical grounding for radical democratic egalitarian vision of an alternative social world'.[52] He makes no mention of André Gorz but offers essentially the same arguments. For anarchists he particularly emphasises how UBI makes a massive subsidy to the social economy and the cooperative market economy, where the main problem is generating a decent standard of living for providers of such services. For instance, 7.5 million people are, without pay, looking after elderly relatives, a partner or a sick or disabled child, the equivalent of 4 million full-time care givers, and of course most of them are women.[53] Scotland is now experimenting with UBI, and not for the first time is showing a dynamism that is singularly lacking in England, as our politicians close their eyes to almost any future unrelated to Brexit.

There are, then, two main paths to a future educational imaginary. Changes to work will be a major influence on the character and timing of the new social imaginary, and the emergent self-managing SISS is the main internal path to it. Both paths are close to the conceptions of the classical and new anarchists.

In 1987 Colin Ward wrote a piece entitled 'The path not taken',[54] in which he cited a Fabian tract of 1886 that had made an unfulfilled prediction that socialism would 'fall into two parties, a Collectivist party supporting a strong central administration and a counterbalancing Anarchist party defending individual initiative against the administration.' He then makes the point that

> it was evident a century ago that there were other paths to socialism beside the electoral struggle for power over the centralised state. In the nineteenth century the British working class built up from nothing a vast network of social and economic initiatives based on self-help and mutual aid … I would claim that the political left in this country invested all its fund of social inventiveness in the idea of the state, so that its own traditions of self-help and mutual aid were stifled for lack of ideological oxygen. How on earth did British socialists allow these concepts to be hijacked by the political right, since it is these human attributes, and not the state and its bureaucracies, that actually hold human society together? … It's going to be a long haul for the political left to unburden itself of all that Fabian, Marxist, managerial and professional baggage and rediscover its roots in the tradition of fraternal and autonomous associations springing up from below. The anarchists ought to be around with our signposts, pointing the way.

Is it now time to take the path not taken?

Notes

1 See Carnie (2003) and in Warpole (1999); Wallace (2009); Wetz (2009).
2 Grant-maintained status was abolished in 1998.
3 See Jackson and Temperley (2006).
4 Hargreaves (2010).
5 Department for Education (November, 2010) *The importance of teaching: the schools white paper 2010*: 12 and 52.
6 Simone Weil makes a similar point, how in adapting to the horrors of her factory life, she came, in spite of herself, to accept submission as natural (Weil, 1951, 2002: 223).
7 *Educational Excellence Everywhere*, HMSO, March 2016.
8 roberthilleducationblog.com, posted 29 June 2017.
9 Adonis (2012: Chapter 10).

10 O'Shaughnessy (2012: 36).
11 O'Shaughnessy (2012: 43, italics added).
12 Greany and Higham (2018: 25, 97).
13 Greany and Higham (2018: 69f).
14 Greany and Higham (2018: 85, 93).
15 Greany and Higham (2018: 95).
16 Bob Black, *The Abolition of Work* (1985), available online: primitivism.com.
17 Clastres (1987: 195).
18 The essay with this title is available free online and at primitivism.com, where there is also a post-script to Sahlins by Bob Black.
19 I rely on James C. Scott (2012) for this point.
20 Godwin (1793: 738).
21 Godwin (1797: 174f).
22 Kropotkin (1906: 119).
23 Kropotkin (1906: 105).
24 Kropotkin (1906: 124).
25 Reported in *The Guardian*, 12 November 2015.
26 IPPR, *Managing Automation*, December 2017.
27 Centre for Cities, *Cities Outlook, 2018.*
28 Graeber (2015).
29 Frayne (2015: 29).
30 Graeber (2018: 270 and 280).
31 Perhaps the best example of this neglect is the chapter on work by Cherkovskaya and Stoborod in Franks et al. (2018).
32 Bowring (2000: 10).
33 Lodziak and Tatman (1997: 6 and 60, original emphasis).
34 Lodziak and Tatman (1997: 11 emphasis added).
35 Lodziak and Tatman (1997: 116 emphasis added).
36 Gorz (1982: 115).
37 Gorz (1982: 11f).
38 Gorz (1982: 13).
39 Gorz (1999: 15).
40 Gorz (1999: 40).
41 Gorz (1999: 54).
42 Gorz (1999: 59).
43 Gorz (1999: 65).
44 Gorz (1999: 79).
45 In France, UBI has been strongly favoured by many on the political left, especially during the presidential elections in 2017. In June 2018 Italy's Five Star Movement leader Di Maio advocated the introduction of a UBI (*reddito di cittadinanza).* A trial of a similar scheme in Finland on 2,000 unemployed persons was abandoned by the centre-right government in April 2018 on grounds of cost and is considering advice from the OECD that a version of Universal Credit might be better. I hope they have some other sources of advice. In July 2018 Ontario's new Conservative government decided to abandon an experimental pilot.
46 A four-day working week was proposed by the general secretary of the Trades Union Congress, 10 September 2018. Two months later it was announced that economist Lord Skidelsky is working on this idea with Labour Shadow Chancellor John McDonnell.
47 Gorz (1999: 94).
48 Gorz (1999: 80).
49 Srnicek & Williams (2016: 120f).
50 Srnicek and Williams (2016: 139).

51 Lowrey (2018: 208). See also Standing (2017) and Frase (2016), which reviews the evidence for the loss of jobs in the light of technological advances, and includes UBI in the solution.
52 Wright (2010: 1).
53 Report of Social Market Foundation, *Caring for Carers*, July 2018.
54 *The Raven*, no. 3, 1987, pp. 195–200 (obtainable from the Freedom Bookshop, Angel Alley, 84b Whitechapel High Street, London E1 7QX) and in *The Guardian*, 12 October 1987. Another version of this argument is in Ward (2000).

11

EDUCATION, NOT SCHOOLING

Realising the new imaginary

> Wisdom in all worldly affairs it seems to me consists not in recognising what must be done but in knowing what to do first and then what comes after.
>
> Leo Tolstoy, novelist, 1860, quoted in Simmons (1968)

> If you don't care to listen now, of course, I must postpone the rest of my story till you are ready to listen.
>
> Nikolai Chernyshevsky, novelist, 1863

It is now over 200 years since William Godwin, giving birth to the philosophy of anarchism in England, declared war against the State and its impending control over schooling. In the turbulent years after the 1960s, vehement opposition to what would be an extraordinary rise of centralisation, that would blind many people to the distinction between education and schooling, was confined to a minority, many of whose voices have been lost in the rhetoric around what the State allegedly needed to do in 'the standards agenda'. There is opposition to what has been happening, and no lack of descriptions of what schools could be like based on different principles. Yet there is a worrying lack of concrete proposals in answer to that glorious question:[1] *What is to be done?*

An anarchist answer to this question means not starting from the assumption of a school system and then asking about what education should be conducted within it – which far too often is the way in which the terms of debate and reform are set – but rather asking what education is desirable for children and young people, and then taking the next crucial step of exploring what system or machinery or action might be needed to provide it. Schools might or not be part of such provision, though for most parents they currently would. But who would be in control of them? Pierre-Joseph Proudhon's view was clear: 'I want the school to be as completely separated from the State as from the Church.'[2] So he envisaged three possibilities: home-schooling, a private school, or a public school set up by the commune:[3]

> A community needs a teacher. It chooses one at its pleasure, young or old, married or single, a graduate of the Normal School or self-taught, with or without a diploma. The only thing that is essential is that the said teacher should suit the fathers of families, and that they should be free to entrust their children to them or not.[4]

Anarchists, then, put parents first (Proudhon, like most men of his era, discounted the wishes of mothers) and generally have confidence in their abilities to make good educational choices without unmerited deference towards professional qualifications. Education starts with parental provision in the home. As children grow, parents decide what further education they want for their children, either by their own continuing provision and/or by choosing provision that they commission or is offered by others as a way of building on parental educational foundations. An assumption of most people is that children must go to school to be educated and for many of them school in some form should begin as soon as possible. This assumption may be questioned. Could and should more children be educated at home and if so for how much of their childhood?

In England, home-schooling – which from now on I shall call home education – is perfectly legal, as it is in the rest of the UK, Australia, New Zealand, Canada and the USA, but illegal in some European countries, including Sweden and Germany. In the USA by 2016 some 2.3 million children were fully educated at home. The evidence indicates that these children score more highly on standardised achievement tests than those at school,[5] which is reassuring. In England some 48,000 children are home educated, a rise of 40 per cent in the last three years, though this is less than 1 per cent of the pupil population. Currently registration is not compulsory, but there are moves to make it so, which would undoubtedly be acted upon should home education increase in popularity and the State feel threatened.[6] In the USA John Holt became a leading promoter of home education, especially in *Teach Your Own* (1981) and *Learning All the Time* (1989), following his disenchantment with school reform in the years after his early books that were critical of conventional schooling. He concluded that home was the right and natural place to educate children, not a fallback position against bad schools, though dissatisfaction with schools remains a common motive for parents who opt for home education.

Many of the objections to home education strike me as ill-judged. For instance, it is said that this deprives children of friends of the same age. I have long believed that age-grading in schools, by which children whose birthdays fall between 1 September and 31 August of the following year are grouped together and segregated for the rest of their schooldays, now usually some 15 years, has detrimental consequences. Age-grading is a product of schooling and the main reason for it is administrative convenience. Small rural primary schools have mixed-age classes, but by the secondary stage age-grading has become rigid, with just a few schools adopting vertical tutoring to ensure a better age mix for a small amount of school time – and reaping the social benefits, such as reduced bullying. Age-grading often continues into higher education, and does not abate until entry to the workplace. Families and kinship groups have for most of human history been the main location of child education, so the mixing of age groups was normal. Age-grading of adolescents is a cause, even the main one, of the growth of youth cultures and fashions, with the huge pressures to peer conformity that are often the source of so much distress, online bullying and self-harming. Members of age-graded peer groups can be extraordinarily mean, even cruel, to one another.

Despite the known adverse effects of strict school-based age-grading, it has become an unquestioned and unquestionable feature of our social and educational imaginaries and it will persist as long as our schools remain in their present form. It serves as a key buttress for age-related national testing, with all its defects, including comparing, grading and labelling children in terms of achievement in limited tests, with their implications for ability and future potential not just attainment, with disdain for the important natural variations and differing states of maturity and motivation that characterise perfectly normal differences, including rates of maturation, among children and young people.

I am sensitive to the matter as I was born in the evening of 31 August. Had my mother delayed my appearance for just a little longer – though I am glad she did not – I would have been in a later age group, and the oldest rather than the youngest member of the cohort, and my school friends throughout my childhood would have been wholly different. How many of us, one wonders, would have led different lives had we been allocated to a different year-group. Home education fosters mixed-age relationships, where older siblings support the learning and development of younger family members and take care of them. In small and single-child families social opportunities with other children of a similar age may be fostered in the neighbourhood or within networks and cooperatives of families committed to home education.[7]

Other common objections are that children need professional teachers and should not be deprived of them and that a teacher's personal attention is invaluable. The fact is, however, that children get relatively little individual attention from teachers, because large class sizes necessarily make it a scarce resource. In a class of thirty pupils in any one hour an equitable allocation of teacher attention, even allowing for little teacher time to be allocated to many other aspects of classroom management, would allow each pupil just two minutes. In fact, a few pupils get more than two minutes and most will get much less time or none at all. Moreover many teacher–pupil contacts are concerned with behaviour management, not learning.

At home, learners do not need *constant* attention from a parent-teacher, but quickly learn the art of self-managed learning, resorting to the parent for help in a way that contrasts with the sanctified classroom system of hand-raising, mainly a control mechanism. Many parents initially – and understandably but mistakenly – approach home education by believing they must act like a teacher and treat their home as if it were a classroom. Most soon abandon this school model of lessons for a much more flexible and variable approach to learning and to adult support, which is why we should avoid the term 'home-schooling'. Human beings have an in-built drive to learn and home educators have to learn how to respect and channel it. So much of what we know about learning from research has, not surprisingly, been motivated by a concern to understand and improve learning in school settings, and relatively little on learning among school-age children in what might be called natural settings. Only in recent times have there been significant advances in our understanding of informal learning (Coffield, 2000) or not-school learning, where teaching and learning are often not the primary purpose (Sefton-Green, 2013), and insights in this area are emerging from non-Western cultures (for example, Sefton-Green and Erstad, 2018). Where home educators lead, learning researchers should follow.

The lessons learned by early adopters of home education were reported in Roland Meighan's *The Next Learning System: And Why Home-schoolers Are Trailblazers* (1997) and Alan Thomas's *Educating Children at Home* (1998) and there is now a growing literature of helpful advice. Today there are ever more useful materials available online as well as opportunities to share ideas and practices with other home educators, groups of whom meet and construct a common pool of shared expertise and experience. Out-of-school activities are not easy for teachers to plan and manage, and so become rare treats, whereas out-of-home visits and activities, especially when shared between families, are much easier to organise and so become more frequent. It is in these activities, so unlike school, that some of the most important informal and incidental learning takes place.[8]

Speaking is obviously an important part of becoming a human being and talking with children is vital for their development. There is plenty of talk in classrooms and certainly more than there used to be: the days of children spending most of their day in enforced silence are happily long past. Yet even today teachers dominate the public talk in classroom, and 'Stop talking' and its equivalents remains a common teacher injunction, as pupils seize on any opportunity to engage in chat with their friends.

The rights to talk are distributed very unequally in classrooms, which gives such talk a very distinctive character.[9] Teachers establish the ways in which they talk in the classroom at the very beginning of their careers and usually reflect the way in which teachers talked to them when they were at school. As a result, these patterns of teacher talk form a stable and set routine that is transmitted across generations and thus highly resistant to change. Much has been learned in the last fifty years about how teacher and pupil talk can be changed to help pupils to think and learn more effectively, but this applied research tends to be side-lined by the much stronger emphasis that is usually given in England to writing rather than speaking (oracy). So for most teachers it takes considerable effort, practice and training to replace ingrained habits of talk, and this cannot be afforded when so much government-led change assumes priority and demands immediate attention.

Robin Alexander's *Towards Dialogical Teaching* (third edition, 2006) usefully summarises many years of research on classroom talk as well as his own investigations, and points the way forward with his conception of dialogic teaching, which in a nutshell is:

- *collective* – adult and learner address the learning task together
- *reciprocal* – adult and learner listen to each other, sharing ideas and different viewpoints
- *supportive* – learners articulate their ideas freely, without worrying about 'right answers'
- *cumulative* – adult and learner build on their own and each other's ideas to chain them into coherent lines of thinking and enquiry
- *purposeful* – adult plans and facilitates dialogical teaching

Parents committing to home education have less unlearning to do than professional teachers, and should find it easier to follow Alexander's guidance, as long as they do not try to imitate the ways in which they were taught at school. For this reason I have substituted *adult* for *teacher* in Alexander's original text. His short pamphlet, written for teachers, is a most valuable resource for home educators and should help them to realise that they have some advantages over professional teachers, not just disadvantages.

The reduction of full-time employment and even, for some, the abolition of work will surely be the greatest game-changer in patterns of education and schooling. If school teaching became largely a part-time occupation – which many teachers would welcome as long as it is not linked to a severe loss of income – it would inevitably lead to more home education. They would be a substantial resource to any group of home educators, especially when parents feel insecure in their own knowledge, such as mathematics, science and modern languages. One effect would be a much better balance of teachers and adults-other-than-teachers in the educational experience of the young.

A further driver of home education is likely to come from unemployed or under-employed graduates. A university education is no longer a guarantee of a professional career. Three-quarters of young people still think going to university is important, but this is a decline of 10 per cent in five years.[10] In a post-work world the possession of a degree is clearly a boost to the self-competence and confidence of any potential home-educator. The next generation of home educators will be unusually well educated.

The response of schools to these changes will also be an important factor. I suspect that more part-time teachers, some of whom will also be part-time home educators, will ease the movement to part-time schooling for many children and young people. Why should there by a zero-sum choice between full-time schooling and full-time home education? Such a choice is as silly as having to choose between shopping online or in a supermarket, when most of us do both, and in addition use specialist shops when needed. There is no sensible objection to part-time pupils who choose to go to school for subjects for which a specialised teacher is considered desirable. For each young person the balance between home education and schooling might well vary from year to year, but a flexible home–school contract could easily be managed, especially where the school has a manager and counsellor to advise and negotiate contracts.

Thirty years ago Roland Meighan (1937–2014), an admirer of John Holt, published a booklet on flexi-schooling (1988), which pioneered the idea of a more flexible way in which home education and schooling might be combined. Flexi-schooling or part-time schooling is permitted, subject to the agreement of the school.[11] Schools could, he argued, become community resource centres. In some ways this might be an extension of the vision of another pioneer, Henry Morris (1889–1961), and his conception of the Cambridgeshire Village College.[12] In later years such neighbourhood community centres were successfully developed in urban settings, and they, like the village colleges, can readily morph into resource centres for the flexi-schooling world of new partnerships with home educators. Indeed, I think this will be an important direction for change in many urban schools if young people are to develop the attitudes and skills that will make them more active citizens in the running of their communities. Lessons from Jane Jacobs in New York to the residents of Grenfell Tower in London are still to be learned.

The financing of a system that combines part-time home education with part-time schooling would not be difficult, for when all schools are directly funded from central government, each child registered with a school might be free to opt out of part of the school's offer and be recompensed with an appropriate portion of the income the school obtains for that child's education, presumably in the form of some kind of voucher. This would also ensure that parents with lower incomes might opt for home education, where at present they are in a minority, and be able to pay for help from other home educators or other sources. Indeed, in the longer term it might allow the creation of working-class schools as existed in the nineteenth century, as described earlier by Phil Gardner and advocated by James Tooley.

Such diversity would offer real choices for parents, as against the pseudo-choices they now enjoy, which are limited to preferring one of several largely interchangeable schools, the final choice often depending on the Ofsted rating and league table position based on tests and public examinations. For it is often these criteria that school leaders use to publicise their schools, not a distinctive educational philosophy. Over the last ten years I have noticed that when head teachers make presentations about their school to fellow leaders, they almost invariably first inform the audience about how, under their leadership, the school's league table position and Ofsted rating have improved. This, it seems, is an essential justification of anything else head teachers then say about what happens in their schools: their philosophy or ethos lacks a self-evident justification, unlike the instrumental and crucial outcome of 'raising standards' by test scores.

Most anarchists reject the very notion of the State common school because it necessarily entails action to ensure that they are all somehow essentially equivalent, allegedly in the interests of social justice. It is true that there is some scope for schools to develop a distinctive ethos, but it is very narrow. A parent asking to see the aims and objectives of all the local secondary schools – rarely more than a set of banalities and platitudes – finds astonishingly little difference between them, which demonstrates the lack of distinctive philosophies and thus the restriction on genuine choice.

Diversity and choice require that schools become truly diverse, each with its own ethos and philosophy and perhaps a subject specialism. (Ninety-five per cent of secondary schools in England adopted a specialism, but the scheme was abolished by Michael Gove in 2010.) Anarchists would want to establish explicitly anarchist schools, but as committed pluralists in this area they would always wish their schools to be just one option from a wider range of progressive schools that includes Steiner Waldorf or Montessori schools, many of which would prefer to be small. There was much greater variety in the past – John Shotton's (1993) review of libertarian education in Britain in the past gives a feel for this. Today at secondary level, standardised comprehensive schools must necessarily be large to make a plausible claim that they can cope with the sheer variety of pupils. Certainly such schools can be sub-divided into mini-schools, but they remain within a single over-arching philosophy.

Anarchist and alternative schools almost always insist on being small, a factor which makes them attractive to some parents and children, but these get ruled out of existence by the insistent claim of the common school that it can cater for all. Whilst there is a case for larger secondary schools in rural areas, like the Cambridgeshire village colleges, in urban areas existing large secondary schools are not the outcome of a serious debate about school size and the desirability of variety to provide choice, but simply the historical consequence of the merging of grammar schools with several secondary modern schools to create comprehensive schools and the view that a comprehensive school should be of sufficient size to maintain its own sixth form. A proper debate about size and variety would, I believe, be welcomed by parents but disliked and opposed by politicians and bureaucrats.

If the school system contained anarchist schools among many other types, what would they be like? It is hard to say, of course, in part because there have been relatively few of them and in part because on anarchist principle it would be a matter for each school to decide for itself, which would be a complex and continuing process of negotiation between the school's founders, staff, parents and students. There are variations between anarchist schools in different places and at different times. The best known of these sprang up in the 1890s in France and a little later in Spain. Their stories are well told by Michael P. Smith

(1983) and Judith Suissa (2006).[13] The best known is probably the *Escuola Moderna* (Modern School) of Francisco Ferrer (1859–1909),[14] whose co-educational school incurred the wrath of the clerical authorities. At this period much of the time in the Church-controlled schools was spent on religious education, whereas Ferrer made his opposition to this quite explicit. The school was denounced as subversive, which in a sense it was. In 1906 it was closed down, and not long after, Ferrer was arrested on false charges and executed by firing squad. The Modern School had considerable influence in the USA – the story of which has been well documented by Paul Avrich (1980) – where incidentally A. S. Neill of Summerhill fame was also far more influential than he ever was in the UK, though he cannot really be counted as an anarchist, despite the popular image to the contrary.

The main characteristics of anarchist schools are easily summarised. The first is the notion of 'integral education', which takes various forms but essentially concerns a rejection of a sharp differentiation between the intellectual or academic and the manual or practical, as we saw earlier in Kropotkin's conception, but it is often given a wider interpretation to mean a broad education to include the development of the emotions and the imagination. Michael Bakunin believed that learners should be exposed to adults other than teachers as a necessary part of integral education:

> The education of children must be integral; that is, must at the same time develop both the physical and mental faculties and make the child into a whole man. This education must not be entrusted solely to a specialised caste of teachers; all those who know a science, an art, or a craft can and should be called upon to teach.[15]

Paul Goodman also advocated that children and young people should enjoy substantial contact with adults-other-than-teachers as a natural part of growing up, though today we are more aware of the need for some safeguarding protection of the young. Yet teachers' unions protest against the employment of unqualified adults in classrooms.

Godwin's successors are faithful to his emphasis on the development of rationality and so science is given an important place in the curriculum, as is his concern for teaching to draw on the intrinsic motivation of the learner in place of external coercion or the use of rewards and prizes. Active learning, and what today we call problem-based and project-based learning, are encouraged, for it is within such a pedagogy that the development of autonomy, self-reliance and independence can be combined with a rich experience of collaboration and mutual aid.

Persuasion is always favoured over compulsion, so if the learner decides not to learn or to stay in a class, the choice will be respected if an appeal to rationality fails. But as every teacher knows, the most difficult area for an anarchist teacher will be the exercise of power and authority, the felt tension between abusing that power and abdicating it irresponsibly, both of which harm the child. It works well when the teacher is able to draw principally upon a mixture of expert and charismatic power, but not all anarchist teachers who aspire to this kind of authority are able to achieve it, especially in circumstances where the cultivation of low status differentials is part of the school's ethos of informality.

Children cannot be plunged into autonomy by a sudden and complete withdrawal of teacher power and authority: it is a process of progressive transfer between teacher and taught, demanding great sensitivity on the part of the teacher as well as a developmental approach whereby the learner gains autonomy in planned stages. Otherwise the learner is abandoned into a structureless world of confusion. In England an unfortunate hiatus can be created in the transition from primary to secondary school, if secondary school teachers ignore the autonomy achieved during the last years of primary school, pressing pupils back into a state of dependence by requiring them to seek permission for trivialities. I am always impressed by Bakunin's treatment of the matter, originally lodged in a footnote to his *God and the State*, written in 1871:

> The principle of authority, in the education of children, constitutes the natural point of departure; it is legitimate, necessary, when applied to children of a tender age, whose intelligence has not yet openly developed itself. But as the development of everything, and consequently of education, implies the gradual negation of the point of departure, this principle must diminish as fast as education and instruction advance, giving place to increasing liberty. All rational education is at bottom nothing but this progressive immolation of authority for the benefit of liberty, the final object of education necessarily being the formation of free men full of respect and love for the liberty of others. Therefore the first day of the pupils' life, if the school takes infants scarcely able as yet to stammer a few words, should be that of the greatest authority and an almost entire absence of liberty; but its last day should be that of the greatest liberty and the absolute abolition of every vestige of the animal or divine principle of authority.[16]

Most accounts of the operation of anarchist schools are by insiders, and there is a lack of ethnographic studies of anarchist classrooms conducted by independent researchers. Ann Swidler's *Organization Without Authority: Dilemmas of Social Control in Free Schools* (1979) is a two-year study of two alternative high schools (in Berkeley, California), one of 200 middle- and upper-class white students from well-educated liberal families, the other, half this size, mostly from racially diverse, working-class families, and with histories of poor attainment, failure and rebellion. The book reveals how difficult it was for teachers, when coercion is abandoned, to rely so heavily on forms of personal authority, especially the personal appeal. The students were free to come and go as they pleased, but nevertheless often seemed bored or indifferent: they liked their egalitarian teachers, and the encouragement of student participation, but the ethos failed to generate their active engagement. The strain on teachers was colossal, as with only limited success they sought coping strategies to solve emergent problems. Unsure how to put the principles behind the school's philosophy into pedagogic practice, they ended up trying to teach traditional lessons without traditional discipline, causing confusion on both sides and leading some students to perceive their teachers as weak and ineffective. It was a recipe for teacher burnout, the heavy price paid for an ill-considered and poorly executed experiment.

Frankly this is what I would have expected, as I imagine you would too. It is a pity that neither the teachers nor their schools' leaders were familiar with Bakunin's good sense. Many of us have witnessed examples of high-flown rhetoric from school leaders that has not been accompanied by the most careful preparation and by high levels of ongoing support for the young teachers on whom falls the burden of trying to live the declared ideals in the rough and tumble of classroom life. At the end of the book Swidler offers an interesting comment:

> In some ways free schools resemble anarchist communes. Looked at from a slightly different perspective, however, they appear like colleges, graduate schools, or research institutes. It is possible to interpret free school pedagogy as training youngsters in the habits of independent enquiry, originality, and self-motivation that characterise the upper reaches of the academic system. Alternative education, rather than representing a rebellion against established educational forms, may simply be an extension of the styles and values of the universities into the elementary and secondary schools.[17]

Curiously this reflects what Bakunin, in his usual punchy style, says next in the quotation I included above:

> The principle of authority, applied to men who have surpassed or attained their majority, becomes a monstrosity, a flagrant denial of humanity, a source of slavery and intellectual and moral depravity … From these schools [for adults] will be absolutely eliminated the smallest applications or manifestation of the principle of authority … [where people are] rich in their own experience, they will teach in their turn many things to their professors, who shall bring them knowledge which they lack. Thus, there will be mutual instruction, an act of intellectual fraternity.[18]

The teachers in Swidler's book simply did not know how to do this. Her account does not undermine faith in anarchist and libertarian ideals and practices, but it does demonstrate convincingly that the right way forward is to build an educational trajectory of a common philosophy that is applied when the children first go to school and that continues until the end of the secondary phase and beyond, with teachers who are confident in their practice and who are fully supported by more experienced colleagues. With our present structure of primary and secondary schooling it is virtually impossible to ensure that a child will be exposed to a consistent educational philosophy in both primary and secondary school. In this regard the emergence of 4–16 schools is to be welcomed. Swidler's report also confirms two of my convictions: that anarchists rightly insist that such schools need to be small, with small class sizes; and that the values be shared by the parents/carers, who preferably adopt a similar approach in some part-time home education. It can then succeed and the outcome of education during the school years would indeed be a superb preparation for higher education, far better than what many schools are now forced to do with their sixth-formers.

You may well be thinking that anarchist schools are very little different from other libertarian or progressive or alternative pedagogies. They certainly overlap, as we have seen whenever I have moved beyond strictly anarchist examples. Judith Suissa rightly points out that the distinctiveness of anarchist practice lies in its ideological basis and political vision.

> It is a serious failing of the work of anarchist educators that they made little systematic attempt to provide a theoretical account of the relationship between child-centred pedagogical practice and their own anarchist goals and values … It would appear that the anarchist educational experiments are unique in the world of "progressive", "libertarian" or "free" education not in terms of their pedagogical practice but in terms of the substantive ideas and motivations behind them. These ideas can only be grasped in the context of the anarchist commitment to undermining the State by creating alternative forms of social organisation and relationships.[19]

Ferrer saw his school as an embryo or microcosm of a future anarchist society, but others, who did not share Ferrer's terrible fate, may have accepted that a degree of discretion is the better part of valour. In any event, there is an inevitable tension between preparing the young for the world in which they have to live as well as for the world as it might be. Proudhon was fully committed to integral education and wanted working-class children to have proper industrial or agricultural apprenticeships. To this end, the school should take on the character of a workshop and even become a small business, so that pupils should qualify as craftsmen:

> [Giving them an integral education] would on the one hand be a practical means of freeing them from dependency in the work-place and in the labour-market, and on the other by developing them as full persons prepare them for the duties of citizenship in the new society.[20]

How would these anarchists of the classical period interpret integral education and its dual purpose for the twenty-first century? My belief is that they would be appalled by the way in which practical crafts and the arts have been demoted in the school curriculum. The notion of the craft has suffered badly in the school curriculum ever since the term was lopped off 'design and technology' (CDT). The sharp differentiation that governments have made between the so-called academic subjects and the rest of the curriculum, including vocational education, became more deeply entrenched than ever with the introduction of the E-Bacc by Michael Gove in 2010. The argument for the crafts is in my view stronger than ever.

In his wise book *The Craftsman* (2008), Richard Sennett offers the best defence of this old concept that he treats as gender-neutral. He shows how misguided it is to think of craftsmanship as an enemy of standards, which has been part of the argument for the E-Bacc:

> "Craftsmanship" may suggest a way of life that waned with the advent of industrial society – but this is misleading. Craftsmanship names an enduring, basic human impulse, the desire to do a job well for its own sake. Craftsmanship cuts a far wider swath than skilled manual labour; it serves the computer programmer, the doctor, and the artist; parenting improves when it is practiced as a skilled craft, as does citizenship. In all these domains, craftsmanship focuses on objective standards, on the thing in itself … Every good craftsman conducts a dialogue between concrete practices and thinking; this dialogue evolves into sustaining habits, and these habits establish a rhythm between problem-solving and problem-finding. The relation between hand and head appears in domains seemingly as different as bricklaying, cooking, designing a playground, or playing the cello … Since there can be no skilled work without standards, it is infinitely preferable that these standards be embodied in a human being than in a lifeless static code of practice. The craftsman's workshop is one site in which the modern, perhaps unresolvable conflict between autonomy and authority plays out.[21]

When I was researching orthopaedic surgeons a few years ago, I asked one of them what led him to choose this specialty. 'Well,' he replied, 'I was very good at woodwork at school, so it seemed a good way to use my skill in medicine.' No doubt his patients have reason to be grateful that his school offered the subject that led him from one craft to another. In a future society where most people will be working part-time, the pleasure of having mastered a craft in youth can be turned into a rewarding use of free time. I came across surgeons who in their spare time were painters, potters and furniture makers.[22]

For Richard Sennett in his later book *Together: The Rituals, Pleasures and Politics of Cooperation* (2012), physical activity and crafts have as much civilising capacity as they had for Kropotkin and Proudhon, for cooperation at work builds mutual respect and mutual aid. The making and repairing in workshops depends on the possession of dialogic skills – listening well, behaving tactfully, finding points of agreement, avoiding frustration as differences are used to solve problems. It is experiment and innovation that thrive in such a climate and so build social capital. Sennett believes modern capitalism has unbalanced competition and cooperation, and made modern forms of cooperation less dialogic. And he cites evidence that young people in the USA and the UK are more likely than those in other countries to report being bullied and be less likely to see their peers as supportive and a source of help in learning. In the highly competitive climate in many English schools, pupils placed by well-meaning teachers in cooperative groups so easily use it to display 'feigned solidarity' by which their superficial cooperativeness is a mask for exhibiting their superiority to an observing teacher.[23]

Government education policy has for years been squeezing creativity from the work of teachers. Anarchists always stress the importance of innovation and experiment, as noted earlier, but the opportunities for developing and exercising these crucial professional qualities have diminished at the very time when they are most needed. If teachers in their practice are not themselves models of innovation, how can pupils be expected to develop the relevant attitudes and skills? In the future of education that I have outlined it will not be a matter of simply disseminating fresh ideas and practices around the profession, but rather finding ways of helping teachers to become active innovators rather than adopters of practices devised and honed by others. Identifying and spreading new pedagogic practice has been the most popular strategy for school improvement, but it has met with limited success: even if a small fraction of the new practices that are now touted in books on school improvement were being widely adopted, most of our schools would by now be radically different, whereas in reality it is just a minority who have undergone the profound change advocated.

That disseminators underestimate the real difficulties of knowledge transfer is only part of the explanation. The main cause is the rigidity of schools and classrooms, by which teachers spend so much of their time working as the one adult with a class of pupils. Teachers certainly plan in teams, but they carry out their work mainly in isolation from colleagues. I have in the past argued that the key to innovation is teachers' engagement in joint practice development (JPD),[24] by which two or more teachers jointly agree on a selected weakness in their practice and then work together to improve it, step by step, within their everyday routines. The problem is this still takes time and patience: it is never a quick fix. And professional time is becoming a scarcer resource as school budgets decline and fewer teachers face larger classes.

When teachers are partners with parents on schemes that are partly school-based and partly home-based, they will work in very different conditions. Teachers will have some usable knowledge from their classroom expertise to assist parents, but it will need sensitivity to get beyond treating the parent as a kind of classroom assistant who happens to be working off-site at the pupil's home, and instead become co-innovators with parents of a different pedagogy in circumstances unconstrained by the rigidity of a school timetable and the crowded, age-graded classroom. Moreover some of the most impressive JPD I witnessed involved the learners as joint partners with teachers. In partnerships between teacher and parent it is more natural to include the learner as an equal partner, which in turn helps to promote learner autonomy. Such innovations should permeate back into schools as learners develop the self-managing skills and the lack of dependency on adults that are a natural product of home education. Both parent and teacher have much to gain from a partnership in which both learn to be better as educators, and it is probably on this basis that their partnership can be extended to involve other adults in shared educational roles. My intuition is that top-down reform of education has had its day, as have schemes for purported transformation designed by expensive consultants.

Exemplars of the sort of collaborative innovations that might serve as inspirational models of what might spring from a creative fusion between home education and self-managing and self-improving school systems can be found, sometimes in unexpected places. One is in the field of post-school art education, for which I am indebted to Sam Thorne's (2017) gripping account of recent developments. In the twentieth century art schools have gone through various transformations as the nineteenth-century model of academic training and imitation gave way to a new valuation of student creativity and a reluctance to teach students in any conventional way, and then to later versions of art education that I hesitate to describe. The driver of the most recent developments with which Thorne is concerned is the high cost of an art education in higher education art schools, mainly caused by huge fees and consequent debt. Rather than being a direct replacement for the art school, these lateral developments are, by contrast, free, self-managed on a part-time basis by artists (and sometimes curators and educators), and are unaccredited. The varieties of these projects make it impossible to capture the essence in a few words, and for me it is their very incoherence that makes them interesting. They are not merely symbolic gestures:

> They are conceived as critical alternatives or para-institutions, small-scale but long-term platforms to explore critical education and community … They are frequently read as reactions to the inflexibilities of fixed institutions, but their impulses are much more varied. Despite that, there are certain shared structures and strategies. Most projects are small and occasionally nomadic, while emphasizing an approach to learning that is collaborative and discursive … Organizationally, these projects are self-directed and anti-hierarchical, frequently not making distinctions between teachers and students – "participants" is the more usual term.[25]

Thorne acknowledges that if the many initiatives that his book describes are the green shoots of longer-term change, they must be able to articulate their benefits more clearly and openly, but he is convinced that the present precarious state of art education is fertile ground. His interviews with project leaders are replete with ideas and practices that might be very suggestive to those interested in the kind of collaborations I have advocated.[26]

If what I propose were to happen, it would be a process of slow and uneven evolution, for it would be a broad direction with some bumpy travel, not a blueprint for short-term or sudden reform. Its occurrence would depend on a variety of factors, including the number of parents who opt for home education in coming years, which I expect to continue to rise, not least as many lose faith in what schools are being forced to do by the State. The responses of teachers to these new opportunities for collaborative partnerships with parents and other adults as well as of schools to part-time schooling would all be critical. Schools that are over-subscribed and high performers in government measures, and this includes grammar schools, would see no obvious incentive to change, at least as long as parents select them. A trend to offer part-time schooling would be started by schools that are either less successful in conventional terms and/or contain or recruit staff who are seeking a very different role or who choose to be part-time schoolteachers. If teachers enjoy much greater professional satisfaction from these new roles, and parents find their children happier and learning better in the new arrangements, then inroads into the current dominance of 'high performing schools' will be made. Conditions are, I contend, more favourable to such a scenario than they were in the 1960s and 1970s. If universal basic income were introduced, perhaps in Scotland first, this would make a significant impact on the speed of change in education too.

The emerging structure of the education system would unquestionably become progressively more complex as individual learners and their parents/carers opted for different and variable patterns of relations with schools and networks of home educators. As a result, provision would become less and less legible by the State, which it would not easily renounce, standing idly by as the testing regime and the league tables start to crumble. Ministers would contend that the emerging system is turning education into confusion, chaos and – dare I say it? – anarchy, so the State's default position of defensive resistance becomes essential for maintaining standards, with the claim that it is acting in the public interest and in response to widespread concern (usually from certain daily newspapers) – essentially the same argument that has buttressed increased centralisation for the last fifty years. A robust system of quality assurance for the emerging system would be needed for protective counter-argument.

I believe the elements of such an alternative are already at hand. As the schools have moved from being isolated, self-contained units to becoming members of inter-school partnerships, mainly but not exclusively in the form of multi-academy trusts and teaching-school alliances, earlier work on school self-evaluation has at the same time blossomed into sophisticated peer review systems. The best exemplar of this has been Challenge Partners, descriptions of whose work are readily available – www.challengepartners.org and Berwick and John (2017) – as are independent evaluations.[27] Their primary goal is school improvement within a self-improving school system, linked to improved accountability as a by-product.

The approach stimulates professional learning and development, enhances the quality of leadership, overcomes the introspective and defensive culture engendered by Ofsted inspection, and provides the glue that binds participating schools into self-managing and self-improving networks.[28] Challenge Partners are implicitly a challenge to Ofsted, which has not adapted its own approach as quickly as it should have done. Frank Coffield's (2017) constructive critique of Ofsted offers not only a better model for Ofsted, but also a better conceptual basis for any post-Ofsted system of inspection and accountability. There is no doubt that these will both require new approaches if the changes I advocate are realised. If schools with Challenge Partner experience take the lead in developing new partnerships between home education and schooling, new ideas for inspection and accountability will be simultaneously co-created in anticipation of the ineluctable suspicion and doubts of the State, ever ready to step in with a threat of new controls. One of the lessons of Challenge Partners is that further development of school-led system change depends on outstanding leadership, of the kind displayed by Sir George Berwick and Dame Sue John, who have sown the seeds of what the future might hold.

The many projects of school reform and school improvement since the 1980s have not been the success that was so fervently desired. Some school reformers and improvers with their international consultancies claim great success; well, they would, wouldn't they? This is, of course, a self-indictment too, as I have come to realise how easy it has been to shore up a waning imaginary rather than courageously welcoming and facilitating the arrival of a new one. Part of the distraction is that the criterion for improvement has too often been the metric of test scores, as demanded by contractors, against which any other metrics pale into insignificance. The basic questions of what is a good education, what might be a better education and how might that be achieved have too often been excluded from mainstream discussion and debate, yet this is fundamental to reform for the next generation. Never has it been more necessary to rehearse the 1970s insistence that *education* and *schooling* are not synonyms and to make consequential changes. However, apart from occasional lectures and articles by a few head teachers, leaders of professional associations and the indefatigable Tim Brighouse, closely argued radical rethinking from the political left has recently been in short supply.

In addition to Coffield and Williamson's *From Exam Factories to Communities of Discovery* discussed in Chapter 9, there are two other important exceptions. *Radical Education and the Common School: A Democratic Alternative* (2011), by Michael Fielding and Peter Moss (Michael is a friend and a former colleague, but I have not met Peter), is a fascinating and thoughtful book that has some distinct resonances with an anarchist perspective, from which I must judge the book, leaving a more general appraisal to others. Its appeal is to the traditional left, and offers the usual bitter critique of neo-liberalism and in particular of the 'marketisation' of education. Their alternative vision is of a common school committed to democratic principles, with a core theme of person-centred, democratic fellowship, and for this their major exemplars are the achievements of Alex Bloom, and his secondary modern school St George-in-the-East after 1945 (reported in Chapter 4), and the influential philosophy and practice in preschool and primary schooling of Reggio Emilia in northern Italy (see www.scuolenidi.re.it if you know Italian, or the Wikipedia entry in English under *Reggio Emilia approach*). Another of Fielding's heroes is the Scottish philosopher John Macmurray, whose work and its application to education deserve a much wider audience.[29]

If you are familiar with progressive education and alternative schools, you will readily follow the broad argument. To judge what is unique in their approach is more difficult, in part because almost every concept they employ is preceded by the adjective 'radical' or 'democratic', or both, which is presumably intended to distinguish their specific argument, but too often they add nothing of substance to the words they qualify. Broad terms such as 'democratic' and 'radical' do not have a self-evident meaning when applied so liberally. There are occasional nods to anarchism, but without any detail and no reference at all to Francisco Ferrer or other anarchist educationists, so one is unsure how much common ground there is. Judith Suissa's point made above about the relationship between anarchist and progressive schools applies here too. If one wandered around their proposed common school it would be impossible by observation to differentiate it from many other schools of a progressive kind, though their rationale for how the staff and pupils were behaving would certainly differ from that of other progressive educators and of anarchists.

Despite some common ground between the Fielding and Moss model and practices advocated by anarchists, there are fundamental ideological differences. The first is that they simply accept in principle the State's role in education and schooling and for the most part that of the local authorities: they simply want them to operate differently. The second is that their State-imposed common school is a fixed model, a new version of the comprehensive school but run in a different way: their system contains very weak differentiation between schools. Parental choice, which they term 'shopping around in an educational market', is rejected, and individual choice is replaced by collective choice, a distinction I fear might mean their common school is somehow a product of 'the will of the people'. They allow the possibility of some choice *within* the common school, which might have 'schools within schools',[30] but this is evidently very limited. I, and many anarchists, believe freedom requires there be schools of different kinds, based on philosophies, forms of organisation and styles of pedagogy that might be sharply divergent. I cannot support a State-imposed single standard school, and more to the point I do not see any government in England entertaining the Fielding–Moss model for the whole school system or garnering wide public support for it.[31]

There is more common ground between Fielding and Moss and anarchism on strategic issues: how we get from here to there. They focus on the potential of prefigurative practice, which has been discussed in previous chapters. Like Benjamin Franks,[32] they trace the term's origin to Carl Boggs, who coined it in

1997, and use it mainly to suggest ways in which educational practices might prefigure their common school, whereas for anarchists the focus is more on how educational practice prefigures the future society. Nevertheless, this sharing of a key concept in strategic thinking is welcome, as is the importance they attach to experimentation, also at the heart of anarchist thinking. They settle on an incrementalist strategy, which inevitably they call *radical* incrementalism, drawing on Erik Ohlin Wright's notion of 'waystations' or institutional innovations that move in the right direction whilst only partially embodying the values of the final destination.[33]

Like anarchists, they are open to a charge of utopianism. Their purpose is 'overtly utopian … to describe and argue for one scenario and alternative'.[34] They are reluctant 'to get down to prescribing detailed directions … [and] for now we admit to not knowing fully about our destination or direction of travel'.[35] To defend their position, they draw extensively on Wright's *Envisioning Real Utopias* (2010), and are willing to subject their vision to his three criteria of desirability, viability and achievability. They acknowledge that their proposals for a common school focus primarily on desirability and viability,[36] declining to face the difficult challenge of achievability, at least at this point.

A third outstanding contribution to radical thinking from the left is Melissa Benn's *Life Lessons: The Case for a National Education Service* (2018). Again, it is passionately written and bubbles with ideas, and so, like the other two books, is essential reading for anybody interested in a very different future for education. The core argument is for a National Education Service (NES) that is in close parallel to the NHS, with an entitlement to free provision from the early years, through further and higher education, to continuous access to lifelong learning opportunities. The NES 'would knit together disparate services, institutions and stages into a more unifying "offer" without compromising the distinct character, demands and autonomy of each part' so that 'the NES will provide us with the education we need, at different times, in different ways, guided by thoughtful, expert educators'.[37]

Whilst there is again much to agree with in her critique of recent education policy, her alternative of an NES to match the NHS is vulnerable to anarchist critique in two ways. First of all, her education proposals necessarily involve huge costs. Although she insists that our society is rich enough to afford it, the costing of the various components of this ambitious plan is unconvincing, and seems to depend heavily on the idea of a permanent tax on all graduates. It also ignores the fact that the NHS is already in dire financial straits and that the ballooning costs of social care over coming years are likely to be a more pressing priority for any government. Are we really rich enough to afford her NES as well, with its investment in 'proper early years provision, spacious school buildings, well-paid teachers, generous special needs provision, and fully resourced further and adult education'[38] in addition to free higher education?

A second and more important objection is one of principle, her assumption that any just and efficient education system requires centralised control by the State. Making a parallel between education and health will attract many, for the

NHS is so widely assumed to be an inherent feature of a civilised society that the Conservatives have had to approach the introduction of private provision into the NHS with stealth lest they lose public support. A claim that we must make education provision match that of the NHS sounds appealing – despite the seemingly endless reorganisations of both services by the State. By contrast, Colin Ward draws attention to the working-class systems of self-help and mutual aid in health that preceded the NHS, as a parallel to Phil Gardner's account of their educational equivalents prior to the introduction of State schooling. He takes the example of the Tredegar Medical Aid Society, to which every employed worker paid a small contribution. The workers thought that the newly-created NHS was going to be a network of Tredegars:

> There once was the option of universal health provision "at the point of service" if only Fabians, Marxists and Aneurin Bevan had trusted the state and central revenue-gathering less, and our capacity for self-help and mutual aid more ... I think it is time to admit that universalism is an unattainable idea in a society that is enormously divided in terms of income and access to employment ... we stifled the localist and voluntarist approach in favour of conquest of the power of the state. We took the wrong road.[39]

As with most left thinkers, Benn believes that the private-sector schools must be abolished and integrated into the NES – which makes an interesting contrast with the NHS, since she does not speak of abolishing private medicine. For over half a century the Labour Party has consistently declined to tackle this issue, and for various reasons, including the rights of parents to spend their money on their children's education. Questions of liberty are ignored, and the 'philosophy of individual freedom' is seen by Benn in narrow terms as an intrinsic feature of the Conservative Party's preference for a hierarchical schooling system.[40] At the same there would be room for parents to set up their own schools 'within a responsive democratic framework ... [and] with the appropriate education authority'.[41] There is no mention of home education. How much room would exist for schools to develop in distinctive ways is unclear, but the impression is of more flexibility than with the Fielding–Moss model, as shown by her short portraits of some of our very best State schools under inspired leaders.

Compared with Fielding and Moss, Benn offers very little on political theory, so it is hard to detect much common ground with anarchism. The main flaw from an anarchist perspective is that the State itself is never challenged, merely those who have recently managed its education policies. With new people in charge, it could all be very different. The path to the future would in her view require much more consultation and debate than we have seen in recent years. True, she wants a commission to make proposals for the integration of academies and free schools into the NES; an independent committee to shape the national curriculum, qualifications and examinations; and an independent trust to advise on how private schools can be integrated into the State system. However, we have had similar bodies or consultations before, and in every case when they have failed to give advice or behave in ways that please central government, they have been ignored or even abolished – I know, for I have successively worked for several of them, though the University of Cambridge seems safe, at least for the moment. Why should this not happen yet again? Although she is clearly unhappy about the rapid increase in centralisation, I believe that getting her NES into being relatively unscathed would necessarily involve considerable centralisation of power – to be followed by the usual reluctance ever to let go of it.

As for many left radicals, the aim is to rid the system of its present messiness and replace all education, not just the schooling sector, with something more integrated, coherent and tidy. For an anarchist, this search for rational planning, clarity and coherence ineluctably demands the political power and control that has resulted in our present system. For an anarchist, there is a desirable and beneficial form of messiness that empowers people to make their own choices and decisions that reflect their values and aspirations. Towns and cities have been important in this book because they are a critically important layer between the State and individuals, families and neighbourhoods. Murray Bookchin has constantly reminded us that the State

> parasitizes the community, denuding it of its resources, and its potential for development. It does this partly by draining the community of its material and spiritual resources; partly, too, by steadily divesting it of the power, indeed of the legitimate right, to shape its own destiny … Municipal freedom, in short, is the basis for political freedom, and political freedom is the basis for individual freedom – a recovery of a new participatory politics structured around free, self-empowered and active citizens.[42]

How could any of this be achieved if the State makes all the key decisions about education and schooling and assumes the major role in the accountability of schools? Rejecting statist control entails giving power to communities, and this must include the opportunity to make distinctive policies for education and schooling.

Wright's triple challenge (desirability, viability and achievability) is one to which we must all face up. What is your response to my proposals and to those of Fielding–Moss, of Benn and of Coffield–Williamson? Do you have proposals of your own that you would now make, whether or not they have been influenced by our encounter with anarchist thinking? I believe my proposals go some way to meeting it, but I leave it to you to take my proposals, those of Fielding–Moss, Coffield–Williamson and Benn, and any ideas of your own, and subject them all to an evaluative template of utopian ideas like the one I suggested in Chapter 8, derived from Wright and Levitas, with five criteria:

1. Would the things you most value in the present education and schooling system survive in the proposed system?

2. Would those things you most dislike in the present education and schooling system be absent in the proposed system?
3. Are there elements of the proposed system to which you would strongly object?
4. On balance, would the proposed system of education and schooling be preferable to the present system?
5. Is such a system of education and schooling achievable, and is it linked to wider social changes that drive in the same direction?

As you respond to the fifth criterion, bear in mind Wright's theory of transformation in the final section of *Envisioning Real Utopias*. He suggests three models of transformation, which he calls *ruptural, interstitial* and *symbiotic*, reflecting the different political traditions with which they are most closely associated. The ruptural is clearly in the Marxist tradition; the symbiotic, the social democratic; and the interstitial, you will not be surprised to hear, the anarchist. Strategically, the ruptural requires a frontal attack on the State, a revolution; the symbiotic sees the State as a field of struggle, for it can be used for different ends; and the interstitial creates developments outside the State to build new social institutions:

> Interstitial success is more like a complex ecological system in which one kind of organism initially gains a foothold in a niche but eventually outcompetes rivals for food sources and so comes to dominate the wider environment.[43]

The process of change is not smooth and free of conflict, for it entails power struggles and unavoidable confrontations. Interstitial innovations must overcome opposition from those whose interests are threatened, and whose opposition will be 'nasty, recalcitrant and destructive'.[44] He quotes Colin Ward on how the alternatives are already here, like spare parts of a future society, tucked away in the interstices of the dominant power structure,[45] as well Martin Buber's observation that 'revolution is not so much a creative as a delivering force whose function is to set free and authenticate … something that has already been foreshadowed'.[46] Wright then points out that there is little in anarchist theory that explores how these cumulative processes build up over time, and offers two possible trajectories. In the first, the anarchist alternatives accumulate within the interstices until these meet limits or opposition, and then new interstices must be sought in which to devise new ways to circumvent them. In a second possibility, the process at some stage runs up against immovable constraints and a revolutionary rupture, though a relatively shallow one, is needed to clear the path to further progress. This is food for thought in relation to my proposals as much as to Fielding and Moss's, which without embarrassment they ought to confess are, in Wright's terms, an anarchist strategy.

Battles of a Jane Jacobs versus Robert Moses variety may indeed have to be fought, but they are not the main path to a new form of order that is bottom-up, not just a different version of the top-down exercise of power. A most vivid account of such a way to this future is to be found in a book by a person who is neither an anarchist nor an educationist, but a social scientist and social entrepreneur, who has captured the essence of the processes of social reconstruction necessary to the emergence of a new social imaginary with a compatible educational imaginary. I end with her intentionally to show that potential allies are to be found in many places, and we should not build alliances only from the usual suspects.

The aim of Hilary Cottam's *Radical Help: How We Can Remake the Relationships between Us and Revolutionise the Welfare State* (2018) is to design ways of promoting human flourishing by means of human connection. Her core conviction is that when people feel supported by strong human relationships, change happens. She sees the point of the welfare state, but argues that it is simply not working in accordance with its original aims, and is beyond repair by conventional means. In terms that immediately endear her to anarchists, she speaks of her work over the last decade as *experiments*, that is, practical innovations in everyday settings: a big-picture vision with smaller steps applied in five areas – family life, growing up, work, health and old age. The relevance of most of these to this book's thesis is obvious. And she never balks at confessing the mistakes she has made and how she learned from them to redesign the experiments.

The adolescents she met are recognisable in many secondary schools: academic failures, sometimes with dreams, yet disenchanted, powerless, with no decent employment prospects. She looked in the community to locate people who might offer, for free, a worthwhile experience for a young person. Almost every person she and her team asked said yes. The reaction of the adolescents was uncomprehending and hostile. As one said, 'An adult hanging out with a young person? That's weird. That's perverted.'[47] This is the price we pay for school's age-grading, and for failing to provide real opportunities for young people to meet with adults-other-than-teachers. So it was back to the drawing board to find ways of making the adolescent–adult interaction more comfortable. I leave it to you to read what happened on her road to some success, which is attributed to the focus on a relational organisation rather than the control of traditional management hierarchies that were so evident in the youth service sector designed to help young people. The incomprehension of her scheme's official partners, their inability to cope with new ways of working with young people and community members willing to help, meant no further development was ever possible.

The story of her projects with the unemployed follows a similar track. She describes how the Jobcentre process fails: the unemployed do not get the decent jobs they want and become angry and bitter; and the agency staff are frustrated too. So a project was designed along quite different lines, based on the fact that most people who get jobs of the kind they want and might actually lead somewhere do so through personal connections, not advertisements or the Jobcentre. The project thus started with an invitation to join an actively managed network in which people could work on their dreams and build the new connections and capabilities. This, of course, enjoyed more success.

Towards the end of the book she offers a telling account of a visit to one of her projects by David Cameron, doubtless with 'Big Society' expectations. Duly impressed, he decided the scheme should be replicated nationally. His officials arrived to plan the follow-up, with their idea of providing money for organisations that could compete for funding. In vain Hilary Cottam and her colleagues explained that it was not a matter of money and new professionals, but of freeing those already at the front line to work in new ways:

> Nothing about this story [of the project] resonated with the civil servants … They could not see the difference that we tried to articulate. An approach based on horizontal relationships and a shift in power towards the families was translated back into a linear programme with outputs that could be measured and controlled. Financial incentives are a modern version of command and control. Local leaders who took part would be rewarded with pocket money, like children.[48]

Fifteen years ago when I was working as a policy adviser in the Education Department, whenever a minister suggested a change in policy and asked the officials to implement it, the immediate question in the next meeting of the officials was always the same: how can we incentivise people to do what the minister wants? A change of government since then, but no change of civil service mentality apparently.[49]

Hilary Cottom's and Sam Thorne's 'experiments' are exactly what I believe teachers should be doing to create the necessary transformation from schooling into education. But, they will say to me, we simply are not free to do this, as we are caught up in the web of performativity from which we cannot escape. If you are not a teacher, you might reasonably ask why they don't rebel. Why don't the teachers stop complaining and simply refuse? They have the numbers – over 400,000 of them. The impact of concerted action is potentially huge, especially when parents have to find alternative means of caring for their children: industrial action by teachers reminds society of the custodial function of the school. But there are two factors inhibiting this: teachers, like nurses and doctors, have a moral objection to industrial action; and teachers' many unions and associations find it difficult to agree on such matters. The potential for teacher involvement in innovative social movements for more radical experimentation in educational provision is probably a better way forward.[50]

This is not, however, a full explanation, which is much more subtle and insidious. Centralising politicians of both main parties realised long ago that if you want to influence what teachers do, don't do so through the local authorities or through the unions: you do it through the head teachers, who are the gatekeepers to the profession. Schools have always been hierarchical institutions, and the larger the school, the stronger the hierarchy. Back in the 1960s schools, even secondary schools, had a head teacher with one deputy. Today a typical secondary school has one head teacher, several deputies and a plethora of assistant head teachers, who are often referred to by the rest of the staff as 'the management' or something more expressive but less polite. Politicians have captured the head teachers and converted them into 'deliverers' of government policies in general and of test and examination results in particular. Failure to deliver means the end of your career as a school leader, which helps to explain the recurring shortage of candidates for primary school headship. In the 1960s an unhappy staff would use the single deputy as a go-between, mediating between staff and head. Today a discontented staff has above them a whole team of managers, all of whom are, by virtue of their managerial office, committed to carrying out the head's policies. The effect is to paralyse classroom teachers from turning their discontent into rebellion. Now head teachers are being replaced by the new breed of 'super heads' in the form of executive head teachers and chief executives, whose control over staff is greater than ever.

What, then, are we left with? What was Hilary Cottam left with? The action she took is close to the principles and commitments for improving city life that were long ago established by Peter Kropotkin, Ebenezer Howard, Patrick Geddes and Lewis Mumford; and her understanding of the complexities of the modern city is as sophisticated as that of Jane Jacobs and Richard Sennett. Yet she still has faith of some kind in the State:

> Only the state, our leaders and political actors can create the pivot we need, developing the new framework, supporting the vision and nurturing the principles that will guide the behavior, funding and activities of others … The state must seek out and support alternative models … The state's role can no longer be that of pulling the mechanical levers of power. Instead they must be like a head gardener: setting out the design, planting, tending, nurturing, and, where necessary, weeding.[51]

Must we in education also conclude that only the State, which has been moving in the opposite direction, can nevertheless initiate such changes? If the State were as good as Hilary Cottam in learning from her mistakes, I might share her optimism. But the State's track record in education over the last fifty years is absolutely against this. Perhaps, in spite of her experience, she could not think of a more positive note on which to end. It is not how I can end, because in an age when one of the most powerful, insidious and deceptive of political slogans is *Taking back control*, I know what it means when in the hands of Boris Johnson and of Michael Gove, a man who as Secretary of State for Education had a brilliant track record of taking back control, namely into his own hands and that of his officials.

The world is in an unusual period of political instability, sometimes clearly on the surface, and sometime bubbling under the surface, in the USA, in Russia, in China, in South America and especially within Europe with the growth of nationalism and populist autocracy in the East (and in Turkey), the desertion by many voters of the traditional parties of left and right in the West, and the increasing fragility of the European Union itself. Younger people experience new vulnerabilities: unemployment and underemployment, not least for new graduates with huge loans to repay, the near impossibility of getting into the housing market, the prospect of longer working lives and lower pensions than those their parents enjoy. Here perhaps is a level of frustration that for the first time in a generation matches that of the young people in Paris and elsewhere in the 1960s: they will have to fight even harder for a better deal for human flourishing. Neither Martin Rees, the former Astronomer Royal, nor the late Stephen Hawking rate the chances of humanity surviving into the next century very highly,[52] so it is on a new generation that the burden of facing up to humanity's greatest challenges now falls. But to whom will they turn for ideas? Milton Friedman once said that it needs a crisis to produce real change, and that the function of intellectuals is 'to develop alternatives to existing policies, to keep them alive and available, until the politically impossible becomes the politically inevitable'.[53] Anarchism has been lying around for a long time, but is alive and available when the time is ripe.

Members of the next generation do not need to be explicit anarchists, but they must have the passion of Michael Bakunin and Paul Goodman and the humanity of Peter Kropotkin and Colin Ward, feeding into a utopian ideal whose ends will also shape the means of realising it. They should bear in mind Murray Rothbard's advice:

> If social change is not always tiny and gradual, neither does it usually occur in a single leap … How, then, can we know whether any halfway measure or transitional demand should be hailed as a step forward or condemned as an opportunistic betrayal? There are two vitally important criteria for answering this crucial question: (1) that, whatever the transitional demands, the ultimate end of liberty be always held aloft as the desired goal; and (2) that no steps or means ever explicitly or implicitly *contradict* the ultimate goal. A short-run demand may not go as far as we would like, but it should always be consistent with the final end; if not, the short-run goal will work against the long-run purpose and opportunistic liquidation of libertarian principle will have arrived.[54]

We should not wait for our leopard of a State to change its spots, but should concentrate on making alliances with all those who, whatever their political beliefs or aversions, share one important conviction: that the State must be pressured to retreat in order to release the creative energy of the leaders in waiting for the creation of that better world. In this regard, anarchists are better versed than most political groups in the necessary tactics, and perhaps especially refusal and resistance. Making an alliance does not mean compromising one's deepest beliefs, but rather not insisting on a purist position to the point where the real possibility of a significant advance is denied – and anarchists are as guilty of purism as any other group. A short-term common purpose can unite groups with unshared long-term goals, as long as there is enough mutual respect to neutralise tensions. Anarchists have their own fissiparous tendencies that they need to anaesthetise temporarily for a strategic good cause. This does involve a risk, but 'refusal to take such a risk generally means sterility and sectarianism',[55] and the risk is low as long as the means adopted do not conflict with the end. Potential allies often share much the same language, even if the dialects vary.[56] As Mark Bray, seeking to learn lessons from Occupy Wall Street, puts it:

> If anarchists can articulate a clearer vision of how these different forms of resistance feed off each other, I think that the next time a similar opportunity arises we can achieve a greater political clarity. I don't think you that you necessarily need the term "anarchism" to do that, but it can help ...[57]

Ruth Kinna points to this longstanding inclusiveness:

> Kropotkin's ambition was not to make anarchists but to create the conditions in which diverse groups and individuals could live anarchistically ... he imagined that anarchism would provide a home for conservatives as well as socialists and people of faith as well as atheists ... Turning anarchism into a sect or seeking to determine who or who was not genuinely anarchist would likely undermine this strategy, alienating anarchists from potential sympathisers.[58]

As we have seen, there are libertarian conservatives in the form of the anarcho-capitalists and in England many libertarian Conservatives are unhappy about the high degree of centralisation in education. There are many on the political left who share common ground with anarchists, not least on matters of liberty. Bold alliances are possible if we choose to make them.

At the opening of this book I told you I was not an anarchist. I am still not an anarchist, though the reading and thinking inherent in the writing have made me more sympathetic to their perspective, which I am convinced is even more relevant to education and schooling in England than it has ever been from the late 1960s and early 1970s through to the present day. If you were not an anarchist when you started reading this book, I think it very unlikely that you have become one. But I hope that I have persuaded you that anarchist ideas and principles are more compelling and more urgent today that they were in the 1960s and 1970s and that anarchism shines a powerful light both on the failings of our present system of education and schooling and on possible alternatives. I hope too that anarchism has helped you, as it has helped me, to question what once were unquestionable assumptions, and to envisage different possibilities for a new social and educational imaginary that might be within our grasp should we so choose.

By 2020 we shall have experienced 150 years of State control over education and schooling, a relatively short period in our history. The rapid centralisation that has taken place during the last fifth of this period is, when seen from a wider historical perspective, astonishing and frightening, in part because there was never a strong case to justify it and in part because we have so quickly come to treat it as largely unquestionable; just imagine how William Godwin and the classic anarchists would be writing about schooling today. It is, I submit, time to turn the tide on centralisation and find a better path to the future in the light of the rapidly changing conditions in which centralisation becomes less and less warranted. In moving beyond the centralised model of schooling, an anarchist perspective should help to illuminate the way and give us the courage to refuse and resist as well as the inventiveness to build and reconstruct.

Notes

1 This is, of course, a reference to the title of Lenin's 1902 pamphlet and to the title of the 1863 novel by Nikolai Chernyshevsky, written in the Fortress of St Peter and St Paul.
2 McKay (2011: 702).
3 Smith (1983: 25).
4 McKay (2011: 593).
5 See the entries in Wikipedia for details. It is difficult to ensure that the comparisons control relevant variables, such as social class and parental interest.
6 See House of Commons Briefing Paper Number 5108, *Home Education in England*, May 2018.
7 See Todd in Haworth (2012). Care would have to be taken that such cooperatives did not become so extensive as to be open to the charge of being an unregistered school.
8 As recognised by Alan Thomas (1998: chapters 7 and 8).
9 Edwards and Westgate (1994).
10 Report of the Sutton Trust, August 2018.
11 House of Commons Briefing Paper Number 5108, *Home Education in England*, May 2018, Para. 1.4 implies that from February 2013 whilst existing flexi-schooling arrangements will be honoured, such arrangements should be denied in future. It seems that this decision was later withdrawn. The impression left is the DfE officials are unsympathetic to flexi-schooling, which complicates established bureaucratic procedures and funding schemes.
12 See Reé (1973).
13 John Shotton's *No Master High or Low* (1993) has good British examples. Joel Spring's *A Primer of Libertarian Education* (1975) is in my view much inferior to Smith, Suissa and Shotton. Raynaud and Ambauve's *L'éducation libertaire* (1978) is also a key source. See also David Gribble in Purkis and Bowen (2004).
14 Francisco Ferrer (1913). An excellent recent account is Bray and Haworth (2018). See also De Cleyre (2016).
15 Dolgoff (1980: 373).
16 Bakunin (1970: 41) and in Maximoff (1953: 333–4).
17 Swidler (1979: 157).
18 Bakunin (1916: 42).
19 Suissa (2006: 85 and 97).
20 Smith (1983: 27).
21 Sennett (2008: 9 and 80).
22 Perhaps the best-known surgeon with such interests is Henry Marsh, through his fascinating books.
23 Sennett (2012: 168) takes this concept from the work of Gideon Kunder (1992), but I am applying it to schools.
24 Fielding et al. (2004), Hargreaves (2012).
25 Thorne (2017: 48).

26 I found the interviews with Pablo Helguera (USA), Sean Dockray (USA), Piero Golia (USA), Olafur Eliasson (Germany) and the leaders of Open School East, London, particularly rich in this regard.
27 Matthews and Headon (2015).
28 Matthews and Ehren (2017).
29 Fielding and Moss (2011: 47–52 especially). If you are unfamiliar with Macmurray's work, a biography (Costello, 2002) is a good starting point.
30 Fielding and Moss (2011: 130–4).
31 I understand the concern that choice often results in inequities. Certainly the middle classes sometimes use choice as an opportunity to enhance their advantages (see, for example, Power et al., 2003). But the only way in which this could be eradicated is by prohibition of any kind of schooling other than that provided by the State and the allocation of pupils to schools be placed under State control, at least in principle. I and anarchists would find this an entirely unacceptable restriction on liberty, which will always result in some inequities that have to be tackled in less draconian ways.
32 Franks in Franks et al. (2018).
33 Fielding and Moss (2011: 140).
34 Fielding and Moss (2011: 39).
35 Fielding and Moss (2011: 37).
36 Fielding and Moss (2011: 142).
37 Benn (2018: 4).
38 Benn (2018: 55).
39 Ward (2000: 16f). Ward also had reservations about government policy on housing and his alternative approach is very interesting – see Ward (1976, 1985).
40 Benn (2018: 132).
41 Benn (2018: 82).
42 Bookchin (1992: 228).
43 Wright (2010: 307).
44 Wright (2010: 321).
45 Ward (1973: 18).
46 Buber (1949: 44).
47 Cottam (2018: 93).
48 Cottam (2018: 250).
49 A report by Peter Walker (*The Guardian*, 2 August 2018) on Cameron's residential youth scheme National Citizen Service ended up using vast sums diverted from traditional youth services but reached few of its intended participants.
50 See for instance, Sitrin (2006, 2012) and Zibechi (2010). Mark Bray provides an overview of horizontalism in Franks et al. (2018). I hope to develop this notion further in my next book.
51 Cottam (2018: 264–6).
52 Martin Rees (2018); Stephen Hawking's views on poor prospects of avoiding disaster in the next hundred years were widely reported and can be found in the bigthink.com interview with Stephen Johnson, 14 March 2018.
53 Milton Friedman, preface to 1982 edition of *Capitalism and Freedom*, University of Chicago Press.
54 Rothbard (1973: 383).
55 Nicolas Walter in Woodcock (1977: 172).
56 De Souza et al. (2016a: 8).
57 Bray (2013: 267).
58 Kinna (2016: 202).

BIBLIOGRAPHY

Adonis, A. (2012) *Education, Education, Education: Reforming England's Schools*. London: Biteback.

Alexander, R. (2006, 3rd ed.) *Towards Dialogic Teaching*. York: Dialogos.

Allen, A. (2014) *Education in and Beyond the Age of Reason*. London: Palgrave Macmillan.

Applebaum, A. (2018) *Red Famine: Stalin's War on Ukraine*. London: Penguin.

Apter, D., and Joll, J. (eds.) (1971) *Anarchism Today*. London: Palgrave Macmillan.

Arshinov, P. (1974) *History of the Makhnovist Movement 1918–1921*. Detroit: Black and Red.

Avrich, P. (1980) *The Modern School Movement: Anarchism and Education in the United States*. Princeton: Princeton University Press.

Bakunin, M. (1916/1970) *God and the State*. New York: Dover.

Ball, S. (ed.) (1990) *Foucault and Education: Disciplines and Knowledge*. London: Routledge.

Ball, S. (2013) *Foucault, Power and Education*. London: Routledge.

Ball, S. (2017) *Foucault as Educator*. New York: Springer.

Bammer, A. (2015) *Partial Visions*. Bern: Peter Lang AG.

Barber, M. (1996) *The Learning Game: Arguments for an Education Revolution*. London: Gollancz.

Barclay, H. (1982) *People without Government: An Anthropology of Anarchism*. London: Kahn and Averill.

Barclay, H. (1997) *Culture and Anarchism*. London: Freedom Press.

Barclay, H. (2003) *The State*. London: Freedom Press.

Barrow, R. (1978) *Radical Education: A Critique of Freeschooling and Deschooling*. London: Martin Robertson.

Beck, J., Jencks, C., Keddie, N., and Young, M. (eds.) (1976) *Toward a Sociology of Education*. Piscataway: Transaction Books.

Bellamy, E. (1888) *Looking Backward (2000–1887)*. Boston: Houghton Mifflin.

Benn, M. (2018) *Life Lessons: The Case for a National Education Service*. London: Verso.

Bentley, T. (1998) *Learning Beyond the Classroom: Education for a Changing World*. London: Demos.

Berkman, A. (1912) *Prison Memoirs of an Anarchist*. Originally Mother Earth Press, now Edinburgh: AK Press.

Berneri, M. (1950) *Journey through Utopia*. London: Freedom Press.

Berwick, G., and John, S. (2017) 'School networks, peer accountability and the brokerage of knowledge and expertise', in Earley, P., and Greany, T. (eds.) (2017) *School Leadership and Education System Reform*. London: Bloomsbury.

Biehl, J. (ed.) (1999) *The Murray Bookchin Reader*. London: Black Rose Books.
Black, B. (1985) *The Abolition of Work*. Available online at primitivism.com.
Bookchin, M. (1992) *Urbanization without Cities: The Rise and Decline of Citizenship*. London: Black Rose Books.
Bookchin, M. (2004) *Post-Scarcity Anarchism*. Edinburgh: AK Press.
Bookchin, M. (2005) *The Ecology of Freedom: The Emergence and Dissolution of Freedom*. Edinburgh: AK Press.
Bookchin, M. (2007) *Social Ecology and Communalism*. Oakland and Edinburgh: PM Press.
Bowles, S., and Gintis, H. (1976) *Schooling in Capitalist America: Educational Reform and the Contradictions of Economic Life*. London: Routledge & Kegan Paul.
Bowring, F. (2000) *André Gorz and the Sartrean Legacy*. London: Palgrave Macmillan.
Branford, V. (1914) *Interpretations and Forecasts*. London: Duckworth.
Branford, V. (1921) *Whitherward? Hell or Eutopia*. London: Williams and Norgate and reprinted in Leopold Classic Library.
Bray, M. (2013) *Translating Anarchy: The Anarchism of Occupy Wall Street*. Winchester and Washington: Zero Books.
Bray, M. (2017) *Antifa: The Anti-Fascist Handbook*. New York and London: Melville House Publishing.
Bray, M., and Haworth, R. (2018) *Anarchist Education and the Modern School: A Francisco Ferrer Reader*. Oakland: PM Press.
Buber, M. (1949) *Paths in Utopia*. Boston: Beacon Press.
Buber, M. (1999) *Pointing the Way: Collected Essays*. New York: Humanity Books.
Bunt, L., and Harris, M. (2010) *Mass Localism: A Way to Help Small Communities Solve Big Social Challenges*. London: NESTA.
Burchell, G., Gordon, C., and Miller, P. (eds.) (1991) *The Foucault Effect: Studies in Governmentality*. Chicago: University of Chicago Press.
Burke, C., and Jones, K. (eds.) (2014) *Education, Childhood and Anarchism: Talking Colin Ward*. London: Routledge.
Butterworth, A. (2011) *The World That Never Was*. London: Vintage.
Caplan, B. (2018) *The Case against Education: Why the Education System Is a Waste of Time and Money*. Princeton: Princeton University Press.
Carlin, M., and Wallin, J. (2014) *Deleuze and Guattari, Politics and Education*. London and New York: Bloomsbury.
Carnie, F. (2003) *Alternative Approaches to Education*. London: RoutledgeFalmer.
Caro, R. (2015) *The Power Broker: Robert Moses and the Fall of New York*. London: Bodley Head.
Centre for Contemporary Cultural Studies. (1981) *Unpopular Education*. London: Hutchinson.
Charkin, E. (2014) '"A parable of the way things ought to be": Colin Ward, the Peckham Health Centre and the deschooling movement', in Burke, C., and Jones, K. (eds.) (2014) *Education, Childhood and Anarchism: Talking Colin Ward*. London: Routledge.
Chernyshevsky, N. (1863) *What Is to Be Done ?* Ann Arbor: Ardis.
Chitty, C. (1989) *Towards a New Education System*. Basingstoke: Falmer Press.
Chitty, C. (2004) *Education Policy in Britain*. Basingstoke: Palgrave Macmillan (and later editions).
Chomsky, N. (2013) *On Anarchism*. London and New York: Penguin.
Christie, S., and Meltzer, A. (1970) *The Floodgates of Anarchy*. London: Kahn and Averill.
Cicourel, A., and Kitsuse, J. (1963) *The Educational Decision-Makers*. Indianapolis: Bobbs-Merrill.
Clark, J. (2013) *The Impossible Community: Realizing Communitarian Anarchism*. London and New York: Bloomsbury.
Clastres, P. (1987) *Society Against the State*. New York: Zone Books.
Coffield, F. (2000) *The Necessity of Informal Learning*. Bristol: Policy Press.
Coffield, F. (2017) *Will the Leopard Change Its Spots? A New Model of Inspection for Ofsted*. London: UCL Institute of Education Press.
Coffield, F., and Williamson, B. (2011) *From Exam Factories to Communities of Discovery: The Democratic Route*. London: Institute of Education, University of London.

Cohen, S., and Taylor, L. (1976) *Escape Attempts: The Theory and Practice of Resistance in Everyday Life*. Harmondsworth: Penguin.

Cole, G. D. H. (1954) *Socialist Thought: Marxism and Anarchism 1850–1890*. London and New York: Palgrave Macmillan.

Collier, P. (2018) *The Future of Capitalism: Facing the New Anxieties*. London: Allen Lane.

Conservative Party (2010) *Invitation to Join the Government of Britain: The Conservative Manifesto 2010*. London: The Conservative Party.

Cosin, B., Dale, I., Esland, G., Mackinnon, D., and Swift, D. (eds.) (1971) *School and Society: A Sociological Reader*. London: Routledge & Kegan Paul.

Costello, J. (2002) *John Macmurray: A Biography*. Edinburgh: Floris Books.

Cottam, H. (2018) *Radical Help: How We Can Remake the Relationships between Us and Revolutionise the Welfare State*. London: Virago.

Cox, B. (1992) *The Great Betrayal*. London: Chapmans.

Dahl, R. (1970) *After the Revolution?* New York and London: Yale University Press.

Dale, R., Esland, G., and MacDonald, M. (eds.) (1976) *Schooling and Capitalism: A Sociological Reader*. London: Routledge & Kegan Paul.

Davis, L., and Kinna, R. (eds.) (2009) *Anarchism and Utopianism*. Manchester: Manchester University Press.

De Cleyre, V. (2016) *Francisco Ferrer*. Schooner & CO. Available on Kindle.

De Jouvenel, B. (1993) *On Power: The Natural History and Its Growth*. Indianapolis: Liberty Fund.

De Souza, L., White, R., and Springer, S. (eds.) (2016a) *Theories of Resistance*. London and New York: Rowman & Littlefield.

De Souza, L., White, R., and Springer, S. (eds.) (2016b) *The Radicalization of Pedagogy*. London and New York: Rowman & Littlefield.

Dean, M. (1999, 2nd ed., 2010) *Governmentality: Power and Rule in Modern Society*. London: Sage.

Deleuze, G. (2006) *Foucault*. London: Continuum.

Dennison, G. (1969) *The Lives of Children: The Story of the First Street School*. Harmondsworth: Penguin.

Dolgoff, S. (1980) *Bakunin on Anarchism*. Montreal: Black Rose Books.

Dreeben, R. (1968) *On What Is Learned in School*. Boston: Addison-Wesley.

Earley, P., and Greany, T. (eds.) (2017) *School Leadership and Education System Reform*. London: Bloomsbury.

Edwards, A., and Westgate, D. (1994) *Investigating Classroom Talk*. London: Falmer.

Elden, S. (2017) *Foucault: The Birth of Power*. Cambridge: Polity.

Elzbacher, P. (2004) *The Great Anarchists*. New York: Dover.

Faubion, J. (ed.) (2002) *Power (Essential Works of Foucault 1954–1984, Volume 3)*. London: Penguin.

Ferrer, F. (1913/2014) *The Origin and Ideals of the Modern School*. Christie Books. Available on Kindle.

Fielding, M., Bragg, S., Craig, J., Cunningham, I., Eraut, M., Gillinson, S., Horne, M., Robinson, C., and Thorn, J. (2004) *Factors Influencing the Transfer of Good Practice*. London: Department for Education and Skills.

Fielding, M., and Moss, P. (2011) *Radical Education and the Common School: A Democratic Alternative*. London: Routledge.

Fishman, R. (1982) *Urban Utopias in the Twentieth Century*. Cambridge: MIT Press.

Flint, A. (2011) *Wrestling with Moses*. New York: Random House.

Florida, R. (2002) *The Rise of the Creative Class*. New York: Basic Books.

Florida, R. (2008) *Who's Your City?* New York: Basic Books.

Foucault, M. (1975) *Surveiller et punir*. Paris: Gallimard.

Foucault, M. (1977) *Discipline and Punish: The Birth of the Prison*. London: Penguin.

Foucault, M. (1978) 'Governmentality', in Faubion, J. (ed.) (2002) *Power (Essential Works of Foucault 1954–1984, Volume 3)*. London: Penguin.

Foucault, M. (1979) 'Omnes et Singulatim: Towards a critique of political reason,' in Faubion, J. (ed.) (2002) *Power (Essential Works of Foucault 1954–1984, Volume 3)*. London: Penguin.
Foucault, M. (1982) 'The subject and power,' in Faubion, J. (ed.) (2002) *Power (Essential Works of Foucault 1954–1984, Volume 3)*. London: Penguin.
Franks, B. (2006) *Rebel Alliances*. Oakland and Edinburgh: AK Press.
Franks, B., Jun, N., and Williams, L. (2018) *Anarchism: A Conceptual Approach*. Abingdon and New York: Routledge.
Frase, P. (2016) *Four Futures: Life after Capitalism*. London: Verso.
Frayne, D. (2015) *The Refusal of Work*. London: Zed Books.
Friedman, D. (1973) *The Machinery of Freedom: Guide to a Radical Capitalism*. New York: Open Court.
Fuller, T. (1989) *Michael Oakeshott on Education*. New Haven and London: Yale University Press.
Gardner, P. (1984) *The Lost Elementary Schools of Victorian England*. Beckenham: Croom Helm.
Geddes, P. (1905) *Civics: As Applied Sociology*. Available free online at www.gutenberg.org/ebooks/13205.
Geddes, P. (1915) *Cities in Evolution: An Introduction to the Town Planning Movement and to the Study of Civics*. London: Williams and Norgate.
Geddes, P. (2004) *The French Connection*. Oxford: White Cockade Publishing.
Godwin, W. (1783) *An Account of the Seminary that Will Be Opened on Monday*. London: Ecco Print Editions.
Godwin, W. (1793/1976) *Enquiry Concerning Political Justice*. London: Penguin.
Godwin, W. (1797/1965) *The Enquirer: Reflections on Education, Manners and Literature in a Series of Essays*. New York: Augustus Kelley.
Goffman, E. (1956) *The Presentation of Self in Everyday Life*. New York: Doubleday Anchor, now Penguin.
Goffman, E. (1961) *Asylums: Essays on the Social Situation of Mental Patients and Other Inmates*. London: Penguin.
Goldman, E. (1969) *Anarchism and Other Essays*. New York: Dover.
Goodman, P. (1950) *Utopian Essays and Practical Proposals*. New York: Vintage Books.
Goodman, P. (1960/1970) *Growing Up Absurd*. London: Sphere Books.
Goodman, P. (1964) *Compulsory Miseducation*. New York: Vintage Books. First UK edition, Penguin Books (1971).
Goodman, P. (1968) *People or Personnel*. New York: Vintage Books.
Goodman, P. (1969) *New Reformation: Notes of a Neolithic Conservative*. New York: Vintage Books.
Goodman, P., and Goodman, P. (1947) *Communitas: Means of Livelihood and Ways of Life*. New York: Vintage Books.
Goodway, D. (2012) *Anarchist Seeds beneath the Snow*. Oakland: PM Press.
Goodwin, B., and Taylor, K. (1982) *The Politics of Utopia*. London: Hutchinson.
Gordon, U. (2008) *Anarchy Alive!* London: Pluto Press.
Gorz, A. (1959/1989) *The Traitor*. New York: Simon and Schuster (then London: Verso).
Gorz, A. (1980a) *Adieux au prolétariat*. Paris: Éditions Galilée.
Gorz, A. (1980b) *Ecology as Politics*. London: Pluto Press.
Gorz, A. (1982) *Farewell to the Working Class*. London: Pluto Press.
Gorz, A. (1985) *Paths to Paradise*. London: Pluto Press.
Gorz, A. (1989) *Critique of Economic Reason*. London: Verso.
Gorz, A. (1994) *Capitalism, Socialism, Ecology*. London: Verso.
Gorz, A. (1997) *Misères du présent: richesse du possible*. Paris: Editions Galilée.
Gorz, A. (1999) *Reclaiming Work: Beyond the Wage-Based Society*. Cambridge: Polity Press.
Graeber, D. (2004) *Fragments of an Anarchist Anthropology*. Chicago: Prickly Paradigm Press.
Graeber, D. (2015) *The Utopia of Rules*. Brooklyn and London: Melville House.
Graeber, D. (2018) *Bullshit Jobs: A Theory*. New York: Simon & Schuster.

Graham, R. (ed.) (2009) *Anarchism: A Documentary History of Libertarian Ideas. Volume 2: The Emergence of the New Anarchism*. London and New York: Black Rose Books.
Greany, T., and Higham, R. (2018) *Hierarchy, Markets and Networks: Analyzing the 'Self-Improving School-Led System' Agenda in England and the Implications for Schools*. London: UCL Institute of Education Press.
Gross, R., and Gross, B. (eds.) (1971) *Radical School Reform*. London: Gollancz.
Guérin, D. (1970) *Anarchism: From Theory to Practice*. London and New York: Monthly Review Press.
Gutting, G. (2005) *Foucault: A Very Short Introduction*. Oxford: Oxford University Press.
Hall, P. (1998) *Cities in Civilization*. London: Weidenfeld and Nicolson.
Hall, S., and Jefferson, T. (1975) *Resistance through Rituals*. London: Hutchinson.
Harber, C., Meighan, R., and Roberts, B. (eds.) (1984) *Alternative Educational Futures*. London and New York: Holt, Rinehart and Winston.
Hargreaves, D. (1967) *Social Relations in a Secondary School*. London: Routledge & Kegan Paul.
Hargreaves, D. (1982) *The Challenge for the Comprehensive School*. London: Routledge & Kegan Paul.
Hargreaves, D. (2010) *Creating a Self-improving School System*. Nottingham: National College for School Leadership.
Hargreaves, D. (2012) *A Self-Improving School System: Towards Maturity*. Nottingham: National College for School Leadership.
Hargreaves, D., Hester, S., and Mellor, F. (1975) *Deviance in Classrooms*. London: Routledge & Kegan Paul.
Haworth, R. (ed.) (2012) *Anarchist Pedagogies*. Oakland, CA: PM Press.
Haworth, R., and Elmore, J. (eds.) (2017) *Out of the Ruins*. Oakland: PM Press.
Henry, J. (1955) 'Docility, or giving teacher what she wants,' in Beck, J., Jencks, C., Keddie, N., and Young, M. (eds.) (1976) *Toward a Sociology of Education*. Piscataway: Transaction Books.
Henry, J. (1963) *Culture against Man*. Harmondsworth: Penguin.
Hicks, D., and Slaughter, R. (eds.) (1998) *World Yearbook of Education 1998: Futures Education*. London: Kogan Page.
HMSO. (1997) White Paper: *Excellence in Schools*. London: HMSO.
HMSO/Cabinet Office. (2009) *Working Together: Public Services on Your Side*. London: HMSO/Cabinet Office.
Holt, J. (1964) *How Children Fail*. Harmondsworth: Penguin.
Holt, J. (1981) *Teach Your Own*. Brightlingsea: Lighthouse Books.
Holt, J. (1989) *Learning All the Time*. Ticknall: Education Now Publishing Cooperative.
Honeywell, C. (2011) *A British Anarchist Tradition*. London: Continuum.
Howard, E. (1902) *Garden Cities of Tomorrow*. London: Swan Sonnenschein.
Hyams, E. (1979) *Pierre-Joseph Proudhon: His Revolutionary Life, Mind and Works*. London: John Murray.
Illich, I. (1971) *Deschooling Society*. London: Calder and Boyars.
Illich, I. (1973a) *After Deschooling, What?* London: Writers and Readers Publishing Cooperative.
Illich, I. (1973b) *Tools for Conviviality*. London: Marion Boyars.
Jackson, D., and Temperley, J. (2006) *From Professional Learning Community to Networked Learning Community*. London: Innovation Unit.
Jacobs, J. (1961) *The Death and Life of Great American Cities*. New York: Random House.
Joll, J. (1964) *The Anarchists*. London: Eyre and Spottiswoode.
Judge, H. (1974) *School Is Not Yet Dead*. Upper Saddle River: Prentice Hall.
Kahn, R., and Kellner, D. (2007) 'Paolo Freire and Ivan Illich: Technology, politics and the reconstruction of education'. *Policy Futures in Education*, 5 (4), 431–448.
Kinna, R. (2005) *Anarchism*. Oxford: Oneworld.
Kinna, R. (ed.) (2012) *The Bloomsbury Companion to Anarchism*. London and New York: Bloomsbury.

Kinna, R. (2016) *Kropotkin: Reviewing the Classical Anarchist Tradition.* Edinburgh: Edinburgh University Press.
Klausen, J., and Martel, J. (eds.) (2011) *How Not to Be Governed.* Plymouth: Lexington.
Kozol, J. (1967) *Death at an Early Age.* Boston: Houghton Mifflin.
Kozol, J. (1972) *Free Schools.* Boston: Houghton Mifflin.
Kropotkin, P. (1892) *The Conquest of Bread.* Harmondsworth: Penguin.
Kropotkin, P. (1897) *The State: Its Historic Role.* London: Freedom Press.
Kropotkin, P. (1898/1974) *Fields, Factories and Workshops Tomorrow.* London: Allen and Unwin.
Kropotkin, P. (1899/1971) *Memoirs of a Revolutionist.* New York: Dover.
Kropotkin, P. (1902) *Mutual Aid: A Factor of Evolution.* Boston: Extending Horizons Books.
Kropotkin, P. (1906) *The Conquest of Bread.* Page references are to the edition independently published by Jonathan-David Jackson, 2017.
Kropotkin, P. (1927) *Revolutionary Pamphlets: A Collection of Writings.* New York: Vanguard Press.
Kuhn, G. (2010) *Gustav Landauer: Revolution and Other Writings: A Political Reader.* Oakland: PM Press.
Kunder, G. (1992) *Engineering Culture.* Philadelphia: Temple University Press.
Landauer, G. (1911) *For Socialism.* St Louis: Telos Press.
Lang, G., and Wunsch, M. (2009) *The Genius of Common Sense.* Boston: David R. Goldine.
Laughlin, J. (2016) *Kropotkin and the Anarchist Intellectual Tradition.* London: Pluto Press.
Lawton, D., and Chitty, C. (eds.) (1988) *The National Curriculum: Bedford Way Papers 33.* London: University of London Institute of Education.
Levitas, R. (1990) *The Concept of Utopia.* Hemel Hempstead: Philip Allan.
Levitas, R. (2013) *Utopia as Method.* New York: Palgrave Macmillan.
Levy, C. (ed.) (2013) *Colin Ward: Life, Times and Thought.* London: Lawrence and Wishart.
Lister, I. (1974) *Deschooling: A Reader.* Cambridge: Cambridge University Press.
Lodziak, C., and Tatman, J. (1997) *André Gorz: A Critical Introduction.* London: Pluto Press.
Lowrey, A. (2018) *Give People Money.* London: WH Allen.
Lukes, S. (1974) *Power: A Radical View.* London: Palgrave Macmillan.
Malatesta, E. (1891/1974) *Malatesta's Anarchy: A New Translation.* London: Freedom Press.
Mansell, W. (2007) *Education by Numbers: The Tyranny of Testing.* London: Politico's.
Manuel, F. (1965/1973) *Utopias and Utopian Thought.* London: Souvenir Press.
Marshall, P. (ed.) (1986) *The Anarchist Writings of William Godwin.* London: Freedom Press.
Marshall, P. (1992) *Demanding the Impossible: A History of Anarchism.* London: HarperCollins.
Marshall, P. (2017) *William Godwin: Philosopher, Novelist, Revolutionary.* Oakland: PM Press.
Martin, R. (1977) *The Sociology of Power.* London: Routledge & Kegan Paul.
Mason, P. (2015) *Postcapitalism: A Guide to Our Future.* London: Allen Lane.
Masters, A. (1974) *Bakunin: The Father of Anarchism.* London: Sidgwick and Jackson.
Matthews, P., and Ehren, M. (2017) 'Accountability and improvement in self-improving school systems', in Earley, P., and Greany, T. (eds.) (2017) *School Leadership and Education System Reform.* London: Bloomsbury.
Matthews, P., and Headon, M. (2015) *Multiple Gains: An Independent Evaluation of Challenge Partners' Peer Reviews of Schools.* London: UCL Institute of Education Press.
Maurer, C. (1971) *Call to Revolution: The Mystical Anarchism of Gustav Landauer.* Detroit: Wayne State University Press.
Maximoff, G. (1953) *The Political Philosophy of Bakunin.* New York: Free Press.
May, T. (1994) *The Political Philosophy of Poststructuralist Anarchism.* University Park: Pennsylvania State University Press.
McCraw, T. (2007) *Prophet of Innovation: Joseph Schumpeter and Creative Destruction.* Cambridge and London: Harvard University Press.
McKay, I. (2011) *Property Is Theft! A Pierre-Joseph Proudhon Anthology.* Edinburgh: AK Press.
McKay, I. (2014) *Direct Struggle against Capital: A Peter Kropotkin Anthology.* Edinburgh: AK Press.

Meighan, R. (1988) *Flexi-Schooling*. Ticknall: Education Now Books.
Meighan, R. (1997) *The Next Learning System: And Why Home-Schoolers are Trailblazers*. Nottingham: Educational Heretics Press.
Miles, S. (ed.) (1986) *Simone Weil: An Anthology*. London: Virago Press.
Miller, D. (1984) *Anarchism*. London and Melbourne: Dent.
Miller, J. (1993) *The Passion of Michel Foucault*. London: HarperCollins.
Miller, M. (1976) *Kropotkin*. Chicago: University of Chicago Press.
Monbiot, G. (2017) *Out of the Wreckage: A New Politics for an Age of Crisis*. London: Verso.
Morris, B. (2007) *Kropotkin: The Politics of Community*. Oakland: PM Press.
Muller, J. Z. (2018) *The Tyranny of Metrics*. Princeton: Princeton University Press.
Mumford, L. (1922) *The Story of Utopias*. New York: Viking Press.
Mumford, L. (1938) *The Culture of Cities*. London: Secker and Warburg.
Mumford, L. (1955) *The Human Prospect*. London: Secker and Warburg.
Newman, S. (2016) *Post Anarchism*. Cambridge: Polity Press.
Nyberg, D. (1981) *Power Over Power*. Ithaca and London: Cornell University Press.
O'Shaughnessy, J. (2012) *Competition Meets Collaboration: Helping School Chains Address England's Long Tail of Educational Failure*. London: Policy Exchange.
Parsons, T. (1959) 'The school class as a social system: Some of its functions in American Society'. *Harvard Educational Review*, 29 (4), 297–318, and in Halsey, A., Broadfoot, P., Cross, P., Osborne, M. and Abbott, D. (eds.) (1997) *Education, Economy and Society*. London: Collier/Macmillan.
Partridge, J. (1966) *Life in a Secondary Modern School*. Harmondsworth: Penguin.
Pinch, A., and Armstrong, M. (eds.) (1982). *Tolstoy on Education: Tolstoy's Educational Writings 1861–62*. London: Athlone Press.
Popper, K. (1945) *The Open Society and Its Enemies*. London: Routledge & Kegan Paul.
Postman, N. (1995) *The End of Education: Redefining the Value of School*. New York: Knopf.
Postman, N., and Weingartner, C. (1969) *Teaching as a Subversive Activity*. New York: Dell.
Power, S., Edwards, T., Whitty, G., and Wigfall, V. (2003) *Education and the Middle Class*. Buckingham: Open University Press.
Proudhon, P.-J. (1840/1970) *What Is Property?* New York: Dover.
Purkis, J., and Bowen, J. (eds.) (1997) *Twenty-First Century Anarchism*. London: Cassell.
Purkis, J., and Bowen, J. (eds.) (2004) *Changing Anarchism*. Manchester: Manchester University Press.
Putnam, R. (2001) *Bowling Alone: The Collapse and Revival of American Community*. New York: Simon and Schuster.
Putnam, R. (ed.) (2002) *Democracies in Flux: The Evolution of Social Capital in Contemporary Society*. Oxford: Oxford University Press.
Quail, J. (1978) *The Slow-Burning Fuse*. London: Granada.
Rawls, J. (1971) *A Theory of Justice*. Cambridge: Harvard University Press.
Raynaud, J., and Ambauves, G. (1978) *L'education libertaire*. Paris: Spartacus.
Read, H. (1925) *Education through Art*. London: Faber and Faber.
Read, H. (1974) *Anarchy and Order*. London: Souvenir Press.
Read, H. (1994) *A One-Man Manifesto and Other Writings*. London: Freedom Press.
Reé, H. (1973) *Educator Extraordinary: The Life and Achievement of Henry Morris*. London: Longman.
Rees, M. (2018) *On the Future Prospects of Humanity*. Princeton: Princeton University Press.
Reimer, E. (1971) *School Is Dead*. Harmondsworth: Penguin.
Richards, V. (1965) *Malatesta: Life and Ideas*. London: Freedom Press.
Ritter, A. (1980) *Anarchism*. Cambridge: Cambridge University Press.
Rockwell, L. (2014) *Against the State: An Anarcho-Capitalist Manifesto*. Auburn: LewRockwell.com.
Rothbard, M. (1973) *For a New Liberty: The Libertarian Manifesto*. Auburn: Ludwig von Mises Institute.
Rothbard, M. (1979) *Education: Free and Compulsory*. Auburn: Ludwig von Mises Institute.

Rothbard, M. (1998) *The Ethics of Liberty*. New York and London: New York University Press.
Rothbard, M. (2009) *Anatomy of the State*. Auburn: Ludwig von Mises Institute.
Rousselle, D., and Evren, S. (eds.) (2011) *Post-Anarchism: A Reader*. London and New York: Pluto Press.
Russell, B. (1938) *Power: A New Social Analysis*. London: Unwin.
Sahlins, M. (1968) 'Notes on the original affluent society', in Lee, R. and DeVore, I. (eds.) *Man the Hunter*. New York: Aldine.
Schütz, A. (1963) 'Common-sense and scientific interpretation of human action', in Natanson, M. (ed.) *Philosophy of the Social Sciences*. New York: Random House.
Schütz, A. (1964) 'The stranger: An essay in social psychology', in Brodersen, A. (ed.) *Studies in Social Theory*. The Hague: Martinus Nijhoff.
Schwan, A., and Shapiro, S. (2011) *How to Read Foucault's* Discipline and Punish. London: Pluto Press.
Scott, J. (1985) *Weapons of the Weak: Everyday Forms of Peasant Resistance*. New Haven and London: Yale University Press.
Scott, J. (1990) *Domination and the Arts of Resistance*. New Haven and London: Yale University Press.
Scott, J. (1998) *Seeing Like A State*. New Haven and London: Yale University Press.
Scott, J. (2009) *The Art of Not Being Governed: An Anarchist History of Upland Southeast Asia*. New Haven and London: Yale University Press.
Scott, J. (2012) *Two Cheers for Anarchism*. Princeton: Princeton University Press.
Scott, J. (2017) *Against the Grain*. New Haven and London: Yale University Press.
Scott, J., and Bromley, R. (2013) *Envisioning Sociology*. New York: State University of New York Press.
Sefton-Green, J. (2013) *Learning at Not-School*. Cambridge: MIT Press.
Sefton-Green, J., and Erstad, O. (eds.) (2018) *Learning Beyond the School*. London: Routledge.
Seltzer, K., and Bentley, T. (1999) *The Creative Age*. London: Demos.
Sennett, R. (1996) *The Uses of Disorder: Personal Identity and City Life*. London: Faber and Faber.
Sennett, R. (2008) *The Craftsman*. London: Penguin.
Sennett, R. (2012) *Together: The Rituals, Pleasures and Politics of Cooperation*. London: Allen Lane.
Sennett, R. (2018) *Building and Dwelling: Ethics for the City*. London: Allen Lane.
Serge, V. (1967) *Men in Prison*. Harmondsworth: Penguin.
Shone, S. (2013) *American Anarchism*. Chicago: Haymarket Books.
Shotton, J. (1993) *No Master High and Low: Libertarian Education and Schooling 1890–1990*. Bristol: Libertarian Education.
Simmons, G. (1968) *Introduction to Tolstoy's Writings*. Chicago: University of Chicago Press.
Sitrin, M. (2006) *Horizontalism: Voices of Popular Power in Argentina*. Oakland and Edinburgh: AK Press.
Sitrin, M. (2012) *Everyday Revolutions: Horizontalism and Autonomy in Argentina*. London and New York: Zed Books.
Slaughter, E. (1996) *New Thinking for a New Millennium*. London: Routledge.
Smith, M. P. (1983) *The Libertarians and Education*. London: Unwin.
Spring, J. (1975) *A Primer of Libertarian Education*. Montreal: Black Rose Books.
Srnicek, N., and Williams, A. (2016) *Inventing the Future: Postcapitalism and a World without Work*. London: Verso.
Standing, G. (2017) *Basic Income: And How We Can Make It Happen*. London: Pelican Books.
Starhawk (1990) *Truth or Dare? Encounters with Power, Authority, and Mystery*. San Francisco: Harper Collins.

Stirner, M. (1842) *The False Principle of Our Education*. Edited with and introduction by James Martin (1967). Colorado Springs: Ralph Myles.
Stoehr, T. (ed.) (1977) *Drawing the Line: The Political Essays of Paul Goodman*. New York: Free Line Editions.
Stoehr, T. (ed.) (2010) *Drawing the Line Once Again*. Oakland: PM Press.
Streeck, W. (2016) *How Will Capitalism End?* London: Verso.
Suissa, J. (2006) *Anarchism and Education: A Philosophical Perspective*. London: Routledge. (Further edition, 2010: Oakland and Edinburgh: PM Press.)
Swidler, A. (1979) *Organization without Authority*. Cambridge: Harvard University Press.
Taylor, C. (2004) *Modern Social Imaginaries*. Durham and London: Duke University Press.
Taylor, C. (2007) *A Secular Age*. Cambridge and London: Harvard University Press.
Taylor, M. (1992) *Community, Anarchy and Liberty*. Cambridge: Cambridge University Press.
Terkel, S. (1972) *Working: People Talk about What They Do All Day and How They Feel About What They Do*. New York: New Press.
Thomas, A. (1998) *Educating Children at Home*. London and New York: Continuum.
Thomas, K. (2009) *The Ends of Life: Roads to Fulfilment in Early Modern England*. Oxford: Oxford University Press.
Thomas, K. (2018) *In Pursuit of Civility: Manners and Civilization in Early Modern England*. New Haven and London: Yale University Press.
Thompson, P. (1983) *The Nature of Work*. London: Palgrave Macmillan.
Thorne, S. (2017) *School: A Recent History of Self-Organized Art Education*. Berlin: Sternberg Press.
Tooley, J. (1996) *Education without the State*. London: Institute of Economic Affairs.
Tooley, J. (2000) *Reclaiming Education*. London: Cassell.
Tooley, J. (2009) *The Beautiful Tree*. Washington: Cato Institute.
Tooley, J., and Stanfield, J. (eds.) (2003) *Government Failure: E. G. West On Education*. London: Institute of Economic Affairs.
Tyrwhitt, J. (ed.) (1947) *Patrick Geddes in India*. London: Lund Humphries.
Voline. (1974) *The Unknown Revolution 1917–1921*. Detroit: Black and Red.
Wallace, W. (2009) *Schools Within Schools*. London: Calouste Gulbenkian Foundation.
Waller, W. (1932) *The Sociology of Teaching*. New York: Wiley.
Walter, N. (1969) *About Anarchism*. London: Freedom Press.
Walter, N. (ed.) (2000) *Charlotte Wilson: Anarchist Essays*. London: Freedom Press.
Ward, C. (1973, 2nd ed., 1982) *Anarchy in Action*. London: Freedom Press (now published by the PM Press, Oakland, California).
Ward, C. (1974) *Utopia*. Harmondsworth: Penguin Education.
Ward, C. (1976) *Housing: An Anarchist Approach*. London: Freedom Press.
Ward, C. (1978) *The Child and the City*. London: Architectural Press.
Ward, C. (1985) *When We Build Again*. London: Pluto Press.
Ward, C. (ed.) (1987) *A Decade of Anarchy (1961–1970)*. London: Freedom Press.
Ward, C. (1989) *Welcome, Thinner City: Urban Survival in the 1990s*. London: Bedford Square Press.
Ward, C. (1991) *Influences*. Bideford: Green Books.
Ward, C. (1995) *Talking Schools*. London: Freedom Press.
Ward, C. (2000) *Social Policy: An Anarchist Response*. London: Freedom Press.
Ward, C., and Fyson, A. (1973) *Streetwork: The Exploding School*. London: Routledge & Kegan Paul.
Warpole, K. (ed.) (1999) *Richer Futures: Fashioning a New Politics*. London: Earthscan.
Watt, E. (1982) *Authority*. London: Croom Helm.
Weber, M. (1922) *Economy and Society*. Abingdon and New York: Routledge.
Weil, S. (1951, 2nd ed., 2002) *La condition ouvrière*. Paris: Gallimard.
West, E. G. (1965, 2nd ed., 1970) *Education and the State: A Study in Political Economy*. London: Institute of Economic Affairs.
Wetz, J. (2009) *Urban Village Schools*. London: Calouste Gulbenkian Foundation.

Wilbert, C., and White, D. (2011) *Autonomy, Solidarity, Possibility: The Colin Ward Reader.* Edinburgh: AK Press.

Wilby, P. (2013) 'Margaret Thatcher's education legacy is still with us – driven on by Gove', *The Guardian*, 15 April 2013.

Willis, P. (1977) *Learning to Labour.* Aldershot: Gower.

Wilson, M. (2014) *Rules without Rulers.* Winchester, UK and Washington, USA: Zero Books.

Wilson, P. (1992) *Freedom by a Hair's Breadth.* Ann Arbor, MI: University of Michigan Press.

Wolff, R. (1970) *In Defence of Anarchism.* London: Harper and Row.

Woodcock, G. (1963) *Anarchism.* Harmondsworth: Penguin.

Woodcock, G. (1977) *The Anarchist Reader.* Glasgow: Fontana/Collins.

Woodcock, G. (1989) *William Godwin: A Biographical Study.* Montreal and New York: Black Rose Books.

Woodward, W. (2008) 'The legacy of Blue Ken Baker,' *The Guardian*, 25 March 2008.

Wright, E. (1989) *Free School: The White Lion Experience.* London: Libertarian Education.

Wright, E. (2010) *Envisioning Real Utopias.* London: Verso.

Wrong, D. (1961) 'The oversocialized conception of man in modern society'. *American Sociological Review*, 26, 183–193.

Wrong, D. (1995) *Power: Its Forms, Bases and Uses.* New Brunswick and London: Transaction Publishers.

Youdell, D. (2011) *School Trouble: Identity, Power and Politics in Education.* London: Routledge.

Young, M., and Wilmott, P. (1957) *Family and Kinship in East London.* London: Routledge & Kegan Paul.

Zibechi, R. (2010) *Dispersing Power: Social Movements as Anti-State Forces.* Oakland and Edinburgh: AK Press.

INDEX